OLD AGE
IN
MYTH AND SYMBOL

OLD AGE
IN
MYTH AND SYMBOL

A Cultural Dictionary

Jennifer McLerran
and
Patrick McKee

Greenwood Press
New York • Westport, Connecticut • London

Library of Congress Cataloging-in-Publication Data

McLerran, Jennifer.
    Old age in myth and symbol : a cultural dictionary / Jennifer
McLerran and Patrick McKee.
      p. cm.
    Includes bibliographical references and index.
    ISBN 0-313-27845-8 (alk. paper)
    1. Old age in literature—Dictionaries. 2. Old age—Mythology—
Dictionaries. 3. Aging in literature—Dictionaries. 4. Aging in
art—Dictionaries. I. McKee, Patrick L. II. Title.
PN56.04M34   1991
809'.93354—dc20   91-9163

British Library Cataloguing in Publication Data is available.

Library of Congress Catalog Card Number: 91-9163
ISBN: 0-313-27845-8

First published in 1991

Greenwood Press, 88 Post Road West, Westport, CT 06881
An imprint of Greenwood Publishing Group, Inc.

Printed in the United States of America

The paper used in this book complies with the
Permanent Paper Standard issued by the National
Information Standards Organization (Z39.48-1984).

10 9 8 7 6 5 4 3 2 1

For Tom

CONTENTS

INTRODUCTION

A perennial task of literature, visual art, and the behavioral sciences is to observe and interpret those aspects of experience which have especially profound significance—what Jung called "archetypes." Old age is such an archetype. Few things resonate with such richly ambiguous meanings, engage more serious interest, or augur a more universal or more compelling destiny.

Like other archetypes, the image of the aging man or woman evokes responses in us which we urgently want to express but which elude direct, literal language. Such responses find their proper expression not in literal statement but indirectly, through the arts of allegory, myth, and symbol. Because of its powerful hold on our deeper emotions, old age has always captured the imaginations of literary and visual artists. Over half of Rembrandt's canvases depict an aged character. One must search to find a Rubens canvas that does not include at least one aged person. Homer's youthful characters find their essential counterpoints in such elderly characters as Priam and Nestor, and several of Shakespeare's most central characters are aged: Lear, Falstaff, and Shylock are examples. Modern literary and visual artists give careful attention to old age, often portraying aging characters in central and/or important supporting roles. Examples are such literary/film characters as Howard in *The Treasure of the Sierra Madre* and General Kutuzov in *War and Peace.*

The long history of art has evolved a rich tradition of symbolic and mythical allusion to the many meanings of old age. Aging characters are often patterned after gods, goddesses, or other traditional mythical figures. A frequent occurrence of this is elderly characters, both men and women, cast in the role of Charon, the old river god of Greek and Roman myth. In this myth an aged god carries the dead across the Styx to the underworld. In numerous allusions to this myth, elderly characters are placed in the vicinity of water, boats, bridges or other "crossings" where they facilitate the passage of a younger person through a crisis such as growing from adolescence to adulthood or through some other difficult journey from one stage of existence to another. Another widely used device is to give elderly characters props or attributes which connect them symbolically to traditional myth, such as the water, boat, and/or oars of Charon, the scythe, knife, or other sharp cutting instrument of Father Time, or the pigs of Demeter, the Greek goddess who oversees the proper succession of the seasons and of the generations of humans.

In the future artists and behavioral scientists will continue to depend on the great expressive and explanatory power of mythical and symbolic imagery of aging. Elderly characters will continue to be presented in such traditional mythical roles as Father Time, Charon, the hearth goddess Hestia, the mother-goddess Demeter, and so forth. And they will continue to be presented with traditional symbolic attributes such as the scythe or sickle or its equivalents, the clock or watch or other time measuring instrument, the musical instrument, and so forth. Such characters cannot be developed in their strongest form, nor their behavior understood, in any other way. A closer acquaintance with the myths and symbols reported below will contribute significantly to a better understanding both of artistic interpretations of old age and of our own lives as we undergo the universal experience of aging.

This compilation of myths and symbols of old age is the result of four years' research on their use in art, literature, and popular culture. Many standard sources were consulted, including such widely used dictionaries of myths and symbols as *The Oxford Classical Dictionary*, Robert Graves' *The Greek Myths*, Pierre Grimal's *The Dictionary of Classical Mythology*, J. E. Cirlot's *A Dictionary of Symbols*, and Ad de Vries' *Dictionary of Symbols and Imagery*.

Short citations in parentheses within or following each entry indicate sources referred to in compiling that entry. These sources may also be consulted for further information on that particular subject. Full titles of all sources can be found in the bibliography following the main text. Names of authors only are cited when only one source by that particular author appears in the bibliography. Where more than one source by an author is listed, the pertinent titles are cited in abbreviated form. Page numbers are given in the citation whenever a particular source was quoted directly.

Asterisks are used for internal cross referencing. An asterisk preceding a term signals a dictionary item entered under that word. Occasionally, readers are referred to another pertinent entry by the word "see."

LIST OF ENTRIES

THE DICTIONARY

A

Abraham: The Biblical character Abraham embodies the Judeo-Christian concept of longevity and fertility as rewards for goodness. He lived 175 years, fathering Isaac at the age of 100, and died at "a good old age." (Genesis 25:7-8)

acacia: The acacia is a symbol of endurance, constancy, and unchangeability, since its wood is very durable and it possesses great reproductive powers. The Biblical "burning bush" was probably an acacia. It was an early Christian symbol of the soul and immortality. The Freemasons use it as a symbol of immortality and conservation. *Mistletoe, a symbol of longevity, grows on the acacia, further establishing it as a symbol related to the aging process. (de Vries; Herder)

Aegeon: Adriana's father-in-law in Shakespeare's *The Comedy of Errors*, Aegeon represents old age, as evidenced by the author's reference to him as "old man." He embodies, as well, a number of complex symbols employed elsewhere by Shakespeare as emblematic of old age ("*sap-consuming *winter," "*night of Life", "wasting *lamps"). (Draper, "Shakespeare's Attitude...") This can be seen in the following passage where Aegeon speaks of old age:

> . . . this grained face of mine be hid
> In sap-consuming winter's drizzled snow.
>
> Yet hath my night of Life some memory,
> My wasting lamps some fading glimmer left.

Aeson: Aeson, the father of Jason from Classical mythology, was restored to youth by the *sorceress *Medea. (cf. Ovid's *Metamorphoses* 7, 159-298) This aged *king, whose name means "ruler," was described by Ovid as "weary and worn by weight of years." (Graves, GM II, p. 378)

As an example of the fulfillment of the desire for eternal youth, the story of Aeson serves, according to Simone de Beauvoir, as a complement to the myth of *Tithonus: "It is the counterpart of the legend of Tithonus—immortality is nothing without youth, but on the other hand the perpetuation of youth would be man's supreme happiness." (de Beauvoir, p. 98)

Ages of Man: The number of the Ages of Man varies from one system of thought to another; however, division into *four ages is most common. It corresponds to the division of the phases of the *moon, the *seasons, and the directions, reflecting a view of the human being as a microcosm of the greater macrocosm.

The four Classical phases of humankind's collective development listed in Ovid's *Metamorphoses* (1, 89-150) can be seen as analogous to human development on the individual level from what has often been perceived as a spiritual to a more material state (*golden, silver, bronze, iron). These progress (or regress) from the purest to the most malleable, and thereby the most corruptible state. By analogy, the last phase of an individual's life can be seen as the phase when most malleability, resulting from the degradation of the material body, is exhibited.

Hesiod's (8th century B.C.) and Lucretius' (94-55 B.C.) systems of division of the collective ages of man similarly end with an iron age. Hesiod lists five ages: *golden, or patriarchal, ruled by *Saturn; silver, or voluptuous, ruled by Jupiter; brazen, or warlike, ruled by Neptune; heroic, or renaissant, ruled by Mars; and iron, or present, ruled by *Plutus. In *Works and Days*, Hesiod describes the *four ages of mankind corresponding to four metals, the first age comprised of a "golden race of mortal men" (110) who did not experience "helpless old age" (114). This first race became the spirits who guide and protect mortals. The gods of Olympus then created a second race, this one of silver, its members remaining children for 100 years, and never growing out of adolescence and its foolishness. This race, called "blessed mortals," resides underground. Zeus created a third race of bronze mortals from ash trees who possessed great strength and a propensity toward war and violence, which caused their own destruction. They now reside, nameless, in Hades. The fourth race, made up of a "divine race of heroes, who are called demigods," also was destroyed by war, some dying in the battles of Thebes and Troy, and some settling at "earth's ends, apart from men." The last race, the fifth, is the race of iron which is burdened with growing cares and whose "lot will be a blend of good and bad." This race will survive until "children are born grey at the temples." In this final age, children will not honor their parents, men will lay each other's cities to waste, they will not honor their oaths, "they will be blighted by envy," and "might will make right." In the end, "Shame and Retribution will cover their fair bodies with white cloaks and, leaving men behind, will go to Olympus from the broad-pathed earth." (197-199)

Lucretius, basing his system upon the metals used for tools during each of the successive ages, lists three: stone, bronze, and iron. (Brewer)

Other systems divide the Ages of Man into *seven, *twelve, and *ten. Animals correspond to the phases in the medieval artistic and literary convention of the Ages of Man which divides a person's life into *ten stages. They are as follows:

	male	female
0-10	calf/puppy	quail
10-20	calf/he-goat	dove
20-30	bull	magpie
30-40	lion	peahen
40-50	fox	hen
50-60	*wolf	*goose
60-70	tom-*cat/*dog	*vulture
70-80	tom-*cat/*dog	*owl
80-90	*ass	*bat
90-100	*Death	*Death
		(de Vries, Sears)

Aion: In Greek, *aion* means "time." In Greek and Egyptian belief, each person was believed to possess a life fluid which constituted his or her soul and allotted life span. The Greeks named this substance "aion."

Early images of Aion are either Mithraic in origin, consisting of a *winged figure with the head and claws of a lion, its body entwined by a *serpent holding a *key; or they derive from the Orphic divinity Phanes, who is portrayed as a handsome young man wrapped in a snake's coils and surrounded by the *zodiac. Aion enters Greek thought as *Chronos. Like many images related to *time and *cyclic change, Aion combines bipolar elements (*wings related to heaven and flight, and *snakes related to the underworld and earthbound existence). (Lurker; von Franz, *Time*) In *Phanes' Birth from the World Egg*, an Orphic relief sculpture from the reign of the Roman Emperor Hadrian (A.D. 117-138), we see a *winged Aion wrapped in *serpents' *coils. He is surrounded by an egg-shaped band bearing the *twelve signs of the *zodiac. (Campbell, MI, p. 34)

In an image reflective of Aion, Shakespeare makes reference in *Hamlet* to material existence as "this mortal coil":

> To die,--to sleep;--
> To sleep! perchance to dream:--ay, there's

the rub;
For in that sleep of death what dreams may come,
When we have shuffled off this mortal coil,
Must give us pause: there's the respect
That makes calamity of so long life;
                    (*Hamlet*, act 3, sc. 1, 71-77)

Alberich: Alberich, King of the Dwarves in Scandinavian Mythology, is described as 500 years old but still the size of a child. In Wagner's *Der Ring des Nibelungen* he is the gnome who, because he steals the *gold guarded by the Rhine Maidens, is seized by the gods. He is freed in exchange for the *gold. (Brewer) As a shapeshifter, he takes numerous forms, including that of a toad and a *serpent. (Walker, WEMS)

alchemist's tree: The alchemist's tree is, in general, symbolic of philosophical thought and, specifically, representative of reflection, wisdom, and integrative understanding. It is also related to the archetype of the *"Wise Old Man." Carl Jung explains: "In the long encounter with life and the world there are experiences that are capable of moving us to long and thorough reflection, from which, in time, insights and convictions grow up—a process depicted by the alchemists as the philosophical tree. The unfolding of these experiences is regulated, as it were, by two archetypes: the anima, who expresses *life*, and the 'Wise Old Man', who personifies *meaning*." (Jung, *Mysterium*, p. 233)
    Titus Burckhardt, in *Alchemy: Science of the Cosmos, Science of the Soul*, presents an alchemist's tree, "the tree of psychic *materia prima* which has its roots in the earth of cosmic *materia prima*," from a medieval manuscript (MS. 428 of the Vadian Library, St. Gallen) as a "Symbolical Representation of the Alchemical Work." (Burckhardt, Plate 5, p. 128)

alchemy: *Faust represents the archetype of the alchemist, attempting to reverse the process of materialization and, thereby, the process of aging. (cf. Rembrandt's etching, *Dr. Faustus in His Study*, 1652) Alchemy is the symbolic *four phased process of turning base metals to *gold and the analogous process of turning the material into the spiritual. The phases of this process and the substances corresponding to those phases are as follows: prime matter (the original soul in its uncorrupted state); mercury (feeling and imagination); sulphur (intuition and reason); lapis or *gold (synthesis, transcendence). (de Vries) When viewed as analogous to the *four Ages of Man, the fourth of these alchemical phases corresponds to old age.

Alecto: Her name meaning "she who is unremitting," Alecto is one of the three *Erinyes or *Furies, the avenging deities of Classical mythology. In Virgil's *Aeneid* 7, 450-455, Juno calls Alecto, or "Old Age," forth from the underworld to start war:

"Lo!" she said, "I, I am she,
Old Age, quite broken down, quite drained of
        truth,
And, 'midst the arms of kings, by idle fear
Deceived. And look thou here. From out the
        home
I come where dwell the sisters terrible,
And bears my potent hand its grasp within
Both war and death.

amaranth: Because it reputedly never fades, the amaranth is symbolic of vitality and resistance to deterioration through age. Shelley (1792-1822) employs it as a symbol of endurance and undiminished integrity in "Prince Athanase," fragment II:

        . . . as daylight finds
One amaranth glittering on the path of frost,
When autumn nights have nipped all weaker
        kinds,
Thus through his age, dark, cold, and tempest-tossed,
Shone truth upon Zonoras;

In *Aesop's Fables*, the *rose, because it is desired by the gods, is the object of the amaranth's envy. However, as the fable points out, a rose, though highly valued for its beauty while in full bloom, fades quickly and thereby loses its value. The amaranth, on the other hand, lives forever; consequently, it retains its value, even in old age. (de Vries)

Ancient of Days: A Jungian archetype or "mana personality" related to the Great Mother (Magna Mater), the Ancient of Days takes the form of a magician, *sorcerer, or sage. He is depicted as an aged man with white hair like unspun wool wearing a white robe and is seated upon a throne of flames with wheels. (Cirlot; de Vries)

The name of the judge in the eschatological scene in Daniel 7:9-10 is variously interpreted as: "a primeval being"; "A Venerable One"; "one crowned with age"; and "Ancient of Days." The passage reads as follows:

        As I looked,
thrones were placed
        and one that was ancient of days
            took his seat;
his raiment was white as snow,
        and the hair of his head like pure
            wool;

his throne was fiery flames,
    its wheels were burning fire.

In *The Interpreter's Dictionary of the Bible*, Stanley B. Frost postulates that the ancient appearing in *Daniel* is representative of the God of Judeo-Christian culture: "The figure is probably intended to be that of God himself, and the attribute of age is ascribed to convey the ideas of dignity, wisdom, and primevality (cf. Job 36:26). . . . " (Buttrick, vol. 1, p. 126)

Angurboda: As Hag of the Iron Wood in Old High German culture, Angurboda is a form of the *crone. Her name meaning "anguish-boding," she is also known as Hagazussa, Priestess of Hel, the underground mother. (Leach) Angurboda was the mother of the *moon *dogs, the psychopomps who carried the dead to the world of the afterlife. (Walker, *Crone*)

Anjana: Anjana is a *witch in Hispanic folklore. As a *sorceress, she sometimes takes the form of an *old woman, and at other times she appears as a young woman with blond hair and blue eyes wearing green stockings and a gown covered with flowers and silver stars. She carries a *staff which causes whatever it touches to turn to riches. The riches which Anjana accumulates through the function of her *staff are stored in underground palaces. (Cirlot)

St. Anthony Abbot: St. Anthony Abbot, an Egyptian *hermit who lived ca. 251-356, was the founder of monasticism. In his youth, he renounced his wealth, gave his money to the poor, and went into the desert where he became a solitary ascetic. He is often depicted in scenes of an episode where he was tempted by demons with "the pleasures of the flesh." (cf. Lucas Cranach the Elder's *The Temptation of St. Anthony*, a woodcut from 1506, and Martin Schongauer's *Temptation of St. Anthony*, an engraving from 1522) He resisted and was consequently beat into unconsciousness by the demons. He is represented as an *old man with a long white beard dressed in a monk's habit. The habit is sometimes marked with a blue "T" standing for *Theos* or God, as in *The Ghent Altarpiece* (by Hubert and Jan Van Eyck, completed 1432), in which he is portrayed leading the Holy Hermits. He is usually shown resting on a crutch and carrying a bell to exorcise demons. (Pierce)

ape: The ape is a symbol of wisdom in the Far East because of its intelligence and cunning. Originally, apes were portrayed as blind, deaf, and dumb as an ironic twist upon the fact that they were supposedly messengers who reported to the gods on the behavior of humans. (Herder)

In Elizabethan literature (cf. Shakespeare's *King Lear*), the ape is a symbol of man's folly in life. Man is a *fool moving about on a *stage for the amusement of the immortals. The ape, in mimicking human behavior, reflects man's image back to him and shows him his folly. He causes man to see himself as the immortals see him, as a *fool lacking wisdom. (Hankins) This can be seen in a passage from the *Zodiake*, an Elizabethan text:

Perhaps thou dost it to that ende our doings to deride,
And makest man thy laughing stocke. For nothing else to be
The life of men on earth doth seem, then staged Comedie.
And as the ape that counterfets, to us doth laughter move:
So we likewise doe cause and move the Saintes to laugh above.

In *Old Fortunatus* (1600), Thomas Dekker employs the ape as a symbol of youthful folly in old age:

When the old traveller my Father comes home, like a young Ape,
full of fantasticke trickes, or a painted Parrot.

apple: The apple is a symbol of *autumn and approaching death. In many tales, heroes refuse the apple offered by the goddess because they realize it indicates impending death. It also symbolizes wisdom, as in the case of the apples of the Hesperides of Classical mythology, which yield knowledge.

Apples often appear in mythology as agents of eternal youth. In Scandinavian mythology, there are tales of attempts by giants to steal the apples of youth growing near Yggdrasil, the world tree. The gods fed upon these apples to maintain their immortality. Briagi, the poet god, was married to Idun, the goddess entrusted with guarding the apples of immortality. Loki (the Trickster) was forced by the giant Thiazi to kidnap Idun and steal her apples. He then stole them (and her) back in order to prevent the gods from suffering old age and death. H. R. E. Davidson suggests that Idun is a character borrowed from either Celtic or Classical mythology, her golden apples borrowed from the apples in the Garden of the Hesperides and the story of their theft finding its origin in an Irish tale, *Sons of Tuireann*: "Apples and nuts from the land of promise, renewing youth and freeing those who ate them from the tyranny of time, are a familiar feature in Irish sagas, and one that goes back to an early date." (Davidson, GMNE, p. 165)

The sorb apple is a symbol of positive value arising from physical decay, since it is sweet and eatable only after it rots. (de Vries)

Artemis at Brauron: Artemis at Brauron was the Greek patroness of the life cycle of women. (cf. Euripides, *Iphigenia in Taurus*)

ashes: Because they are the purified remains of *fire, ashes symbolize the transitory nature of life leading to death; but they also represent resurrection and purification. They symbolize renunciation of the physical world, as evidenced by the practice of Indian yogis who cover their bodies with ashes as a symbolic act of renunciation. (Herder) In the Old Testament, covering of the body with ashes as an imitation of burial is an act intended to avert death (cf. Job 2:8).

In "Past," John Galsworthy (1867-1933) uses ashes as symbolic of weakening of desire in old age:

> The hot desires burn low, and wan
> Those ashy fires, that flamed anon.

In Dylan Thomas' (1914-1953) "It is the Sinner's Dust-tongued Bell," Time, along with his familiar *hourglass, carries a *torch. With its ashes, he "marks a black aisle."

asphodel: The asphodel, a member of the lily family, is a symbol of approaching death and the afterlife because in Classical mythology fields of asphodel were thought to grow in the underworld, their roots serving as food for the dead. (Graves, GM I, p. 121) Shelley alludes to Classical mythology in his poem, "The Witch of Atlas," when he places the *witch's *cauldron in a field of asphodel:

> Where in a lawn of flowering asphodel,
> Amid a wood of pines and cedars blended,
>   There yawned an inextinguishable well
> Of crimson fire--full even to the brim,
> And overflowing all the margin trim.

In "Asphodel, That Greeny Flower," the contemporary poet William Carlos Williams (1883-1963) uses the asphodel as a symbol of approaching death.

In Gerrit Dou's painting *Old Woman in a Window* (1669), the artist places an asphodel just outside the window through which an *old woman leans. Representative of the afterlife, its placement may indicate that her bridging of the *threshold from interior to exterior is intended to symbolize passage from one realm of existence to another. The empty bird *cage placed on the other side of the window's exterior, which can be viewed as symbolic of escape from the restriction of the aged body in passage to the afterlife, further reinforces this interpretation. (McKee and Kauppinen)

ass: In the *Ages of Man, the medieval artistic and literary convention dividing an individual's life into *ten stages, an ass represents a man of 80 to 90 years old. (cf. Jorg Breu the Younger's *Steps of Life*, 1546) (Sears, Plate 98) It is an attribute of *Saturn, who is the Greek god related to old age and the passage of time (the precursor of *Father Time). (Cirlot) It is also a symbol of longevity, possibly through the phrase "donkey's years." In Elizabethan times "years" and "ears" were spelled the same; consequently, long "ears" (of a donkey) became long "years." (de Vries)

Atropos: In Greek mythology, Atropos was the oldest of the Three *Fates. She took the form of the *crone who cut the *thread of life which was drawn and measured by her two younger sisters, Clotho and Lachesis. She therefore governed the last phase of life, ending in death. (cf. Homer's *Iliad* 24, 49 and Hesiod's *Theogeny* 217 ff. & 904) Her name meaning "she who cannot be turned," she was described as the shortest and "most terrible" of the Three *Fates. (cf. Hesiod's *Shield of Heracles*; Graves, GM II, p. 383)

Atropos, as the *crone, became the prototype for the *witch. The designation of witches as fays or *fairies is evidence of this connection, as Barbara Walker explains: "the terms for fairies and witches were interchangeable, and both were called fays, fates, or *fatidae*." (Walker, Crone, p. 103) Rather than perceiving her in her original conception as the expression of a necessary element in the natural process of birth, growth, decay, and rebirth, as one aspect of a repeated cycle, the crone became a personification of the modern Western concept of old age and death as wholly undesirable, to be avoided at all costs.

In *Richard II*, Shakespeare refers to Atropos as "blindfold Death," since she is sometimes portrayed as blindfolded:

My oil-dried lamp and time-bewasted light
Shall be extinct with age and endless night;
My inch of taper will be burnt and done,
And blindfold Death not let me see my son.
(*Richard II*, act 1, sc. 3, 221-224)

Shakespeare refers to Atropos in *King John* (act 4, sc. 2, 91), calling her *scissors "the shears of destiny," and in *Pericles, Prince of Tyre* (act 1, sc. 2, 108) he makes further reference to the Fates: "till the Destinies do cut his thread of life." (Hankins)

autumn: In the human life cycle, autumn represents middle or old age, the time of physical decline and cessation of growth. In "Elegies 9, The Autumnal," a poem by John Donne, the author uses autumn as a metaphor for aging: "No spring nor summer beauty hath such grace As I have seen in one autumnal face." In Tennyson's *The Princess* IV, "Song," autumn is the time of review of one's past: "Tears . . . Rise in the heart . . . In looking on the happy Autumn fields, And thinking of the days that are no more."

In Christianity, autumn is the time of *pilgrimage, the time for disengagement from ordinary life in the search for one's center. The process of the inward *journey and search for a center typical of life review in old age is analogous to the *pilgrim's outward search for the holy center.

Avalon: The Isle of Avalon, a mythical island whose residents enjoy eternal youth, is an example of the medieval obsession with the theme of physical rejuvenation and avoidance of old age. In Arthurian legend, it is the island to which the mortally wounded King Arthur is taken. (cf. Geoffrey of Monmouth's 12th-century Latin *History of the Kings of Britain* and Malory's *Morte d'Arthur*, ca. 1469) Its existence originally based upon oral legend, this "Island of Life" was purported to hold a magical object or elixir with rejuvenating powers. However, its effects were restricted to those residing on the island. As soon as residents left Avalon and set foot on another land, they lost their youth and reassumed the physical aspects of old age. (de Beauvoir)

B

---

baboon: The baboon, like the *ape, is a symbol of approaching death. It is also a symbol of enlightenment and wisdom. It is found on ancient Egyptian water *clocks as a symbol of time. Later, it came to symbolize stupidity, as an inversion of its earlier representation of wisdom.

In Egypt, the baboon was a messenger of the gods and was involved in the weighing of a man's soul against a feather after death, thereby passing judgment upon that individual's life. Consequently, the baboon serves as a reminder to aged persons that they will soon be held accountable for their actions in this life and must, therefore, not dally. (de Vries)

ball: In Classical mythology, the ball is an attribute of Tyche (whose name means "fortune"). Tyche's function, similar to that of the *Fates, is intimately connected with that of *Nemesis, who is the forerunner of the Roman goddess *Fortuna. Tyche had the power to determine the fortunes of mortals. She would dispense gifts and good fortune upon some from her horn of plenty, and upon others she would impose deprivation. Her ambivalent, uncaring attitude is exemplified in the action of juggling, as described by Graves: "Tyche is altogether irresponsible in her awards, and runs about juggling with a ball to exemplify the uncertainty of chance: sometimes up, sometimes down."

Tyche is scornful of those who do not show gratitude for the gifts she bestows. If someone she has favored fails to share his or her good fortune by sacrificing a portion of it to the gods or to charity so as to benefit the common good, Nemesis enters to punish that individual. Nemesis carries an apple bough in one hand. In the other hand she carries a *wheel. This latter attribute links her to the Roman goddess *Fortuna and to the concept of fate. Graves explains: "That Nemesis' wheel was originally the solar year is suggested by the name of her Latin counterpart, Fortuna (from *vortumna*, 'she who turns the year about')." (Graves, GM I, pp. 125, 126)

As a *circular form, the ball represents *cyclic movement and is thereby related to the passage of time and aging. As a *sphere, it is related to age as a symbol of completion or perfection. (de Vries)

Among the Yakima, Native Americans of the northwestern United States, a "time ball" is used to record important events of a woman's life. Called *ititamat*—"counting the days" or "counting calendar"—it consists of lengths of hemp tied together and wound into a ball. A knot or bead is tied onto the string to mark major events in the owner's life: first courtship, marriage, birth of a child, birth of a grandchild, etc. Each year, a new length of string with major events marked is added and wound into the ball. When the woman dies, the time ball is buried with her. (Yakima Nation Museum)

bat: In the *Ages of Man, the medieval artistic and literary convention dividing an individual life into *ten stages, the bat symbolizes a woman of 80 to 90. It is a symbol of longevity because bats are believed to live a long time. In *Aesop's Fables*, the bat symbolizes wisdom. (de Vries)

Baubo: Baubo, the figure from Classical mythology whose name is interpreted by some as meaning "soother," cheered *Demeter during the latter's search for her daughter, Persephone. (Graves, GM II, p. 384) An *old nurse in the household of King Celeus of Eleusis and his wife Metaneira, Baubo, according to the Classical myth, entertained *Demeter on her visit to the household. She joined Iambe (daughter of Celeus and Metaneira) in this effort, Iambe singing lascivious songs with comic effect: "careful Iambe . . . moved the holy lady with many a quip and jest to smile and laugh and cheer her heart." (Hesiod, "Homeric Hymn to Demeter") Baubo is often portrayed with prominently displayed genitals, a characteristic derived from descriptions of her attempts to entertain Demeter. According to such stories, Baubo lifted her skirts, exposing her genitals, and allowed Iacchus to spring from between her legs.

As an *old nurse, Baubo is, according to Graves, a form of the *crone: "Old nurses in Greek myth nearly always stand for the goddess as Crone." (Graves, GM I, p. 95) Graves further asserts that Baubo, Iambe, and *Demeter together form the Virgin/Mother/*Crone complex: "Iambe and Baubo personify the obscene songs, in iambic metre, which were sung to relieve emotional tension at the Eleusinian Mysteries, but Iambe, Demeter, and Baubo form the familiar triad of maiden, nymph, and *crone."

bead: The bead is a symbol of time through its association with the *rosary. "Bead" is derived from the Old English word *gebed*, which means "prayer." (de Vries, p. 37) The *rosary, which consists of a string of prayer beads, was originally a measure of time, the closed *circle of beads symbolizing the *cyclic progression of time. Pope in his *Essay on Man*, Ep. 2, relates beads to old age: "And beads and prayer-books are the toys of age."

Belisarius: Though a historical character, Belisarius, a renowned Byzantine general, became more a stereotype than an historical individual in the Middle Ages. Through the experience of great renown and good fortune at one point, followed by extremes of hardship and ill fate later in life, he became the object of Christian teaching. As explained by de Beauvoir, he came to illustrate "the scriptural 'vanity of vanities': on this earth, nothing was sure; man must set his trust in God alone." (de Beauvoir, p. 144) Though he was instrumental in winning Italy back from the Goths, he was later the object of scandal and disgrace. Accused of plotting against Justinian in 562, his possessions were seized and he was restricted from traveling beyond the bounds of his palace. Though historical accounts document Belisarius' release and the return of his property following his trial in 563, fictionalized versions of the story from the Middle Ages present him as suffering blinding as a form of punishment and passing the rest of his years as an aged beggar.

bird: The *caged bird is a common symbol of the restriction of old age. However, Edward Arlington Robinson (1869-1935), in "The Poor Relation," presents a view of such restriction as a desirable state because of the comfort it affords: "safe in a comfortable cage."

In "Meditations of an Old Woman," Theodore Roethke (1908-1963) describes old age as "Nervous and cold, bird-furtive whiskery."

black: In the *Ages of Man, the medieval artistic and literary convention which divides an individual's life into *ten stages, black corresponds to the last stage. It also corresponds to *Saturn, another form of which is the Grim Reaper or *Father Time with his *hourglass and *scythe. Through association with the dark underworld, it symbolizes wisdom, hidden knowledge. In the *alchemical system of thought, it symbolizes the recluse's or *hermit's withdrawal and thereby shares in the symbolism of the *hermit. (de Vries)

blindness: Blind, aged characters often possess inner vision and foresight, either in the form of wisdom or in more occult form as the gift of prophecy. In Classical mythology, blindness is often the punishment for mortals who have seen, whether accidentally or purposefully, the goddess unveiled (cf. the myth of Tiresias). But such a punishment often brings with it the compensatory gift of prophecy whereby the offender obtains the "inner eye" of the seer. (de Vries)

Blindness is a symbol of the physical decline and withdrawal from the world often experienced in old age; however, as the above-cited mythology expresses, such decline and withdrawal are often perceived as bringing with them the compensatory qualities of wisdom and inner vision. As well, blindness is representative of and often attendant upon disengagement leading to detachment in old age. This detachment is believed a necessary condition for the form of wisdom which derives from being able to perceive a number of sides to things. It is the result of non-investment in a *single* viewpoint, the single viewpoint being necessary when one is engaged, when one is invested in, and hopes to profit from, that viewpoint. The aged person, as a liminal figure, has the freedom to engage different viewpoints, thereby gaining insight surpassing that of a single viewpoint.

boat: The boat is a symbol of passage through life, as Ralph Waldo Emerson's (1803-1882) "Terminus" exemplifies:

> As the bird trims her to the gale,
> I trim myself to the storm of time,
> I man the rudder, reef the sail,
> Obey the voice at eve obeyed at prime . . . .

There is a symbolic connection between the boat and the human body as the vessel of the soul. As a symbol of rebirth, it represents the cradle rediscovered and the mother's womb. In ancient Egyptian culture, a funerary boat accompanied the mummy to facilitate its passage through the underworld to rebirth on the other side. The coffin later replaced the boat as the vessel of transport. In numerous cultures the boat symbolizes the passage from the world of the living to the world of the dead. In Classical mythology, *Charon, depicted as an old man with a white beard, ferries souls across the River Styx into the underworld.

For several reasons, the boat and the *moon share in each other's symbolic meaning. First of all, because it journeys across the sky each *night, the *moon's *journey is viewed as analogous to the individual's journey through life, a journey or "voyage" of which the boat is symbolic. Second, the *crescent shape of the *moon is similar to the curved form of the boat; therefore, through visual association, the boat is often related to the *crescent moon. The *moon is a symbol of *cyclic change and the passage of time since, through waxing and waning at regular intervals, it undergoes repeated, predictable *cycles. Through association, the boat becomes a symbol of *cyclic change and the passage of time.

Because it can travel in either direction (its front and back are interchangeable), the boat is related to the two-faced Roman god, *Janus, the god associated with transition, with the passing from one phase to another, one *cycle to another. (Herder)

Another example of the boat as a symbol of the individual's *journey through life is found in *The Voyage of Life* (1839-1840), a series of four paintings by the 19th-century American artist Thomas Cole. Cole presents images of *four successive stages of life: childhood, youth, manhood, and old age. Each of the four pictures contains a boat carrying its voyager down the Stream of Life. Cole describes the boat's symbolism: "The Boat, composed of Figures of the Hours, images the thought that we are borne on the hours down the Stream of Life." The first painting in the series, "Childhood," shows a laughing infant accompanied by an angel who steers the boat. In the second work of the series, "Youth," the infant has become a lone adolescent who steers the boat through a verdant landscape. The guardian angel now stands on the shore. Cole says that the images in this painting "figure forth the romantic beauty of youthful imaginings, when the mind magnifies the Mean and Common into the Magnificent, before experience teaches what is the real." In the third image, "Manhood," the landscape has become rugged and forbidding. The sky is filled with storm clouds, and the stream rushes torentially through a shadowed ravine toward the ocean. The boat, which is now rudderless, contains a middle-aged man who looks toward heaven for help. Demonic forms hover in the sky, and the guardian angel sits among the clouds. Cole explains the imagery in this piece: "It is only when experience has taught us the realities of the world, that we lift from our eyes the golden veil of early life: that we feel deep and abiding sorrow; and in the picture, the gloomy, eclipse-like tone, the conflicting elements, the trees riven by tempest, are the allegory; and the Ocean, dimly seen, figures the end of life, to which the voyager is now approaching." In the final image of the series, "Old Age," the boat, battered and decrepit, glides across the ocean at *midnight. The figures of the Hours are damaged and nearly unrecognizable. The voyager, now an old man, is accompanied and directed by the Guardian Spirit. The old man looks toward the sky, from which a brilliant light emanates. The clouds form stairs upon which angels descend, welcoming the traveler to what Cole calls the "haven of Immortal Life." Cole explains this last image: "The Stream of Life has now reached the Ocean, to which all life is tending. The world, to Old Age, is destitute of interest. There is no longer any green thing upon it. The broken and drooping figures of the boat show that Time is nearly ended." (Merritt, pp. 35-37)

book: The book symbolizes the individual life story. As such, it is related to the process of life review. It is a symbol not only of the totality of an individual's life, but of the totality of the universe, as well—a unified whole consisting of individual pages (individual lives). (Herder) The title of Edmund Waller's poem about old age, "Of the Last Verses in the Book," indicates his use of the book as a symbol of a lifetime, in this case the last verses signifying old age. The book as a symbol of a lifetime is used also in Oliver Wendell Holmes' (1809-1894) "The Old Man Dreams":

> Off with the spoils of wrinkled age!
> 　　Away with Learning's crown!
> Tear out life's Wisdom-written page,
> 　　And dash its trophies down!

The book is a symbol of wisdom and knowledge, in part through association with the wise female elder, the *crone. In pre-Christian European culture, elder women were scribes, keeping historical accounts, vital records, and calendars for religious purposes. (Walker, Crone) They were therefore regarded as repositories of wisdom and knowledge and as those responsible for the continuity of culture. The *Sibyl of Cumae from Classical mythology exemplifies this culturally vital aspect of the wise female elder. As a wise prophetess living to the age of 1,000 years and as the originator of the Sibylline books which contained instructions for various rites and actions appropriate to specific situations, she performed a role vital to the propagation of the accumulated wisdom of a culture. The *Sibyl of Cumae is portrayed with a book in her lap in Michelangelo's Sistine Chapel frescoes.

bridge: The bridge symbolizes states of transition—between phases of life, between life and death, between two worlds, etc. Demeter, the earth goddess of Greek mythology, is called the "Lady of the Bridge." This designation may be related to her aspect as the *crone, since the *crone is associated with the transition from life to death. (de Vries; Herder)

In Scandinavian mythology, the gods must cross over Bifrost, the "rainbow bridge" made of fire, air, and water. It arches from Yggdrasil, the world tree, to Asgard, the world of the afterlife.

These mythological associations of the bridge to passage from one realm of existence to another are similar to the common association of the bridge with states of transition in personal narrative. We find expression of this in contemporary culture in the film *Hoosiers*. At the beginning of the film, the aging main character, an ex-basketball hero who returns to his hometown to coach the high school basketball team, must cross over a bridge at the town's edge. Such a passage expresses transition to a new life which offers a "last chance" for redemption, an opportunity for the protaganist to make his life's story cohere to the narrative which he desires.

Brigit or **Brigid**: The Irish Saint Brigit is a later version of the Celtic Goddess Brigit, the *Triple Goddess incorporating Virgin, Mother, and *Crone, her *crone form being Cerridwen, who personified the wisdom behind poetic inspiration. (Walker, Crone) Brigit's name is derived from the Irish *brig*, meaning "power" or "authority." She is the patroness of smiths, poets, and doctors. Appropriated by Christianity, she became the patron saint of Ireland, who tended the holy fire with the assistance of nineteen nuns. (Lurker, pp. 68-69)

buzzard: The buzzard is a symbol of old age, the decline of the physical, and death. In the *Ages of Man, the medieval literary and artistic convention which divides an individual's life into *ten stages, it corresponds to a woman of 60 to 70. (de Vries)

C

cage: The cage is often employed as a symbol of the restriction of old age. In "The Poor Relation" Edward Arlington Robinson (1869-1935) describes his aged subject as "safe in a comfortable cage."

In Gerrit Dou's painting *Old Woman in a Window* (1669), the artist places an *asphodel and an empty bird cage on either side of the window through which an *old woman leans. As a symbol of the afterlife, the *asphodel's placement may indicate that the *old woman's bridging of the *threshold from interior to exterior represents imminent passage from one realm of existence to another. The empty bird cage placed on the other side of the window's exterior, when viewed as a symbol of escape from the undesirable restriction of old age in the passage to the afterlife, further reinforces this interpretation. (McKee and Kauppinen)

In Shakespeare's *King Lear*, the cage is symbolic of a desirable state of restriction and disengagement for the aged Lear. (H. Luke, pp. 25-33) Lear entreats his daughter, Cordelia, to join him in prison:

> Come, let's away to prison:
> We two alone will sing like birds i' the cage
> When thou dost ask me blessing, I'll kneel down
> And ask of thee forgiveness: so we'll live,
> And pray, and sing, and tell old tales, and laugh
> At gilded butterflies, and hear poor rogues
> Talk of court news; and we'll talk with them too,--
> Who loses and who wins; who's in, who's out;--
> And take upon's the mustery of things,
> As if we were God's spies: and we'll wear out,

In a wall'd prison, packs and sects of great ones,
That ebb and flow by th' moon.
                          (*King Lear*, act 5, sc. 3, 8-19)

Caillech: Variously signifying *old woman, *hag, nun, or "veiled one," the
Caillech was the ancient Celtic version of *Kali, the *crone. Her veil probably
represented the crone's role as the aspect of the *Triple Goddess related to
fate and death, to the individual's future which is veiled and cannot be known
in advance. Caillech is synonymous with *old woman in present-day Ireland
and Scotland. (Walker, WEMS)

candle, candlestick: The burning candle is a common symbol of the individual
soul and the relationship between the spiritual and the material, the *flame
representing the eternal soul and the candle representing the material body
which is consumed. It becomes, thereby, a symbol of the transitory quality of
human life. (Herder)

In John Bunyan's *Pilgrim's Progress*, the burning candle, as a reminder of
the transitory nature of material existence, becomes instructive of the value of
a virtuous life:

Matt: Why doth the fire fasten upon the candlewick?
Prud: To shew that unless Grace doth kindle upon the heart, there will
        be no true Light of Life in us.
Matt: Why is the wick, and tallow, and all spent, to maintain the light of
        the candle?
Prud: To shew that Body and Soul, and all should be at the service of,
        and spend themselves to maintain in good condition, that Grace
        of God that is in us. (pp. 274-275)

The face of an aged person is often compared to a candle. In "The Old
Woman" Joseph Campbell (1879-1944) likens the subtle beauty and serenity
of "an aged face" to a votive candle. Campbell's comparison may find its
source in the Apocrypha (Ecclesiasticus 26:22): "As the clear light upon holy
candlesticks, so is the beauty of the face in ripe age." (Griffin)

Shakespeare often employed the dying or extinguished candle as a symbol
of old age and death, as in the following:

Out, out, brief candle! (*Macbeth*, act 5, sc. 5)

Here burns my candle out, ay, here it dies,
Which, while it lasted, gave King Henry light.
                          (*3 Henry VI*, act 2, sc. 6, 1-2)

The fading candle as a symbol of old age can be found in a number of other Elizabethan sources, including the following from the *Zodiakus Vitae*, a philosophic text in verse used in Elizabethan classrooms:

> . . . A fiery spirit doth raine,
> Which quickneth every living thing, in world which doth remaine.
> This heat doth lively moisture feede, as flame of Candle bright,
> . . .
> At length it makes an end and stayes, when spent is all the heate,
> Which fading, body fades: as shewes in them whose yeares are great,
> For wasted they like pined Ghostes, their aged lymmes doe crooke,
> And stouping low with hollowed eyes upon the earth doe looke.
> For fyre is gone, and lively heate, and moysture doth decay,
> Without the which no lyfe remaines: as Lampes no longer may
> Give out their light than oyle doth serve, but dies and darknesse brings.
>   (Hankins)

A number of modern poetic references to the candle exist as well, as in W. B. Yeats' (1865-1939) reference to the "candle-end" as an image of old age in "The Wicked Old Man."

The seven-branched candlestick, the Hebrew Menorah, symbolizes the *seven planets, the *seven heavens, the *seven days making up the week, the *seven archangels (and, by extension, the *Seven *Ages of Man). In Christianity, it further represents the *seven gifts of the holy spirit: "counsel, knowledge, peace, piety, strength, understanding and wisdom." (de Vries, p. 79)

cane: Because its use is the result of the physical decline accompanying old age, the cane is a symbol of the *support* which such decline necessitates, the direct physical support which the cane offers being emblematic of the general support of others necessary for the infirm to maintain functionality. The cane shares in the symbolism of the *staff. (de Vries)

In several works the Spanish artist Francisco Goya (1746-1828), employs the cane to express the infirmity of age. In *Two Old Friars* (1819-1823), an aged, bearded man leans on a cane and another aged man, grotesque in appearance, peers over his shoulder from behind. (McKee and Kauppinen) In *Aun Aprendo* (I Am Still Learning), a chalk drawing from 1824-1828, which shows an old man with long, white hair walking with the aid of two canes, Goya presents an image of engagement despite infirmity. Goya lived to the age of 82, executing *Aun Aprendo* in the last four years of his life. This work may be seen as an expression of Goya's attitude toward his own old age. Though deaf since the age of 47 as the result of a serious disease and suffering the infirmity of old age, he remained highly prolific in his later years.

He expresses in *Aun Aprendo* an optimistic view of old age as a time of continued growth and widened understanding.

cape: The cape is an attribute of the *pilgrim; therefore, it shares in the symbolism of the *pilgrim. Like the *cloak, it simultaneously represents superior or dignified status and disengagement from the world; consequently, it is a common symbol of old age. (cf. Isaak Dinesen's *The Cloak*; Cirlot)

carp: The carp is a symbol of longevity because it may live to the advanced age of 200 years. It is also a symbol of endurance and perseverance because it struggles upstream, against the current, and can stay alive out of water for long periods of time. (de Vries; Herder) It is represented as the "steed of the immortals" by virtue of its longevity.

The carp is sometimes employed as symbolic of the wisdom of the deep, as in Virginia Woolf's *Between the Acts* (1941). Mrs. Swithin, while gazing into a lily *pool, observes the "great carp" rising from the *pool's depths. Seldom seen and, when visible, only briefly glimpsed, the carp is symbolic in Woolf's work of an age-old, essential force running through all of life. It is apprehended only in the process of self-reflection (symbolized by the action of staring into a deep *pool), as in the process of life review.

casket: The casket is a symbol of death and impending death in old age. A recurring motif in numerous legends consists of three caskets, the first and second holding goods and riches and the third dispensing storms, devastation, and death. This image reflects a common division of life into three stages, the first two containing desirable and the last undesirable conditions (as in the Three *Fates or Virgin/Mother/*Crone complex), representing youth, middle age, and old age. (Cirlot)

In Shakespeare's *The Merchant of Venice* (act 2, sc. 7), we see an example of the hero choosing a casket. Three suitors much choose one of three caskets: one *gold, one *silver, and one *lead. Whoever chooses the one containing Portia's image wins her hand. The first (the Prince of Morocco) chooses the *golden one, the second (the Prince of Arragon) chooses the *silver one, and the third (Bassanio) selects the *leaden one. The *leaden casket contains Portia's image, and Bassanio thereby wins her hand. The three caskets bear the following inscriptions: the *gold says "Who chooseth me shall gain what many men desire"; the *silver reads "Who chooseth me shall get as much as he deserves"; and the *lead is inscribed with "Who chooseth me must give and hazard all he hath."

cat: In the *Ages of Man, the medieval artistic and literary convention which divides an individual's life into *ten stages, a man of 70 to 80 is a tom-cat. In Jorg Breu the Younger's *Steps of Life* (1540), a cat corresponds to the ninth of *ten stages of life. (Sears, Plate 98) The cat symbolizes longevity by virtue of folklore which affords it nine lives.

As the *witch's familiar, the cat is seen in many depictions of *witches. *Hecate, the *crone from Classical mythology, transformed herself into a cat. The chariot of Freya, the Teutonic goddess of witchcraft, was drawn by two cats. (de Vries)

cauldron: Cauldrons of regeneration (restoring youth or health) are common in Celtic myth. Both the *Tale of Kilwych* and Olwen and the *Tale of Peredur Son of Evrawc* contain a cauldron of regeneration, which was found by a giant at the bottom of a *lake in Ireland. (Graves, GM II, p. 220) In Celtic mythology, the Cauldron of Regeneration, believed to lie under the ocean or on Apple-Land (*Avalon) across the Western Sea, functions not only as a symbol of regeneration but as a symbol of wisdom as well. In the tale of Gwion-Taliesin, three drops from the cauldron of Cerridwen gave Taliesin vast knowledge and poetic inspiration. Cerridwen, Taliesen's mother, boiled in her cauldron her own attributes (produced from her own body--the cauldron representative of her uterus): "life, wisdom and inspiration." She distilled three drops from this mixture, the "Grace of Inspiration," which provided her son with the inspiration for his poetry. (Walker, *Crone*, p. 106)

The cauldron is a symbol of regeneration in Classical mythology as well. In Ovid's *Metamorphoses* 7, 159-298, *Medea convinces King Pelias that her cauldron will make him young again and thereby tricks him into willingly submitting to his own death by boiling. Her claims for the regenerative power of her cauldron were not, however, always the basis for trickery, since she did restore Jason's aged father, *Aeson, to youth.

The cauldron is an attribute of the *crone, the aspect of the Triple Goddess related to old age. Through its relationship to the *Triple Goddess, the cauldron signifies the womb, source of regeneration and rebirth. Just as everything is dissolved and recombined in boiling, so everything in the cosmos (symbolized by the cauldron) perpetually dissolves and recombines in a cyclic fashion. Barbara Walker explains: "The cauldron symbolized creation that occurred not just once, as in the Bible story, but constantly, as long as the universe lasted." (Walker, *Crone*, p. 111)

Cauldrons accompany *witches in numerous literary and artistic images. In *The Magic Circle* (1886) by the pre-Raphaelite painter, John William Waterhouse, a *witch holds a wand in one hand and a *sickle in the other as she stands over a boiling cauldron. In *Macbeth*, Shakespeare presents one of the best-known literary portrayals of *witches at their cauldron. The three Wyrd Sisters stand over their boiling pot chanting:

Double, double toil and trouble;
Fire, burn, and cauldron bubble"
        (*Macbeth*, act 4, sc. 1)

cave: As the *hermit's typical dwelling, the cave represents disengagement from the world, as in old age. As the result of worship of ancestors buried in caves, the cave came to be viewed as the entrance to the underworld. (de Vries) Through Earth Goddess worship, the cave became symbolic of the entrance to the passage to rebirth, to the womb of the Earth Mother, the dwellingplace of the "underground *crone." It was, thus, seen as the source of life and afterlife. The meaning of *hellir* in Old Norse was "a cave." The Black Goddess (or *crone) was manifested in Scandinavian mythology as the goddess Hel, Queen of the Shades. Our word "hell" came from her; although Hel's subterranean world, unlike our hell, was not a place where souls were sent for punishment. It was, rather, the earth's womb to which the dead returned in order to experience rebirth. (Walker, *Crone*, p. 85)

The cave figures prominently in *alchemy as a symbol of the unconscious. According to Paracelsus, the 16th-century philosopher and reformer of medicine and pharmacology whose treatise *De Vita Longa* addresses the prolongation of life through *alchemy, the transformation which occurs through immersion in the unconscious, symbolized by the cave, results in prolongation of the natural life span. (Jung, *ACU*)

celandine: Wordsworth, in "The Small Celandine" (1807), employs the celandine as a symbol of endurance and the necessity of hardship in old age:

'It doth not love the shower, nor seek the cold:
This neither is its courage nor its choice,
But its necessity in being old.

'The sunshine may not cheer it, nor the dew;
It cannot help itself in its decay;
Stiff in its members, withered, changed of hue.'
And in my spleen, I smiled that it was grey.

To be a Prodigal's Favourite--then, worse truth,
A miser's Pensioner--behold our lot!
O man, that from thy fair and shining youth
Age might but take the things Youth needed not!

Celestina: Celestina is the aged heroine of Roja's play of the same name written in 1492. An example of the old bawd or old prostitute, so popular in French theater of the time, she was an ex-prostitute who thoroughly enjoyed her profession. Describing her as lewd and *witchlike, Simone de Beauvoir in *The Coming of Age* says that "In her are summed up all the vices that had been attributed to old women since classical times. . . . " (p. 148) She views Celestina as exemplary of the attitude in the Middle Ages toward the aged who freely expressed their sexuality.

cell: The cell symbolizes old age as isolation and imprisonment, as in George Peele's (1558-1597) "A Farewell to Arms (To Queen Elizabeth)": "And when he saddest sits in homely cell. . . . "

In a similar image from Shakespeare, *King Lear speaks of the restriction of prison as desirable in old age:

> Come, let's away to prison:
> We two alone will sing like birds i' the cage
> (*King Lear*, act 5, sc. 3, 8-9)

Cerberus: Cerberus, as the dog at the entrance to the underworld of Classical mythology, symbolizes death and the impossibility of atonement for sins after death. He is assigned the task in the underworld of preventing souls from returning to earth where the possibility of atonement and salvation still exists. (cf. Ovid's *Metamorphoses* books 4, 7, 9, 10) Consequently, he is a reminder of the urgency of atoning for past misdeeds in old age before death comes. (Cirlot; Herder)

Cerberus appears three-headed in a depiction on a Caeretan hydria, a Greek black-figure vase (ca. 530 B.C.). In the scene depicted, Heracles is shown delivering Cerberus to Eurytheus. (Boardman, p. 81)

chair: The chair is a symbol of rest and old age (de Vries), as a passage from Shakespeare's *1 Henry VI* (act 4, sc. 5) exemplifies:

> When *sapless age and weak unable limbs,
> Should bring thy father to his drooping chair.

chalice: The chalice, representative of the Holy Grail, is the Christian form of the *cauldron. It appears in Psalms as the source of abundance and life:

> thou anointest my head with oil,
>   my cup overflows.
> Surely goodness and mercy shall
>   follow me
>   all the days of my life;
>   (Psalms 23:5-6)

Early Christianity appropriated the elusive and long-sought-after *cauldron of regeneration of pre-Christian times, giving it the form of a chalice, a form likewise representative of the womb. Just as the *cauldron symbolized the source of life, constantly forming, dissolving, and reforming, so the chalice represented the source of life as the vessel of life, the cup of Christ, filled with wine (Christ's blood). However, the Grail's connection to the *cauldron was repressed by the Church because its symbolism undermined Christian theology in its representation of a universe consisting of *cyclic recurrence as opposed to linear progression. (Walker, *Crone*)

In James Joyce's short story "Sisters," the chalice dropped and broken by the aged Father Flynn becomes a symbol of the priest's decline in old age. After he drops the chalice, he rapidly degenerates physically and mentally. Only after his death is the chalice restored to perfection. Here the chalice functions as a symbol of the human body as the frail, easily broken container of the life force.

Charon: Charon, as the ferryman on the River Styx which runs through the underworld in Classical mythology, is a symbol of approaching death. He is portrayed as an ugly *old man with a gray beard dressed in a disheveled cloak and round hat. (cf. *The River Styx*, 1510, by Joachim Patinir; *Charon*, 1876, by Arnold Bocklin)

First mentioned in Aristophanes' *The Frogs* (late 5th century B.C.), Charon is described in Virgil's *Aeneid* (6, 297-304):

> And horrible the ferryman who serves
> These miry waves and floods, Charon his name,
> In squalor wrapt, upon whose chin grows thick
> The long white beard neglected, and whose eyes
> Stand out in fire, while from his shoulders hangs,
> Tied in a knot, his 'kerchief old and foul. His boat
> He poles and manages with sails,--sails, pole
> And boat encrusted o'er with rust, the rust
> An aged rust,--but new and fresh his age
> Seemed like a God's, so strong the old man was.

The custom of placing coins on the eyes of the dead derives from the belief that one must pay Charon for his service upon entering the underworld. (Grimal, *DCM*)

Chronos: As the Greek personification of time, Chronos evolved into the image of *Father Time. Chronos became confused with the Roman god *Kronos (or *Saturn), who devoured his own children because he had been warned by Zeus that one of them would someday kill him. Through this mistaken association, Chronos took on *Saturn's attributes as the god of agriculture (the *scythe, or *sickle, and *hourglass). He also became representative of the devouring nature of time, the Grim Reaper. Chronos also functions as the Revealer of Truth. (Panofsky)

chrysalis: The chrysalis is a symbol of transformation, of disengagement from the world by virtue of being on the point of entry of a new developmental level; consequently, it can be viewed as emblematic of disengagement prior to death. Through its relationship to the *cicada, into which it is metamorphosed, it is a symbol of the soul leaving the body. (Herder, de Vries)

The chrysalis functions symbolically in Goethe's *Faust*. *Faust* is the allegory of a man looking for enduring, eternal values confronted with a world of constant flux and change. His search for lasting forms is constantly frustrated by the transitory qualities his experience of the world yields. This constant change is expressed in a number of symbols representative of metamorphosis in *Faust*, for example, the butterfly unfolding from the chrysalis and the *leaf emerging from the bud and in the phrase: "Formation, transformation, Eternal mind's eternal recreation." His desire for lasting forms is further expressed in *Faust's desire to transcend the process of aging. He sells his soul to the devil in return for twenty-four more years of life; however, though rejuvenated, he does age and finally dies. (Dieckmann)

cicada: The cicada is a symbol of resurrection, immortality, metamorphosis, and eternal youth. In ancient China cicadas made of jade were put in the mouths of corpses for the purpose of assuring immortality. Through the Classical myths of *Tithonus and the *Sibyl of Cumae, the cicada is related to old age and the foolish wish for eternal youth. Both *Tithonus, who was granted immortality but not eternal youth, and the *Sibyl of Cumae, who was granted a lifespan of 1,000 years, grew withered and decrepit and finally turned into cicadas. (Cooper)

As the "demon of *light and darkness," the cicada is symbolic of the *cyclic interplay of periods of *light and darkness. (Cooper) In the prologue to Goethe's *Faust*, Mephistopheles compares man to a cicada "that alternately flies and falls down." (Dieckmann, p. 43)

circle: The circle is often used to symbolize the completion of a *cycle, resulting in wholeness and unity. It thereby symbolizes the *cyclic activity of the days, the months, the *seasons, and human life. As an endless line, it is a symbol of time and infinity. In the form of the *ouroboros (the *dragon, *snake, or *fish devouring its own tail) it symbolizes the devouring nature of time. In ancient Greek culture, the Pythagoreans named the *ouroboros surrounding the cosmic egg *"Chronos." *Chronos was married to Necessity, which also encircled the universe, the two together representing *Time and *Fate as circular and conjoint. The Circle of Necessity represented *Fate as manifested in the process of birth, growth, decline, and death in an individual life.

The Cosmic Solar *Wheel, a circle enclosing a cross, resulting in a circle divided into *four equal parts, represents the animating force within the universe and is a symbol of good fortune and change. Its divisions representing the *four quarters of the earth, the *four divisions of the cosmic *cycle, the *four *seasons and the *four ages of man, it reflects a view similar to that expressed in the *zodiac: that man, the microcosm, reflects the macrocosm, the universe. The circular *zodiac, giving attributes and characteristic qualities to each of a succession of *twelve phases of an individual's existence (corresponding to *twelve equal divisions of a circle), represents the *cyclic nature of time, correlating the progression of the individual's life through *four major divisions (divided into three houses each, totaling *twelve houses) with the *four quarters of the earth and the *four *seasons. The Buddhist *Round of Existence, representing the phenomenal world, reflects a similar view of temporal existence as *cyclic. (Cooper; de Vries)

In Jungian terms, the circle is a symbol of the self and of life's wholeness as reflected in man's environment. This is explained by Aniela Jaffe in *Man and His Symbols*:

> It expresses the totality of the psyche in all its aspects, including the relationship between man and the whole of nature. Whether the symbol of the circle appears in primitive sun worship or modern religion, in myths or dreams, in the mandalas drawn by Tibetan monks, in the ground plans of cities, or in the spherical concepts of early astronomers, it always points to the single most vital aspect of life--its ultimate wholeness. (Jung, *MHS*, p. 240)

The *wheel, as a form of the circle, shares in the circle's function as a symbol of completion of a *cycle, as in old age. A notable example of this is Shakespeare's comparison of the course of the aged *King Lear's life to a circle: "The wheel has come full circle." (*King Lear*, act 5, sc. 3)

Numerous other forms of the circle have varied meanings, most reflecting a sense of unity or completion. The circle with a dot in the middle symbolizes a complete *cycle and resulting perfection, the "resolution of all possibilities in existence." (Cooper, pp. 36-37) Three concentric circles symbolize the conjoining of past, present, and future. In Buddhism, three concentric circles are symbolic of the highest level of enlightenment, reflecting the harmony of spiritual powers. Concentric circles in Christian symbolism represent spiritual hierarchies or levels of creation, and three interlocked circles represent the Christian Trinity. The circle within a square is a symbol of the "divine spark hidden within matter" in the *Kabbala*. (Herder)

claws: Claws are symbolic of the metamorphosis of the human body through the action of the aging process, or deformity through aging. W. B. Yeats (1865-1939) uses this symbol in "The Old Men Admiring Themselves in the Water": "They had hands like claws."

Shakespeare presents age as a clawed being in the conversation between two gravediggers (the clowns) in *Hamlet* (act 5, sc. 1):

> But age, with his stealing steps,
> Hath claw'd me in his clutch,

And hath shipp'd me intil the land,
As if I had never been such.

cloak: The cloak is a symbol of both dignified, superior status and of disengagement from the world. It is a veil that, either by virtue of voluntary elevation from the mundane or by forced isolation, causes separation from the everyday world. The cloak of the sage Apollonius is an example of this image's function as expression of isolation from the mundane. (Cirlot)

The cloak figures prominently as a symbol of the disengagement of old age in Isaak Dinesen's (1885-1962) *The Cloak*. In Pieter Brueghel the Elder's *The Misanthrope* (1568), the cloak symbolizes the aged misanthrope's withdrawal from the world. In this circular canvas, Brueghel shows an old, bearded man in a hooded cloak passing through an idyllic, pastoral scene. The hood of the traveler's cloak is so large that it blocks his view of his surroundings. All that is visible to him is a narrow stretch of path ahead in which several thorns lie. His gaze lowered to the path, the *old man is oblivious to the fact that he is being robbed of his purse. A strange, dwarf-like man in a clear bubble reaches under his cloak to steal his money pouch. John Canaday points to the moral of this allegory of disengagement: "The misanthrope is doubly robbed: wrapped in the false security of his symbolic cloak and hood, he robs himself of the world--but he cannot escape the world even so, for it in turn robs him." (Canaday, vol. 1, p. 348)

clock: The clock is a symbol of the passage of time and the *cyclic nature of existence as reflected in the *seasons and in the daily phases of the sun. It functions as a reminder of time's passage and thereby comes to signify man's slavery to time and destiny and the irreversibility of the process of aging. The clock as a reminder of the transitory nature of life became a symbol of death in the Middle Ages, a *memento mori*, reminding one that time was short and that those who desired salvation should not dawdle, but should proceed with good deeds and the virtuous life without delay. (Panofsky)

The clock is a symbolic expression of the Western concept of a mechanical universe, set in motion by the Creator and progressing in an objective, ordered, and measurable fashion. This is expressed in Leo Tolstoy's *War and Peace* in the image of "whirring and chiming in the higher spheres." The clockwork model of the universe is an expression of experience as quantitative (measurable), rather than qualitative. Consequently, it reflects a view wherein the process of aging is quantified in years rather than determined subjectively or qualitatively. Aging, in this view, becomes a linear progression towards death, rather than a deepening of experience through perception of the simultaneous existence of past, present and future in subjective experience. (Boyle and Morriss, pp. 92-94)

In folklore, a change in the rhythm of a clock's ticking portends death. Also, a clock stopping when the owner dies signifies the existence of the dead beyond time. (de Vries)

Audrey Flack, in her painting *Time to Save* (1979), presents an ironic view of time. Flack fills her still-life with images of the temporal and transitory, including a butterfly, an *hourglass, and a clock. The clock, which also serves as a bank, bears the inscription "Time to Save." Flack expresses in this work the irony of the idea of being able to save something which is fleeting and ephemeral.

cobweb: Cobwebs symbolize decay through disuse. For example, "cobwebs in the attic" is a term expressive of deterioration of mental faculties through years of disuse. (de Vries)

In John Galsworthy's (1867-1933) "Past," the "cobweb chime" of *clocks is symbolic of memories of the past in old age:

> The clocks are chiming in my heart
> Their cobweb chime;

cocoon: see CHRYSALIS.

coil: *Aion's coils, the *snakes twining about his body, are symbolic of mortality as a consequence of earthbound, temporal existence. This is similarly expressed by Shakespeare in *Hamlet* (act 3, sc. 1, 71-77).

cold cup: In "Three Seasons," Christina Georgina Rossetti (1830-1894) divides life into three stages, characterized by first hope, then love, and finally memory, a "cold cup":

> 'A cup for memory!
> Cold cup that one must drain alone:
> While autumn winds are up and moan
>   Across the barren sea.

coot: The coot is a symbol of understanding and wisdom because it dips into the *water to catch the symbol of wisdom, the *fish. The terms "bald as a coot" and "old coot," often used to describe an aged man, refer to the commonest species of the coot, the bald coot. It possesses a bill which extends onto the forehead to form a white plate resembling a bald head. (de Vries)

cornel: see DOGWOOD.

coyote: The coyote, a trickster figure in Native American mythology, is sometimes referred to as *"Old Man." He embodies opposite qualities, such as strength and weakness, wisdom and folly, childishness and malice. He is thereby representative of the contrasting qualities of wisdom and folly existing simultaneously in aged characters. (cf. "Coyote Angel" in John Nichols' *The Milagro Beanfield War*) Coyote, the trickster, embodies the state of liminality often experienced by the aged. No longer bound by convention, operating within an undefined social space, the aged character often performs a function similar to Coyote, showing us through absurd example the limits of permissible behavior. Karl Kerenyi, in a commentary accompanying Paul Radin's *The Trickster, A Study in American Indian Mythology*, explains:

> Disorder belongs to the totality of life, and the spirit of this disorder is the trickster. His function in an archaic society, or rather the function of his mythology, of the tales told about him, is to add disorder to order and so make a whole, to render possible, within the fixed bounds of what is permitted, an experience of what is not permitted. (Radin, p. 185)

crab: The crab is a traditional symbol of death and regeneration, of transcendence of the temporal world through devouring what is transitory, thereby effecting regeneration. (de Vries) The term "crabbed age," referring to irritability, probably refers to the irascible nature of the crab. This quality is reflected in the title of an Elizabethan lyric of unknown author, "Crabbed Age and Youth," which consists of a series of oppositions between age and youth. (Benet, p. 220)

In Theodore Roethke's (1908-1963) "Meditations of an Old Woman," the crab is symbolic of regeneration, of the spirit seeking "another life."

crane: The crane is a symbol of longevity as a result of the ancient Chinese and Japanese belief that it could live 1,000 years. (Herder) It occurs as an attribute of a number of Japanese and Chinese figures associated with longevity, including *Fukuro Kuju, the Japanese god of good luck; *Jurojin, the Japanese god of longevity; and *Shou Lao, the Chinese god of long life. (Lurker)

crescent moon: Through visual association with the form of the *boat, the crescent *moon represents the individual's *journey through life. The *moon in its three major phases (waxing, full, and waning) is symbolic of the *Triple Goddess, the waning phase corresponding to the *crone aspect of the goddess. The waning *moon, as a form reflecting loss of vitality through *cyclic change, is symbolic of the diminishment of physical power with age.

cricket: The cricket is a symbol of loquacity and often takes the role the *Wise Old Man (as in Homer's *Iliad* 3, 151). (de Vries) It is connected with aging through *Tithonus, a character from Classical mythology who was turned into a *cicada or cricket (depending upon the source consulted) after having been granted immortality but not eternal youth.

The cricket is viewed as a harbinger of death, especially when it abruptly leaves a home. In Shakespeare's *Macbeth* (act 2, sc. 2), it portends death: "I heard the owl scream and the crickets cry." In China it is a symbol of death and resurrection because it lays its eggs in the earth and, after passing through the stage of a larva, it apparently returns to the surface in the state in which it left. (Herder)

The cricket appears as the *Wise Old Man, advising the headstrong youth in Collodi's *The Adventures of Pinocchio* (1883), a popular children's tale. The cricket, described by Collodi as a "wise old philosopher," introduces himself to the marionette, Pinocchio, as the "Talking Cricket" who has resided in his current home for "more than one hundred years." When Pinocchio demands that he leave, the cricket replies that he won't leave until he has told Pinocchio "a great truth." Pinocchio agrees to listen, and the cricket tells him that boys who disobey their parents and run away from home always suffer great misfortune and come to regret their actions. In fact, the wise old cricket informs Pinocchio that, if he continues with his mischief, he'll grow up to be a donkey. After much arguing, Pinocchio throws a hammer at the cricket and believes him dead. As the story unfolds, the cricket's prophecies prove true. Pinocchio does turn into a donkey and suffers other misfortunes as a result of his bad behavior; however, he is repentant at the end of the story. He comes to respect and revere his elders, and is rewarded by being transformed into a "real boy." The cricket, not dead after all, reappears at the story's end to fulfill his function as the *Wise Old Man. He brings home the story's moral in the following: " . . . in this world of ours we must be kind and courteous to others, if we want to find kindness and courtesy in our own days of trouble." (Collodi)

crocodile: In Egypt, the crocodile, because it devours everything, is a symbol of the devouring nature of *time. It is commonly employed in ancient Egyptian headpieces as a symbol of *time. (de Vries)

The passage across the sky of the Egyptian sun god, *Ra, is marked by his transformation into a succession of animals identified as attributes of each passing hour. *Ra descends as a crocodile, thereby causing identification of the crocodile with the end of a *cycle. (von Franz, *Time*)

crone: The crone, a form of the *Triple Goddess (Virgin/Mother/Crone), appears as an *old woman in numerous myths and tales. The word "crone," which is one variation of the word *"crown," originally designated and represented the power of the tribal matriarch who wrote the first laws and punished the first transgressors, indicating a position of unquestionable power. (Walker, *Crone*, p. 14)

The *Triple Goddess was variously depicted as three-faced, three-headed (for example, Hebe-Hera-*Hecate of ancient Greece), or as three separate but related individuals who formed such complexes of images as the Roman Capitoline Triad (Juventas the Virgin, Juno the Mother, and *Minerva the Crone) or the Three *Fates of Classical mythology (Clotho the Virgin, Lachesis the Mother, and *Atropos the Crone). The crone, as the dealer of death (the goddess who cuts the *"thread of life"), was considered the most powerful of the *Triple Goddess's three manifestations.

The Huntress (Artemis in Greece and Troy, Diana in Rome, Astarte in Byblos, Aphrodite in Syria, Isis in Egypt) was originally associated with the crone aspect of the *Triple Goddess. Death was often portrayed as the huntress, as man's fate pursuing and hunting him down. (cf. Sati, the Huntress, in Egypt)

A product of matriarchal culture, the crone as one form of the Great Goddess resulted from a naturalistic world view which perceived all phenomena as inextricably linked to their opposite—birth to death, dawn to dusk, dark to light, etc. Consequently, she who gave life—the Great Goddess or Great Mother—also took it away. She was the original creator of the universe and each individual life, but she was also the crone—the destroyer who ended each individual life, and who would destroy the whole universe at doomsday (but would then create it again, initiating a new cycle of birth and death).

The Great Goddess in her form as Virgin/Mother/Crone or Creator/Preserver/Destroyer is viewed by some as a precursor of the Christian Trinity. (Walker, *Crone*) This *Triple Goddess form is found in India, Arabia, Egypt, the Middle East, and in the cultures of the Aegean and Mediterranean, as well as in the Celtic and Teutonic cultures of northern Europe. The goddess, through her power as the agent directing *cycles of birth and rebirth, was a powerful and pervasive force.

A product of matriarchal culture, the *Triple Goddess did not survive intact in later patriarchal civilization. The virgin and mother aspects of the complex were assimilated to Christianity, but the crone, as a threatening and powerful image of death, was rejected and repressed. Separated from the complex, she took satanic form, becoming wholly malevolent in the form of the *witch. Suppression of the crone, which took most overt form in witch hunts, is viewed by some as reflecting a general suppression and denial of death in patriarchal culture. Patriarchal culture, as compared to matriarchal culture which views life as *cyclic and thereby always inextricably intertwined with death, views life as a linear progression, its final ending (death) to be avoided at all costs. The crone as a figure whose physical form reflected the ravages of age and the inevitable decay of the body was a too potent reminder of the kind of aging and death that modern Western culture wished to repress: death as the result of slow degeneration and decline. Reduced to the *witch, she became wholly a force of evil to be suppressed and eliminated. (Walker, *Crone*) In contrast, in matriarchal culture the crone was the embodiment of wisdom. Menstrual blood in matriarchal culture was considered the blood of life, the life-giving force. When older women ceased menstruation, it was believed that this blood, named "wise blood," was retained within them, giving them power and wisdom, making older women the wisest of humans. (p. 49; Walker, WEMS, p. 642) The status of older women in pre-Christian European culture, in which they performed religious ceremonies, reflects this view. In the Middle East and Egypt, they performed religious rites, were doctors and midwives, and were scribes, keeping historical accounts, vital records and calendars for religious purposes.

Theodore Roethke's (1908-1963) poem "Meditations of an Old Woman" reflects a mixed view of the crone. In one passage she is viewed as a *hag, but in a following line she is a wise *old woman: "I need an old crone's knowing."

The crone figures prominently in numerous tales. In the Finnish epic, the *Kalevala*, she is *Louhi, the *crone of Pohja, who guards the Sampo, the world pole. Engaging in battles over its possession, she displays her powers of sorcery. *Morgan Le Fay, the sorceress of Arthurian legend, takes the form of the crone, as does *Medea of Classical mythology.

crossroads: The crossroads is traditionally a symbol of transition to a new phase of existence (birth or rebirth, one stage of life to another) and is viewed as a meeting place upon which otherworldly powers subtend (gods, spirits, the dead). (Herder) The crossroads relates to old age as a state of transition, as part of a continual process of change and choice and to the old person as a *pilgrim, encountering numerous crossroads on his or her *journey.

In Robert Frost's (1874-1963) "The Road not Taken," the crossroads is symbolic of a life decision which reflection in later life reveals as essential to the current conditions of that individual's life. It functions, thus, as a symbol expressive of the concept that awareness of the necessary conditions of one's past are essential to full adult development. This view finds expression in the psychologist Erik Erikson's concept of "integrative understanding." This cognitive style develops in the eighth and final stage of Erikson's developmental schema. He describes it as a form of wisdom resulting from the aged individual's choice of integrity over despair when faced with imminent death. The anxiety resulting from the prospect of one's own dissolution leads to despair; however, if this final stage of development is passed through, the aged individual realizes the "integrity of experience." Integrity wins out over despair and results in "the detached and yet active concern with life itself in the face of death itself." (Erikson, "Dr. Borg's Life Cycle," p. 23) In the process of life review, the aged person comes to accept that the conditions, events, and choices of their life "had to be and that, by necessity, permitted no substitution." (Erikson, *Insight and Responsibility*, p. 139)

crow: The crow is a symbol of longevity, since it is believed to live three times longer than a human. (It is referred to as "the treble-dated crow.") Hesiod asserted that it lived nine times as long as man. It is symbolic of the *hermit, since it lives a life of solitude and elevation above the common plane of existence. (de Vries) It is the divinatory bird of *Kronos, whose name means "crow." (Graves, GM II, p. 387)

crown: The crown is traditionally a symbol of union with God or the spiritual. Bodies buried with crowns symbolize union with God after death. In Christian symbolism, it is a symbol of closeness to god as a reward for having lived a good and virtuous life: "Much experience is the crown of old men, and the fear of God is their glory" (Ecclesiasticus 25:3-8), "Old age is a crown of dignity, when it is found in the ways of justice" (Proverbs 16:31). It functions similarly as symbolic of immortality won through virtue in Bunyan's *Pilgrim's Progress*:

> . . . be faithful unto Death, and
> my King will give a Crown of Life.
> (Bunyan, p. 370)

Christian martyrs are often portrayed wearing or carrying crowns. These symbolize their victory over death through closeness to God (immortality through having lived a virtuous life). (Pierce) Jung suggests that the crown's indication of closeness to God may be related to Parmenides' description of God as "'crown,' a circle consisting of glowing light, (which he calls stephane)." (Jung, ACU, p. 326)

The symbolism of the crown is related to the head and its functions, since it surmounts it. It is thereby a symbol of the transcendence of ordinary thought, of wisdom, insight, and elevated thought: "Wisdom crowns a man". (de Vries)

According to Barbara Walker, the crown (of which the word *"crone" is one variation) originally designated and represented the power of the tribal matriarch, who wrote the first laws and punished the first transgressors, indicating a position of unquestionable power. (Walker, *Crone*)

cuckoo: The cuckoo's call is connected with longevity. If its call is long, a long life is indicated; if its call is short a short life is foretold. (Herder)

The cuckoo's role as spring's messenger plays a part in a comical 19th-century English tale in William Clouston's *The Book of Noodles*. In this story, the Wise Men of Gotham attempt to cage the cuckoo to effect perpetual springtime. (Leach, p. 267)

curtain: A dropped curtain symbolizes death. A dropping curtain symbolizes old age, nearing death. Since the *stage is a common symbol for life (cf. Shakespeare's *As You Like It*), the lowering of the curtain on a *stage represents the end of the play of one's life, as seen in the following passage from Ernest Dowson's (1867-1900) "Dregs":

> With pale, indifferent eyes, we sit and wait
> For the dropped curtain and the closing gate:
> This is the end of all the songsman sings.

cycle: The cycle is symbolic of *time. Its graphic representation often takes the form of two signs or images facing opposite directions, as in the case of the last sign of the *zodiac, Pisces. Pisces, represented by two *fish swimming in opposite directions, forms the last constellation of stars forming the progression through the *zodiac before initiation of a new cycle. (Cirlot; de Vries)

A number of circular forms, such as the Buddhist *Round of Existence and the zodiac, express a cyclic view of existence. The Buddhist Round of Existence, or Wheel of Becoming, symbolizes the totality and cyclic nature of phenomenal existence. It is diagrammatic of all phases of life from birth to death, the outer *circle containing *twelve divisions in which are pictured the *twelve phases of man's life. Similarly, the *zodiac is divided into *twelve *houses which correspond to phases in an individual life, its entire circuit representing the totality of a human lifespan.

D

dakini: Hindu priestesses, usually elderly, the dakini (their name meaning "skywalker") comforted and cared for the dying. Their relationship to death and transition to the afterlife extended to responsibility for funerary rites and preparation of the dead for burial. (Walker, *WEMS*, p. 206)

During the Middle Ages, the Palace of Lotus Light in Urgyan, Pakistan, was a well-known place of pilgrimage. Nagas, giant, often malevolent *serpents which are believed to inhabit *springs and other sources where they store treasures, were thought to have originally populated the *lake at Urgyan. Converted to Buddhism by the bodhisattva, Vajrapani, they became dakas and dakinis (warlocks, and witches; or "skywalkers"). An account of the journey of the yogi, Urgyan-pa, to Urgyan and his encounter there with a dakini can be found in Tucci's *Tibetan Painted Scrolls* (Libreria dello Stato, Rome, 1949). (Tatz and Kent, pp. 148, 211, 219)

Darby and Joan: Darby and Joan, characters in a British ballad from 1735 by Henry Woodfall, became a stereotypical expression of the aged husband and wife who lead a close, contented life together. (Brewer)

Death (Tarot): The 13th enigma in the Tarot, Death, is another form of *Saturn, *Chronos, *Father Time and the Grim Reaper. He represents *time, *Fate, transition from one state to another (as in death), and mortality. He is typically represented as a skeleton in armor on a white horse who carries a *black banner with an image of a *rose on it. In the background, a *ship sails and a *sun rises or sets. (de Vries)

Death and the Maiden: "Death and the Maiden" is a traditional Germanic theme representing the conjunction of opposing principles—male and female, life and death—uniting seemingly irreconcilable elements. This conjunction, symbolic of the productive powers of nature made manifest through the reconciliation of opposites, forms one of the root metaphors of the northern Romantic tradition, reflecting that tradition's view of death as the source of vitality in nature and in human life as a part of nature. Aging, in this view, becomes not merely a process of greater and greater decay but also a process which generates its opposite, greater vitality. The youthful maiden is dependent upon death for the perception of value in her beauty. If such beauty and vitality were not in danger of diminishment through age, they would not possess as great a value.

In Hans Baldung's *Death and the Maiden* (1510-1511) in the Kunsthistorisches Museum, Vienna, the artist presents an image of the beautiful, young maiden admiring herself in a *mirror which is supported by an *old, decrepit woman who stands in the shadows. The maiden is partially wrapped in a cloth which traverses the picture from left to right, held on the left by an infant and on the right by Death, a decrepit figure resembling a skeleton. Death holds an *hourglass over the maiden's head, his upraised arm held in check by the *old woman.

Deluge: The Deluge is symbolic of the final stage of a *cycle. (Cirlot) The French painter Nicholas Poussin's (1594-1665) *Winter* or *The Deluge* has been viewed as an expression of that artist's experience of the last stage of his life, since he painted it between 1660 and 1664 between the ages of 66 and 69.

In the Manichaean hymn called *The Ship of God*, a description of doomsday shows the correlation between the dissolution of the world and the dissolution of the body through the aging process:

> Every hand, link, and shutter of the *prison (body) becomes weakened. All the comets quivered, and the stars were whirled about, and each of the planets turned awry in its course. The earth shook, my foundation beneath, and the height of the heavens sank down above. All the *rivers, the veins of my body, dried up at their source. All my limbs have connection no longer. . . . The reckoning of my days and months is ended. Harm befell the course of the *zodiac's *wheel. The seal of my feet and the joints of my toes--each link of the life of my soul was loosed. Each joint of my hands and of my fingers--each was loosed and its seal taken off. All the gristly parts--their life grew feeble. And cold became each one of my limbs. (Barnstone, p. 321)

Demeter: Mother Earth, goddess of fertility, Demeter is related to all things *cyclic. When her daughter, Persephone, was abducted by Hades, the god of the underworld, she traveled the countryside in search of her daughter as an old lady. Demeter is described on her search for Persephone in the Homeric Hymn to Aphrodite (101 ff.) as "like an ancient woman who is cut off from child-bearing and the gifts of garland-loving Aphrodite, like the nurses of king's children who deal justice." Called "old mother" by the young women at the Maiden Well where she stops to rest, she becomes a nurse (an occupation seen fit for an old woman) in the home of Celeus and Metaneira. In her disguise as an old lady she is possibly a manifestation of the *crone, the final stage of the *tripartite goddess manifested as Virgin/Mother/*Crone. (Graves, *GM* II, pp. 92-93)

Demogorgon: Represented as an *old, moss-covered man living underground, the Demogorgon is symbolic of the nutritive power of the soil and the sustenance of plant life. Often invoked in the practice of magic, he is viewed by some as related to Hades, the underworld of Classical mythology, and its ruler, Pluto. (de Vries)

The Demogorgon appears in Shelley's *Prometheus Unbound* (act 2, sc 3, 5-8) as the personification of Eternity:

> Hither the sound has borne us--to the realm
> Of Demogorgon, and the mighty portal,
> Like a volcano's meteor-breathing chasm,
> Whence the oracular vapour is hurled up
> Which lonely men drink wandering in their youth,
> And call truth, virtue, love, genius, or joy,
> That maddening wine of life, wose dregs they drain
> To deep intoxication . . .

He makes an appearance in Spenser's *Faerie Queene* (book 4, pt. 2, 477) as a demon who occupies a great abyss with three "Fatal Sisters" :

> Where Demogorgon . . . he hideous
> Chaos keepes, . . .

Dhritarashtra: Dhritarashtra is the aged *king of Vedic epics. (Cirlot)

Disir: A collective designation for the goddesses of fertility and destiny, the Disir are the form of the Three *Fates found in Germanic mythology. They are goddesses of destiny and fate, as well as of battle, as evidenced by the fact that in the *Edda* both the Valkyries and the *Norns are described as disir. (Lurker)

distaff: A cleft stick which holds the wool or flax for *spinning, the distaff is a symbol of time and the *Fates. (Cirlot) Associated with The Three *Fates of Classical mythology through the action of *weaving, it is specifically an attribute of Clotho the Virgin, who draws out the *thread of life. (de Vries) In turn, Lachesis measures the *thread and *Atropos cuts it. The *Fates were usually believed either to complete their *spinning at birth, determining the life cycle completely beforehand, or to continue to spin throughout the individual lie until the *thread had been used up and the distaff was empty, bringing the life to termination. Consequently, an empty distaff symbolizes the end of an individual life.

The distaff and spindle are seen in numerous images from the Middle Ages. *Decrepitas* (old age), personification of the fourth age of man in an Anglo Saxon manuscript from the early 12th century, a *Tractatus de quaternio*, spins with a distaff and *spindle. (Sears, pp. 23-24)

In Biblical terms, the distaff is an attribute of the "good wife": "She layeth her hands to the spindle, and her hands hold the distaff." (*Proverbs* 31:19)

Doctor: One of two stock old man characters from the commedia dell'arte (the other being *Pantaloon), the Doctor is portrayed as a fat old pedant. Similar to *Pantaloon, who believes himself worthy of high respect and special favor by virtue of his wealth, the Doctor believes himself worthy of such high regard as a wise elder possessing great wisdom. However, gross overestimation of his own mental faculties causes the Doctor to appear the *fool. His recurrent verbal and social blunders cause others to perceive him as, in fact, ignorant and cloddish. Like his friend, *Pantaloon, he is the object of much ridicule. (de Beauvoir)

The old "quack" doctor is a popular stereotype in tales of early Western and Midwestern America in the form of the "snake oil salesman." This character, usually aged, travels the country, usually on the run, selling hope in the form of worthless elixirs. Dorothy encounters such a "snake oil salesman" in *The Wizard of Oz*. This character later, in Dorothy's dream, becomes the wizard who similarly cons people.

We see a similar portrayal of the fraudulent old "doctor" in Gerrit Dou's *The Quack Doctor* (1652). In this painting the aged "doctor" sells his elixirs from a table and umbrella temporarily set up on a busy city street.

dog: In the *Ages of Man, the medieval artistic and literary convention which divides an individual life into *ten stages, a grown dog symbolizes a man of 70 to 80. In Germanic mythology, a dog accompanies the *Norns, who are equivalent to the Three *Fates in Greek mythology. (de Vries)

dogwood: (or cornel) The dogwood is related to the Classical myth of the blind seer, *Tiresias, whose dogwood *staff enabled him to walk like a person with sight. (cf. Apollodorus 3,6,7; de Vries) It is also related to *Saturn, the Roman god closely related to old age and decrepitude, as explained by Graves: "Its Latin name *cornus* comes from *cornix*, the crow sacred to Saturn." (Graves, *WG*, p. 172)

door: The door represents transition from one state of being to another. The Roman god of transitions and changes, *Janus, was the god of Death's door. In the Biblical Apocrypha, the door is "the place of wisdom": "He that awaketh early to seek her, shall not labour: for he shall find her sitting at his door." (Wisdom of Solomon 6:14)

In "A Winter's Tale," Dylan Thomas (1914-1953) uses the complex image of a "dark door" as symbolic of the past, death, sex, and perception. (de Vries) The symbolic meaning of the door is similar to that of the *gate and *bridge. (Herder)

dragon: "Dragon" is derived from the Greek word *derkein* ("seeing"), reflecting perception of the dragon as endowed with exceptional sight. As a result of this belief, the dragon became symbolic of prophecy and wisdom.

The dragon is a variation of the *ouroboros; consequently, it is a symbol of time and *cyclic movement. It is often found in *alchemical texts in ouroboric form (cf. "Symbolic Representation of the Alchemical Work" from the alchemical manuscript, MS. 428, in the Vatican Library, St. Gallen; Burckhardt, Plate 5, p. 128). The dragon is a symbol of wisdom because it possesses chthonic wisdom as guardian of underground riches. (de Vries)

The dragon corresponds to the *twelfth in the *cycle of *twelve years of the Chinese calendar; hence it symbolizes totality, completion. (Herder)

dregs: Ernest Dowson (1867-1900) in his poem "Dregs" employs dregs, that which remains after the "golden wine" is consumed, as symbolic of old age:

> The golden wine is drunk, the dregs remain,
> Bitter as wormwood and as salt as pain.

dust: Dust is a symbol of the transitory nature of human life, of disintegration, dissolution, and death, as expressed by the well-known words of the Christian prayer of interment, "earth to earth, ashes to ashes, dust to dust." (de Vries; Herder) Shakespeare similarly employs ashes as a symbol of the transitory in *Cymbeline* (act 4, sc. 2):

> Golden lads and girls all must
> As chimney-sweepers come to dust.

Dylan Thomas (1914-1953) uses dust as a symbol of death and rebirth: "that to which we return: re-creation, or universal renewal."

E

---

eagle: The eagle is a symbol of longevity, as seen in the following passage from Shakespeare's *Timon of Athens* (act 4, sc. 3): "These moist trees, That have outlived the eagle."

Elders of the Apocalypse: The iconography of the Middle Ages includes a depiction of old age in the image of the 24 Elders of the Apocalypse. They are believed a representation of time as the 24 old men who correspond, in Babylonian culture, to the *zodiac's 24 signs and the day's 24 hours. Dressed in white robes and wearing *gold *crowns, they surround Christ in depictions of the Biblical Apocalypse. (de Beauvoir)

Eleazar: The martyrdom of the aged Biblical character Eleazar serves as a parable of Christian piety and virtue in old age. The story of Eleazar's martyrdom is told in 4 Maccabees 5:1-7:23. The tyrant Antiochus was executing Hebrews who refused to eat pork and sacrificial food. Eleazar, described as "a man of priestly family, learned in the law, advanced in age, and known to many in the tyrant's court because of his philosophy" (4 Maccabees 5:4), was brought before the king for failure to comply. Antiochus, out of respect for Eleazar's age and reputation, advised him to eat the pork rather than face execution. Eleazar refused and took the opportunity to publicly espouse his philosophy of self-control and obedience to the law. Saying that a benevolent God established the law, he viewed transgression of it as irreverent and ungrateful, and vowed that he would never break it: "I am not so old and cowardly as not to be young in reason on behalf of piety. Therefore get your torture wheels ready and fan the fire more vehemently! I do not so pity my old age as to break the ancestral law by my own act." (4 Maccabees 5: 31-33)

Eleazar is subsequently tortured, but still refuses to break the law. He thus becomes an example of the triumph of reason over emotion and of a pious man who, though advanced in years, "became young again in spirit through reason." (4 Maccabees 7:13-14)

elf: The elf or dwarf is a form of the *Wise Old Man, a Jungian archetype. In Scandinavian folklore, elves are often described as aged in appearance. (Porteous)

Of the two types of elves found in folk tales and legends, light elves and dark elves, the light elf, also called Liosalfar, symbolizes old age. It is described as "agelessly old."

Danish legend speaks of the Elle-folk, who are believed the offspring of Adam and Lilith. They inhabit mounds or alder (*elle*) trees. The males are described as aged in appearance and are often found sunbathing. They lure maidens into their company. The females, described as beautiful creatures who dance the "Elle-dance" by moonlight, attract youth with their music and dance. The results of such seduction are fatal. (MacCulloch, pp. 224-225)

Elli: In the northern European tale of the journey of Thor (god of strength and of thunder) and Loki (the Trickster) to Utgard, Thor's strength and power, usually unchallengeable, are overcome by several figures, including Elli. The victors over Thor and his companions are Logi (Fire) "which consumes all things more swiftly than any man or god," Hugi (Thought), "swifter than any man in its flight," and Elli (Old Age), "who can overcome the strongest." (Davidson, GMNE, pp. 33-34)

elm: The elm is a common symbol of longevity. (de Vries)
In Classical mythology, the elm grows in the nderworld. It is described as the seat of ghosts in Virgil's *Aeneid* (6, 282-284):

> And in the midst an aged elm immense
> And dark, and like huge arms its branches spread,
> The chosen seat, 'twas said, of hosts of Dreams . . .

embers: Embers are a symbol of old age as the last vestige of the *fire of life (de Vries), as in Thomas Campion's (1567-1620) "Though You are Young":

> Though you are young and I am old,
> Though your veins hot, and my blood cold,
> Though youth is moist, and age is dry;
> Yet embers live, when flames do die.

In Guariento's depiction of the *ages of life from the Church of the Eremitani in Padua, the elderly figures of a man and woman flanking *Saturn (the planet and Roman god corresponding to old age) attempt to warm themselves over the embers of dying fires. (Sears, Plate 48)

Emma: Emma (or Yama-raja) is a Japanese god of the underworld similar to Pluto of Classical mythology. The Buddhist belief in transmigration of souls has engendered numerous myths of the journeys of the soul. In one tale, the soul encounters a stream, Sansu-no-Kawa ("River of Three Routes"), which forks in three directions. The soul is unable to decide which fork to take: that leading to the hells, that leading to the "beast life," or that leading to the land of "hungry ghosts." After examination by various judges along the way, the soul finally encounters Emma (Yama-raja), who exacts final judgment and determines the soul's subsequent course. Emma appears as an aged, malevolent character in numerous depictions similar to Western representation of the Biblical Last Judgment. (Anesaki, p. 238, Plate XIV)

Erinyes: The Erinyes, the "daughters of the night" from Classical mythology, were the precursors of the *Eumenides. These avenging goddesses who emerge from the underworld to pursue sinners, but especially to pursue those responsible for the deaths of their own family members, sprang from the drops of blood spilled on the earth when *Kronos mutilated his father. Portrayed with *snake-covered heads and carrying *torches, there were three of them: *Alecto ("she who is unremitting"); Tisiphone ("she who avenges murder"); and Megaira ("she who is envious"). (Lurker, p. 112) Graves says the Erinyes are older, even, than Zeus. He describes them as "crones, with snakes for hair, dogs' heads, coal-black bodies, bats' wings, and blood-shot eyes. In their hands they carry brass-studded scourges, and their victims die in torment." (Graves, GM I, p. 122) Later versions of the Erinyes took a somewhat less demonic form as the *Eumenides ("the well-disposed") or the Semnai ("the venerable ones"). The Furiae ("the mad ones") or the *Furies were the Roman version of the Erinyes.

The aged horseman, Phoenix, in Homer's *Iliad* 9, 454-457, describes how his father invokes the Erinyes when Phoenix dishonors him. He says his father "cursed me mightily and invoked the dire Erinyes that never should there sit upon his knees a dear child begotten of me; and the gods fulfilled his curse."

In Greek mythology, the Erinyes pursue and torment Orestes, who murders his mother, Clytaemnestra. In *Les Remords d'Oreste* (1862), the French painter Bougereau portrays both Orestes' murder of Clytaemnestra and the subsequent pursuit of the murderer by the avenging Erinyes.

Es: Es is the sky god of the Ket people of Siberia. Although he is invisible, he is personified as an aged man with a black beard. Creator of the world, he shaped the first humans from clay. Lurker further describes him: "whatever he threw with his right hand towards the left became a man, and what he threw with his left hand towards the right became a woman." (Lurker, p. 113)

Eumenides: The Eumenides were a later version of the Erinyes, the avenging deities of Classical mythology. They punished those who violated the respect which should be accorded elders and the aged. Their name meaning "the kind ones," they were called "the dread Eumenides three" in Virgil's *Aeneid* (6, 250). (Graves, GM II, p. 391) Other variations of the Eumenides are the *Furies and the Semnai.

In Euripides' drama *Orestes* (408 B.C.), Orestes is pursued and tormented by the Eumenides after killing his mother. In Aeschylus' trilogy, the *Oresteia* (458 B.C.), consisting of *Agamemnon*, *The Libation Bearers*, and *Eumenides*, the Eumenides also appear as avenging dieties.

evening: Since the evening is the end of the *cycle of the day and is the time when *light (symbolic of life) fades, it is symbolic of old age as the end of a *cycle. (de Vries) Moses describes old age as evening in Psalm 90:

> Thou dost sweep men away; they are
>   like a dream
>   like grass which is renewed in the
>   morning:
> in the morning it flourishes and is
>   renewed;
>   in the evening it fades and
>   withers.

A painting by the British artist, Hubert Von Herkomer *Eventide--A Scene in the Westminster Union* (1878), shows a group of aged women in a London workhouse. They are gathered around a table sewing, performing the menial labor by which they must earn their keep. The faces of the old seamstresses, in the foreground of a scene which is otherwise dimly lit, appear illuminated by an unknown source. In the background, two aged figures, leaning on one another for support, occupy the end of a deep, tunnel-like space. They are silhouetted against a window through which evening *light filters. (Rosenblum and Janson, p. 368, figure 290)

F

fairy: In the European Middle Ages, "fairy" became synonymous with *Fate, reflecting the Fairy Godmother's origin in the Three *Fates, who were believed attendant at every child's birth. (Walker, *Crone*, p. 99) Lurker explains the origin of the word "fairy": "The word 'fairy' comes via Old French *feie, fee* from Latin *fatua* = (female) seer, and *fatum* = fate, destiny." (Lurker, p. 116) This origin reflects the fairy's connection to the Three *Fates who were believed to determine the fate, or individual destiny, of each individual.

Shelley presents the fairy, Queen Mab, as a wise *crone:

I am the fairy Mab: to me 'tis given
The wonders of the human world to keep:
The secrets of the immeasurable past.
          (Shelley, "Queen Mab," 167-169)

Fates: The Three Fates, symbolic of the lifespan of an individual, represent a concept of life as directed by some hidden force which is immune to the efforts of both gods and mortals to affect its course. The word "fate" is derived from the Latin *fatum*, meaning "something spoken, a prophetic declaration, an oracle, a divine determination." (Eliade, ER, vol. 2, pp. 290-297) As Kees W. Bolle explains in the following, representations of fate seem to remain fairly consistent throughout the history of cultures: "More conspicuously than in the case of other symbolisms, individuals do not make up novel ideas concerning fate. Instead, old ideas dominant in a culture come to the surface from time to time. They may appear new and striking, yet on closer scrutiny they are rather like irrepressible sounds made when old strings vibrate anew." (Kees W. Bolle in Eliade, ER, vol. 2, p. 297)

The original Greek conception of fate took the form of Moera, derived from the word *moera* meaning "lot," a term from older matriarchal culture used to designate the landholding of a female owner. Later personified and split into a threefold representation, Fate took the form of the *Moirai, their collective name reflecting their function as the dispensers of men's allotted portions in life. Lachesis, meaning "apportioner of lots," the name of one of the three representations, further reinforces this concept. (Tripp, p. 246) The split of Fate into a threefold representation has caused some to regard her as a manifestation of the Triple Goddess. Clotho, often represented as the youngest, is believed to correspond to the Virgin, Lachesis to the Mother, and *Atropos, often represented as an *old woman, is believed to be another form of the *Crone.

In Classical mythology, the Fates were represented as all-powerful, directing even the fate of the gods. Both Homer and Virgil present an image of Zeus as *executor* rather than determiner of destiny, holding and reading the scales in which the lots of heroes are weighed, indicating their fates. (Grant and Hazel)

In Roman culture, the *Moirai became the *Parcae, which means "those who bring forth the child." (Grant and Hazel, p. 175) They were believed attendant at the birth of every child, determining that individual's fate. Numerous customs resulted from the belief in their presence at the birth of a child. In one such custom, three *knives were placed on the table at night in the home of a newborn, an action intended to appease the Fates and to discourage them from using their own *knives, from cutting the child's *"thread of life." (Walker, *Crone*, p. 99)

The Fates as *spinners and cutters of the *thread of life became a common personification. Sometimes depicted as three *old women and sometimes as sisters of three ages (Virgin, Mother, and *Crone), Clotho drew out the thread, Lachesis measured it, and *Atropos cut it off. The Fates were usually believed to either complete their *spinning at birth, determining the life *cycle completely beforehand, or to continue to *spin throughout the individual life until the *thread had been used up and the *distaff was empty, bringing the life to termination. In the *Odyssey*, the *spinning is depicted as occurring at two times in a life: at birth and at marriage (*Odyssey*, 4, 207). In a similar image of *spinning from the *Odyssey*, the gods *spin the "great realities—death, trouble, riches, homecoming" as a *thread around a man, his body like a spindle. (*Odyssey*, 7, 197)

In the Middle Ages, "Fate" became synonymous with *"fairy," forming the source of the Fates' later representation as the "fairy godmother" who is attendant at a child's birth and oversees that individual's later destiny. Also known as the *Weird Sisters, the Fates were honored at the beginning of each year in the Middle Ages. Food, drink, and three *knives were put out as offerings and appeasement. This practice was greatly opposed by the Church, as evidenced by the Bishop of Exeter's 12th-century excoriation of such practices. However, such practices persisted in "fringe" groups, as Barbara

Walker indicates: "Gypsies never ceased to lay three pieces of bread on a baby's bed, 'one for each Goddess of Fate.'" (*Crone*, p. 99)

*Atropos, portrayed as the eldest of the Three Fates, became the prototype for the *witch or *crone. The designation of *witches as fays or *fairies is evidence of this connection, as Barbara Walker explains: " . . . the terms for *fairies and *witches were interchangeable, and both were called fays, fates, or *fatidae*, ... " (*Crone*, p. 103) Rather than perceiving her in her original conception as the expression of a necessary element in the natural process of birth, growth, decay, and rebirth, as one aspect of a repeated *cycle, the *crone became a personification of the modern Western concept of old age and death as wholly undesirable, to be avoided at all costs.

T. S. Eliot refers to the ancient concept of the pattern of one's life as determined by Fate as akin to the perception necessary to achievement of the state of mind wherein one reaches closure, a state of grace. He says that we discover the "kind of pattern which we perceive in our own lives at rare moments of inattention and detachment, drowsing in sunlight. It is the pattern drawn by what the ancient world called Fate; subtilized by Christianity into mazes of delicate theology; and reduced again by the modern world into crudities of psychological or economic necessity." (Woodward, *at last*, p. 194)

In Ralph Waldo Emerson's *"Merlin" (1847), we see an image of the Fates as *weavers of man's destiny:

> Subtle rhymes, with ruin rife,
> Murmur in the house of life,
> Sung by the Sisters as they spin;
> In perfect time and measure they
> Build and unbuild our echoing clay.

In Shakespeare's *Midsummer Night's Dream*, the Three Fates appear in the form of the three fairies Peaseblossom, Cobweb, and Mustard-seed.

Fate personified as three women, a form common to Indo-Germanic cultures, occurs under the following names (Lurker):

*Disir	--	Germanic	*Moirai	--	Greek
*Fairies	--	European	*Norns	--	Germanic
*Fatit	--	Albanian	*Parcae	--	Roman
*Gul-Ses	--	Hittite	*Urme	--	Polish,
*Laimos	--	Lithuanian			Russian, Serbian

Father Time: In Renaissance and Baroque art, Father Time is *winged and nude. His common attributes include the *scythe or *sickle, an *hourglass, an *ouroboros (*snake or *dragon biting its own tail), the *zodiac, and crutches (cf. *The Triumph of Time* from Petrarch, by Gregorio de Gregori, 1508).

Classical and late antique representations present two images which are later merged to form the image of Father Time which predominates from the Renaissance onwards. The first of these images is Time as Kairos: "the brief, decisive moment, which marks a turning-point in the life of human beings or in the development of the universe." (Panofsky, p. 71) This was personified by Opportunity, depicted as a male nude, usually young, with *wings on his shoulders and heels. Early depictions include the attribute of scales balanced on the edge of a shaving knife, and later versions include one or two *wheels. He is often depicted with a forelock, by which one "seizes opportunity." After the 11th century, Kairos merged with images of *Fortuna.

The second image is that of *Aion, the Iranian concept of Time: "the divine principle of eternal and inexhaustible creativeness." Images of *Aion are either Mithraic, in which case they consist of a *winged figure with the head and *claws of a *lion, its body entwined by a *snake holding a *key, or they depict the Orphic divinity Phanes, who is portrayed as a handsome young man wrapped in a *snake's coils and surrounded by the *zodiac. We find no images of decay or decrepitude in these images of time, as opposed to later images of Father Time.

The introduction of later specific attributes of Father Time—the *sickle or *scythe and the *hourglass—resulted from the confusion of *Chronos (the Greek expression of Time) and the Roman god *Saturn. *Saturn, as the god of agriculture, was depicted carrying a *sickle. As the eldest of the Greek and Roman pantheon, he was always depicted as aged and was associated with the planet which was the slowest-moving, *Saturn. Original features of *Saturn were reinterpreted and augmented in the 4th and 5th centuries A.D. so as to make his image more reflective of concepts of time. He was given the *ouroboros (the *serpent or *dragon biting its own tail) as an attribute, his *sickle (originally related to agriculture) was reinterpreted as an attribute of Father Time as the Grim Reaper (death), and the myth of *Saturn devouring his own children became an expression of the devouring nature of time.

Father Time operates both as a destroyer and a revealer of the continuity of natural *cycles, creation and destruction alternating in a never-ending cycle. Time as destroyer became associated with Death, becoming Death's assistant, providing him with victims. This association is reflected in the fact that in the late 15th century, Death acquires Father Time's characteristic *hourglass. Time as revealer is reflected in numerous allegorical themes as "Truth revealed or rescued by Time," "Virtue vindicated by Time," "Innocence justified by Time," etc. (cf. *Time Unveiling Truth*, a painting by Jean Detroy, 1732)

The Renaissance conception of Time as both destroyer and revealer is explained by Panofsky: "Only by destroying spurious values can Time fulfill the office of unveiling Truth. Only as a principle of alteration can he reveal his truly universal power." (pp. 82 and 93)

Fatit: The Fatit are the Albanian version of the Three *Fates. They come to the child's cradle on the third day after birth to determine the child's destiny. Also called *miren* (derived from the Greek *Moirai), they are depicted as riding on butterflies. (Lurker)

Faust: The old scholar, Faust, symbolizes the desire to transcend the material world and to obtain absolute knowledge. Faust, depicted as an ugly, bearded, wealthy *old man (cf. Rembrandt's etching of 1652, *Dr. Faustus in His Study*), represents the archetype of the *alchemist, one who wishes through his own manipulation to transcend the limitations of the material world and achieve immortality; he is, thus, a symbol of the desire to transcend old age and death. (de Vries)

According to Lisolette Dieckmann, author of *Goethe's Faust: A Critical Reading*, "The fundamental purpose of *Faust* is to represent, in a work of art, man's place within the confines of life on this earth, more specifically biological and physical life." (p. 7) She says, further, that *Faust* constitutes "a relentless effort to explore man's potential and limitations within the natural laws to which he is subjected." She views the neo-Platonic myth of the soul's entrance into the body, endurance of the hardship of physical existence, and subsequent welcome release from the burden of material existence in a return to the source "from whence it came," as central to the story. (p. 19) This principle is expressed symbolically in images of constant motion, change, and metamorphosis such as *water, butterflies, and *cicadas.

Goethe's Faust sells his soul to the devil in return for renewed youth and 24 additional years of life. The scholar's thirst for knowledge, as well as the *old man's desire for youth, causes Faust to lose his soul. The young scholar's excitement at the discovery of new insights and deeper knowledge has died in the aged Faust. He sells his soul to Mephistopheles in the hope that the restored youth he receives in return will not only rejuvenate his aged body, but will also restore his enthusiasm for scholarship. (de Beauvoir)

Carl Jung regards Faust as a form of the archetype of the *Wise Old Man, "the helper and redeemer, but also the . . . magician, deceiver, corruptor and tempter." (Jung, *The Spirit*, pp. 103-104)

fire: In Chinese culture, fire is used as a measure of time (as in incense *clocks), as opposed to Western cultures, which have traditionally based their time measuring devices on the flow of *water. (Von Franz, *Time*)

Fire is often viewed as a purifying and renewing element through its power to destroy. (Herder) T. S. Eliot employs fire as a restorative symbol in "Little Gidding" (1943): "restored by that refining fire." (Woodward MSM) In "Do Not Go Gentle Into That Good Night," Dylan Thomas (1914-1953) employs fire as symbolic of the life force which need not necessarily diminish with age: "Old age should burn and rave at close of day."

fire, wheel of: The wheel of fire symbolizes the decline of the *sun, the solar hero, and by analogy the individual in old age. In ancient Celtic rites, a wheel of fire was rolled downhill at midsummer, an action symbolic of the lowering course of the *sun at that time of *year. (de Vries)

In Shakespeare's *King Lear*, the aged *king describes himself as bound to a *wheel of fire (act 4, sc. 7):

> I am bound upon a wheel of fire, that mine own tears
> Do scald like molten lead.

The wheel of fire to which Lear describes himself as being bound indicates his role as a solar hero in decline. Like the burning *wheel, the aged king is nearing the horizon, nearing death. He is bound to an endlessly turning *wheel representative of material existence, his earthbound state further amplified by the description of his tears as molten *lead (*lead being symbolic of the physical limitation of material existence, especially in old age). The burning of the *wheel can be viewed as an expression of *Lear's desire and attachment to the material, as contrasted to his daughter Cordelia, who is described as "a soul in bliss."

fish: The fish is a symbol of wisdom, especially in the form of the *salmon, which guards the *Tree of Life and Knowledge. The fish sometimes takes the form of the mystic *"Ship of Life," which is a symbol of *cyclic existence. (de Vries)

Fisher King: The Fisher King is the aged, infirm *king of Arthurian legend whose health and fertility (and, because he is *king, the health and fertility of his country, as well) can be restored only by the Grail-knight. The Fisher King, because he has been wounded, must pass his time *fishing, while the young Grail knight, through asking "the" question, attempts rejuvenation of the *king and his kingdom. (de Vries; Weston)

In T. S. Eliot's *The Wasteland*, the author employs a more contemporary form of the legend of the Fisher King in which there appears no answer.

fishing: Fishing symbolizes the pursuit of wisdom and exploration of the unconscious. Through its association with *water, fishing is related to the representation of all things *cyclic. (de Vries) Fishing is related to old age through the Fisher King of Arthurian legend, the aged, infirm monarch whose health and fertility can be restored only by the young Grail knight.

In Ernest Hemingway's *Old Man and the Sea* (1952), the aged fisherman's pursuit of his catch is representative of the endless struggle of human existence, a struggle that does not diminish with age.

flame: The flame is a symbol of wisdom and the life force. In East Indian culture the flaming *circle is a symbol of *Prakriti, "that which evolves, produces, brings forth." (Cooper, p. 37) It is a symbol of purification and the purity of the soul which passes through the impure material world.

In imagery of old age, the flame represents the *fire of the individual which burns less intensely through long duration. Shakespeare employs the flame as a symbol of the life force which lacks fuel in old age:

"Let me not live," quoth he,
"After my flame lacks oil."
                    (*All's Well that Ends Well*, act 1, sc. 2, 58-59)

The *oil of the *lamp, like another of Shakespeare's metaphors, the *sap in a *tree or vine, symbolizes the "radicall humor," the substance which was believed by the Elizabethans to course through the body, giving it life. (Hankins)

flower: The flower is a traditional symbol of the transitory nature of life, the soul, and the *cyclical nature of life, as expressed in Shelley's "Mutability":

The flower that smiles to-day
    To-morrow dies;
All that we wish to stay
    Tempts and then flies.

Since it is valued by virtue of its transitory quality, the flower represents the concept that death is necessary for life to have value. (cf. Peter Beagle's "Come Lady Death")

fool: Shakespeare repeatedly refers to the aged *King Lear as a fool by virtue of having aged, calling him "the natural fool of fortune" (act 4, sc. 6, 195), and by making reference to fools and foolishness in the following passages from *King Lear*:

Old fools are babes again.
                    (act 1, sc. 3, 19)

This cold night will turn us all to fools and madmen.
                    (act 3, sc. 4, 81)

Lear: "I am a very foolish fond old man. . . . I am
old and foolish."
                    (act 4, sc. 7, 60, 84)

*Lear calls life a *"stage of fools," reflecting the view expressed elsewhere in Shakespeare's work that humans are fools moving about on a *stage for the amusement of the immortals in heaven. They lack the wisdom that the higher powers possess; consequently, those higher powers find amusement in the humans' folly. Hotspur, on the verge of death in *1 Henry IV* (act 5, sc. 4, 81), further expresses this Shakespearean view: "But thought's the slave of life, and life time's fool." (Hankins)

footman: Death is the "Eternal Footman" seen by the aging narrator of T. S. Eliot's "The Lovesong of J. Alfred Prufrock" (1915): "I have seen the eternal Footman hold my coat, and snicker."

Fortuna: Fortuna, known as Fata Scribunda, "the Fate Who Writes," was originally the Roman goddess of women. (Walker, *Crone*, p. 99) Later in Roman culture, she became the goddess of good fortune (her name came from the Latin word *fors*, meaning "luck"), and was portrayed with the attributes of rudder, cornucopia, and *globe. The cult of Fortuna was widely popular in Hellenistic culture. Fortuna was revived in the Renaissance accompanied by the *Wheel of Fortune or *Wheel of Life as emblematic of the *cyclic nature of luck, and her role in directing the course of the *wheel was emblematic of belief in her as the power that determined the course of events. (Lurker) Eliade sums up her symbolic meaning: "The epithets for Fortuna in popular use all amount to a transparent allegorical naming of the mysterious power that determines the course of nature and history." (Eliade, ER, vol. 2, p. 294)

In book 2 of *Consolation of Philosophy* from the 6th century, Boethius describes Fortuna as a two-faced, *blind, deaf woman who is fickle and unpredictable in dispensation of both good and bad fortune. Turning a *wheel on the rim of which a man is bound, she proclaims: "this is my nature, this is my continual game: turning my wheel swiftly I delight to bring low what is on high, to raise high what is down."

Artists' personifications of Fortune often show her blindfolded, turning the crank of a *wheel to which four men (usually four—sometimes more) cling, one ascending, one sitting atop, one descending, and one lying beneath the wheel. The figure at the top usually is portrayed as a *king wearing a *crown, and some depictions bear the successive inscriptions "I shall rule, I rule, I have ruled, I am without rule." Figures on the *Wheel of Fortune are not normally differentiated by age, the inference being that an individual ascends and descends numerous times throughout the course of a life (cf. "Wheel of Fortune" from MS. of John Lydgate's *Troy Book and Story of Thebes*, England, ca. 1455-1462). (von Franz, *Time*, Plate 13) Only later, when the *Wheel of Fortune takes a variant form in the *Wheel of Life, do we see depictions of successive *ages of man. (Sears)

fortune-teller: The aged are often portrayed in folk literature as possessing unusual foresight and/or occult powers, hence the common image of the old fortune-teller. In Gaspare Traverse's painting *The Fortune-Teller* (1760), an aged woman reads a delighted young woman's palm, while an old man peers over the fortune-teller's shoulder.

fountain: The fountain symbolizes the life force which is immune to the process of aging (Cirlot), as seen in William Wordsworth's poem "The Fountain" (1800):

> In silence Matthew lay, and eyed
> The spring beneath the tree;
> And thus the dear old Man replied,
> The grey-haired man of glee:

> "No check, no stay, this Streamlet fears;
> How merrily it goes!
> 'Twill murmur on a thousand years,
> And flow as now it flows."

Dylan Thomas employs the fountain as symbolic of the life force, which time depletes and feeds upon, in "The Force that through the Green Fuse Drives the Flower": "The lips of time leech to the fountainhead."

In Jungian interpretation, the fountain represents the soul as the symbol of the center and source of inner life and energy, the need for which arises when the person's life is "inhibited and dried up," as in old age. (Cirlot) Since it springs from the underworld, it is a symbol of death and rebirth. It is also a symbol of wisdom and truth.

fountain of youth: The fountain of youth was a popular artistic theme in 15th century Europe. The myth of a fountain of youth propagated by these images was so strong that, according to de Beauvoir, it prompted Ponce de Leon's 1512 expedition to Florida. Lucas Cranach the Younger's *A Fountain of Youth*, a painting of 1546, shows a large *pool to which aged, helpless women are being carried. They enter old and infirm on the left, and emerge young and rejuvenated on the right. (de Beauvoir)

four: The number four is related to aging through the system of thought which divides the human lifespan into *four ages, corresponding to the four directions, the four elements, and the four *seasons. Four corresponds to the planet *Saturn, the "time-keeper", the planet related to old age. (de Vries)

four ages of man: The tetradic division of the human lifespan reflects a view of the individual as a microcosm of the macrocosm, the human body correspondingly possessing *four directions and the lifespan possessing *four *seasons. Cosmograms consisting of a *circle divided into four quadrants with a human at the center reflect this view. The best examples of these, though they existed in antiquity, come from the Middle Ages. A crypt in the cathedral at Anagni holds one such tetradic diagram. A lone figure appears at the core of a circle at the intersection of a cross marking the four quadrants. Each quadrant bears a bust of a man of one of the four ages. (Sears, Plate 5)

The division of the human lifespan into four ages and the position of the individual as a model of the universe is reflected in *Plaint of Nature* by the 12th-century poet Alan of Lille. Drawing a parallel between the *four seasons of nature and the four *seasons of human life, he described old age: "And when his day sinks to the West and old age gives notice of life's evening, the Winter's cold forces man's head to turn white with the hoarfrost of old age." (Sears, p. 37)

Philippe de Novarre's *Des IV tenz d'age l'ome* in Paris' Bibliothéque Nationale consists of a series of manuscript illustrations of the four ages. The figure personifying the fourth age is an aged man who walks with the aid of crutches. (Sears, Plates 35-38)

The four phases of humankind's collective development listed in Ovid's *Metamorphoses* (1, 89-150) can be seen as analogous to human development on the individual level from what has often been perceived as a spiritual to a more material state (*Golden, *Silver, Bronze, Iron Ages). These progress, or regress (depending upon one's viewpoint), from the purest to the most malleable, and thereby the most corruptible, state. Hindu belief divides humankind's collective development into four stages, as well. They call these four ages *yugas*. As the world progresses (or regresses) through the four yugas, which are comparable to the Greek *Gold, *Silver, Bronze, and Iron Ages, people become more and more unhappy and warlike. (Walker, *Crone*, p. 150)

In the Hindu text *Laws of Manu*, the Hindu sage Manu divides individual life into four proper stages, as follows:

1. Studenthood.
2. Householder (marriage, family and career; the period of "social responsibility").
3. *Hermit (a period of liberation from practical concerns and worldly pleasures in early old age).
4. Ascetic (late old age).

During the final stage of this schema, that of the ascetic, the attentions should be properly restricted to the regimen and discipline of daily existence. This disengagement from the wider social sphere, successfully achieved, results in "'true insight into the nature of the world' (see section 74 of Manu's text) and achievement of the inner happiness and fulfillment that is appropriate in the final stages of life." (McKee, PF, pp. 4-5)

In Lakota (Native American) belief, an individual life is comprised of four "generations": childhood, adolescence, adulthood, and old age. Each of these generations possesses a corresponding soul. Upon death, one of the individual's four souls "travels along the Wanagi Tacanku ('spirit path,' i.e., the Milky Way) southward, where it meets with an old woman who adjudicates its earthly virtues, directing it either to the spirit world, a hazy analog of earthly life where there is an unending supply of buffalo and where people rejoin their kin, or back to earth where they live as ghosts to haunt others and entice the living to join them." (Eliade, ER, pp. 435-436)

Frankenstein: David Luke suggests that Mary Shelley's *Frankenstein* (1818) is "a diminished parable of the supposed horrors of old age, a parable of the old man as monster." The monster is described by Shelley as stemming from Dr. Frankenstein's desire to "examine the case and progress of decay" and to "renew life where death had apparently devoted the body to corruption." (D. Luke, pp. 221-240) Compared to a "hideous mummy" with "yellow skin" and "shrivelled complexion," Luke points out that the Frankenstein monster "seems to have been born old." Luke says, further, "He seems to represent, as it were, the quintessential birth of the Romantic old man. And he also seems representative of his Romantic age in that his most remarkable narrative feature is the fact that, in the words of one commentator, he 'is more human than his creator.'"

frost: Frost is a symbol of the process of aging which leaves the "frost of age" (*graying) on *hair. An example is Okura's "An Elegy on the Impermanence of Human Life," in which the poet describes "ample tresses" as turning "white with the frost of age." (Lyell)

Another example, contrasting the heat of youth with the frost of age, comes from Walter Savage Landor's (1775-1864) "To Age":

He who hath braved Youth's dizzy heat
Dreads not the frost of Age.

Fukuro Kuju: The name of the Japanese god of good luck, Fukuro Kuju, means "luck, riches, long life." (Lurker, p. 122) Commonly portrayed as an *old man with a very short body and a contrastingly large head with an absurdly long cranium, he is accompanied by common Japanese symbols of longevity, the *crane and the *tortoise. The variety of luck which he represents is characterized by a combination of wisdom and longevity.

Fukuro Kuju is one of the *seven gods that make up the *"Seven Gods of Happiness" (*Shichi-fukujin). Usually portrayed in a comical fashion, these *seven gods are often shown together on a *boat, the "Treasure Ship"

(Takarabune). Fukuro Kuju pilots the *boat, which is filled to overflowing with precious objects. Pictures of this group of gods are often hung in commercial establishments in Japan, particularly around New Year's, to serve as good luck charms. (Grimal, *Larousse World Mythology*)

In an ink drawing/painting on paper by Hakuin Ekaku (1685-1769), Fukuro Kuju appears as the lone occupant of the treasure *boat. The written character *kotobuki* ("long life") forms the *boat which carries *four objects serving as symbols of good fortune: a raincoat; a straw hat which affords invisibility from those who seek to part one from one's money (tax collectors and thieves); a mallet; and a treasure sack. The work's inscription reads: "Those who are loyal to their lord and filial to their elders will be presented with this raincoat, hat, mallet, and bag."

Furies: The Furies are the Roman version of the *Erinyes of Classical mythology. Like the *Erinyes, these avenging deities would rise from the underworld to pursue and torment those responsible for the deaths of members of their own families. Their allegiance to elders is expressed in the following from the *Iliad* (15, 203-204): "You know the Furies, how they forever side with the elder."

Graves says the three Furies, *Alecto ("she who is unremitting"), Tisiphone ("she who avenges murder"), and Megaira ("she who is envious") "are older than Zeus or any of the other Olympians." He describes them further as *"crones, with *snakes for *hair, *dogs' heads, coal-black bodies, *bats' wings, and bloodshot eyes. In their hands, they carry brass-studded scourges, and their victims die in torment." (Graves, GM I, p. 122)

G

---

gate: The closing gate (because the gate is a symbol of the passage between life and death, as in "Heaven's Gate") symbolizes old age, nearing death. (de Vries) Ernest Dowson (1867-1900) uses the closing gate as a symbol of old age in "Dregs":

> With pale, indifferent eyes, we sit and wait
> For the dropped curtain and the closing gate:
> This is the end of all the songs man sings.

Geras: In Greek mythology, Geras is the personification of old age. Typically portrayed as an emaciated, nude, weaponless figure with thinning *hair and wrinkles, he is most commonly found on figure vases in battle with Heracles (Hercules). His characteristic attribute is a thick, knotted *stick. Though he is always portrayed as advanced in years, he is nonetheless represented as remarkably agile. It is speculated that the fight between Hercules and Geras represents Hercules as the god of healing triumphing over disease (represented by Geras). Geras is always portrayed as malevolent. However, he is sometimes gruesome and monstrous, and thus threatening, while, at other times, he is pitifully ugly and enfeebled.

In a vase painting in the Louvre by the Greek artist dubbed the "Old Age Painter," Geras is depicted as a shriveled, hunched *old man leaning on a cane. He is swarfed by his opponent, Hercules, who holds him at arm's length, preparing to strike him with his club. (Richardson, Figure 1)

Geras' name and our term "gerontology" both derive from *gera* or *geron*, a word which was used by the Greeks to refer specifically to the aged among them who were deemed worthy of honor. It referred to "the privileges of age, the rights of seniority, representative position." (Stahmer, in Spicker, et al., p. 33) This demonstrates the fact that the Greeks did not automatically bestow honor and respect upon the elderly; rather, they bestowed honor and respect upon those aged who had, as they perceived it, earned such dignified status.

ghost: The ghost is often employed as a poetic symbol of lost youth, of the former self as recollected by an aged person. In "A Shadow Boat" Arlo Bates describes the ghost of his past as "some gracious shape of my lost youth."

In "The Little Ghosts" Thomas S. Jones, Jr. refers to such specters of one's past as "the little ghosts of long ago," and in "Dregs" Ernest Dowson presents such ghosts as images of others: "This was a mistress, this, perhaps, a friend." In "Meditations of an Old Woman," Theodore Roethke (1908-1963) describes a playful spirit, a voice which enters the narrator's sleep as "A ghost from the soul's house."

girdle: In "Troia Fruit," Reginald Wright Kauffman (1877-1959) describes the limitations of old age as "A girdle 'round the narrow sphere" of his existence.

Glaukos: Glaukos was a Greek sea god who possessed the gift of prophecy. (cf. Ovid's *Metamorphoses*, book 13) Sometimes referred to as the *"Old Man of the Sea," he was believed to have once been a fisherman who was transformed into a god after eating a magic herb and jumping into the sea. (Lurker)

globe: As a form of the *circle, the globe shares in the symbolism of the *circle, representing perfection, wholeness, and all things *cyclic. It represents the completion of a *year's *cycle as well as the completion of the *cycle of an individual life as in old age. In Neoplatonic philosophy, the soul is represented as a *sphere. The soul's substance is deposited as "quintessence" around the *four elements, which lie in concentric *spheres beneath it. In Plato's *Timaeus*, primordial man is described similarly. (Cirlot)

The globe is an attribute of *Fortuna, the Roman goddess who determines human fate. *Fortuna's Greek forerunner, Tyche, juggles a *ball, the course of which, sometimes up and sometimes down, is indicative of individual fate. (Graves, GM I)

goat: In astrological symbolism, the goat corresponds to Capricorn, the sign of the *zodiac under which the *winter solstice occurs. Because of its correspondence to the solstice, Capricorn is located at the point of (and, thus, through association, is representative of) the soul's entry and exit from the *"wheel of birth." (de Vries, p. 81)

When the zodiacal system of *twelve houses is viewed as corresponding to *twelve ages in the human life *cycle, Capricorn, the sign of the goat, corresponds to the tenth age, or the first stage of the fourth age (the first house of the fourth quadrant). It thus corresponds to early old age. Capricorn,

derived from the Latin *caper* ("goat") and *cornu* ("horn"), corresponds to
*Saturn, the planet related to the restriction and decrepitude of old age.

gold: Gold is a symbol of wisdom as an elusive, concealed treasure which,
when discovered, is in perfect and complete form. In *alchemy, it is the end
product of the *alchemical process of transformation to a higher, purer state,
the Ultimate Wisdom. (de Vries)

In "Rabbi Ben Ezra" by Robert Browning (1812-1889), gold symbolizes
Ultimate Wisdom ("I shall know, being old"):

> Youth ended, I shall try
> My gain or loss thereby;
> Leave the fire ashes, what survives is gold:
> And I shall weigh the same,
> Give life its praise or blame:
> Young, all lay in dispute; I shall know, being old.

Gold is symbolic of divine *light, reflected in the similarity of the Latin word
for gold (*aurum*) and the Hebrew word for *light (*aor*). (Cirlot)

goose. In the *Ages of Man, the medieval literary and artistic convention
which divides an individual's life into *ten stages, a goose is a woman of 50 to
60. The goose is a symbol of the earth mother, maternity, fertility, creative
energy, and the "good housewife." An *old woman plucking a goose is
sometimes employed as a metaphor for *snow (e.g., Mother Carey). The
goose was regarded as the *witch's steed in the Middle Ages. (de Vries)

Robert Frost (1874-1963) in "Lines Written in Dejection on the Eve of
Great Success" speaks of being older: "we are goosier now."

Graiae: Their name literally meaning "the gray ones," the Graiae of Classical
mythology are the personification of age. Born with *gray *hair and with only
one eye and one tooth among the three of them, they are the sisters of the
Gorgons and the children of Phorcys and Ceto. (cf. Ovid's *Metamorphoses*,
book 4) Their names, Enyo ("warlike"), Pemphredo ("wasp"), and Deino
("terrible"), reflect their role as a manifestation of the Triple Goddess in her
capacity as destroyer. Their description as *"swan-like" is further evidence of
their malevolent character, since the *swan symbolizes death in European
mythology. (Graves, GM I, p. 129)

The Graiae figured prominently in the Classical myth of Perseus, since
only they knew where the Stygian nymphs lived. Perseus needed to know the
whereabouts of the nymphs, since they possessed the winged sandals, magic
wallet, and helmet of invisibility which he needed to slay Medusa. Perseus
surprised the Graiae while seated on their thrones at the foot of Mt. Olympus,
stole their eye and tooth, and demanded to be told where the nymphs resided

in return for the eye (the Graiae's only source of vision) and tooth. The Graiae complied; Perseus returned their eye and tooth and continued his quest. (Graves; Stapleton)

The Graiae appear as the Three Gray Women, "three very strange old ladies" who "have but one eye among them, and only one tooth," in Nathaniel Hawthorne's "The Gorgon's Head." In this tale, which is one of the stories making up his retelling of Classical mythology in *A Wonder Book for Girls and Boys* (1851), Hawthorne retells the story of Perseus. He gives the three old ladies the names Nightmare, Scarecrow, and Shakejoint. They are humorous characters who quibble incessantly over possession of the eye which they must share. They nearly fool Perseus into believing they cannot help him find the nymphs by playing old and helpless. However, at Quicksilver's insistence, Perseus perseveres in his questioning of them, and they do finally tell him where to find the nymphs. He returns the eye, and they resume their incessant quarreling. Hawthorne draws the following humorous moral from this incident: "As a general rule, I would advise all people, whether sisters or brothers, old or young, who chance to have but one eye amongst them, to cultivate forbearance, and not all insist upon peeping through it at once." (Hawthorne, pp. 34-37)

grasshopper: In the Bible, the grasshopper, since it drags itself dramatically in a state of exhaustion when it is close to death, is a symbol of weakness and decline in old age: "the grasshopper shall be a burden and desire shall fail; because man goes to his long home." (Ecclesiastes 12:5) The grasshopper in Ecclesiastes is interpreted, further, in the *New Oxford Annotated Bible* as a "figure for the stiff-legged gait of the aged." (May and Metzger, p. 814)

Some versions of the Classical myth of *Tithonus state that he was turned into a grasshopper rather than a *cicada. (de Vries)

gray: Gray hair is a symbol not only of age itself, but of certain perceived attendant qualities, such as wisdom and retrospection. In Judeo-Christian terms, gray hair is tacit evidence of goodness and virtue, since old age is a reward for these qualities: "Grey hair is a crown of glory, and it is won by a virtuous life." (Proverbs 16:31)

Shelley presents contrasting images of those old and gray. In one poem, "The Daemon of the World," he presents the graying character as undeformed by "avarice, cunning, pride, or care."

How vigorous now the athletic form of age!
How clear its open and unwrinkled brow!
Where neither avarice, cunning, pride, or care,
Had stamped the seal of grey deformity
On all the mingling lineaments of time!
        (Shelley, "The Daemon of the World": part 2, 186-190)

In "Queen Mab," on the other hand, he presents an image of "hoary-headed hypocrites":

> Then grave and hoary-headed hypocrites,
> Without a hope, a passion, or a love,
> Who, through a life of luxury and lies,
> Have crept by flattery to the seats of power,
> Support the system whence their honours
>   flow. . . .
>
>   (Shelley, "Queen Mab," 203-207)

Gul-Ses: Their name meaning "scribes" or "determiners of fate," the Gul-Ses are the Hittite version of the Three *Fates. (Lurker)

H

---

hag: Now a pejorative term through its connection to *witchcraft, "hag" was formerly a word designating a wise woman. Its former meaning, "a holy one," was derived from the Greek word *hagia*, the root word of hagiolatry (the worship of saints). (Walker, *Crone*, p. 53)

In the Middle Ages "hag" meant the same as *"fairy," designating a woman who practiced *"fairy religion" (*witchcraft). The *witches in Shakespeare's *Macbeth* are an example: "How now, you secret, black, and midnight hags." (*Macbeth*, act 4, scene 1) (see CRONE)

hair: *Father Time is characterized by distinctive hair, possessing either one long forelock, called the "Lock of Horus," or a single hair on an otherwise bald head. Francis Quarles' etching *Emblem* from 1639 shows *Father Time with his characteristic forelock. (von Franz, *Time*, Plate 28)

A widow's peak on a woman is believed to indicate a long life and, concomitantly, that she will live to be a widow. (de Vries)

harvest: The time of harvest is representative of old age, of optimum ripeness or maturity immediately preceding death. (de Vries) John Keats (1795-1821) presents such an image of ripeness in old age in "Ode to Autumn." We see another example in Shelley's (1792-1822) "Queen Mab":

Youth springs, age moulders . . .
They rise, they fall; one generation comes
Yielding its harvest to destruction's scythe.

Harvest is the time of the death of the grain spirit which, in many rituals, takes the form of either an old man or an old woman. (de Vries)

hawk: In Egypt, the hawk is a symbol of immortality and longevity. W. B. Yeats (1865-1939), in "At Hawk's Well," employs the hawk as a symbol related to old age and immortality. In this poem, the *well of immortality (Hawk's Well) is guarded by the hawk-woman who entices Cuchulain (a Celtic hero) away from the *well with her seductive dance. In contrast, the *old man in the poem waits for the *well to rise, hoping thereby to gain immortality. But he waits in vain, because each time it does rise he is asleep. (de Vries)

hearth: In ancient Greek homes, the hearth, which formed the center of life in the household, was always *circular. It, like the *sun which provides the source of warmth and nourishment for the solar system, formed the focal point for the activity of, and provided the warmth and nourishment for, the household. The hearth also traditionally represents the inner center of life and being in an individual, which is often represented as a *circle or *globe (for example, the soul in Neoplatonic philosophy is represented as a sphere). By extension, a waning hearth *fire represents the waning of energy in old age (cf. "The Revolt of Mother," by Mary Wilkins Freeman).

*Hestia, whose name means "hearth," is the Greek goddess who never leaves the interior of the home. Entrusted with the perpetuation of the vitality of the household, as well as of the wider culture, her primary task is to keep the hearth fire burning. *Vesta is Hestia's Roman counterpart.

The ancient Chinese believed that their Hearth Goddess, a beautiful, aged woman dressed in red, inspired and dispensed knowledge to female elders. These elders, in turn, used this knowledge as the source of innovation in *alchemy, medicine, nutrition, and culinary arts. (Walker, *Crone*)

The Tungus, natives of the northern Asiatic region, express the close tie between the *old woman as clan ancestress and guardian of the hearth and home. Their hearth spirit takes the form of a very *old woman who, despite her years, possesses great vitality, strength and cleverness. According to Abramova, a representation of this goddess is found in the home of every Tungus.

Hecate: Hecate, as the *crone, is a form of the *Triple Goddess (Virgin/-Mother/Crone) in her aspect as destroyer. As an indication of this role, she possesses three heads (*lion, *dog, and mare) which preside over birth, life, and death or past, present, and future. (Cirlot) She is sometimes represented as a female trinity: "Selene, the Moon, ruler of heaven; Artemis or Diana, the Huntress, ruler of earth; and Persephone, the Destroyer, ruler of the underworld." (Walker, *Crone*, p. 116)

The name of one of the oldest goddesses of Egypt, Heqit or Hekat, derived from the root word *heq* ("intelligence"), also signifying a pre-dynastic tribal ruler. *Hekau* ("words of power") came from her, determining all things, all creation, and all destruction. Hekat, or Heqit, was regarded by the ancient Egyptians as the carrier of female wisdom. As such, she knew all of the secrets of nature. Thus we see in her early Egyptian representation all of the qualities of the *crone as wise *old woman.

In Greek culture, Hecate was goddess of both life and death. In the *Theogeny*, Hesiod portrays Hecate as a threefold goddess associated with the earth, the sea, and the heavens. In Ovid's *Metamorphoses* (7, 159 ff.), the *sorceress *Medea invokes the aid of Hecate in restoring Jason's aged father, *Aeson, to youth. *Medea calls Hecate "the three-formed goddess." Hecate was sometimes regarded as the daughter of *Demeter; and, as a fertility goddess, she was linked with *Demeter in ritual. Hecate, the goddess of both life (fertility) and death (goddess of the soul in the underworld), was associated with the passage from the world of the living to the world of the dead. She was, in fact, the goddess of all dangerous transitions—life to death, childbirth, and so on. Consequently, her three-faced image stood at *crossroads and on *thresholds. On moonless nights, she was believed to accompany baying *dogs and the spirits of those who were murdered, were not ready to die, or were buried inappropriately. To the Greeks, she came to represent all of the potentially fearsome aspects of femininity.

As the patroness of *sorceresses, Hecate became linked with *witchcraft. In later Christian culture, she was Queen of the *Witches. Becoming solely identified with her *crone aspect, Hecate formed the prototype of the *witch. She was subsequently portrayed as an ugly, *witchlike *old woman, who was believed to cause lunacy. We see her in this role, as queen of the *witches, in Shakespeare's *Macbeth*.

Hecate, as the *crone, is goddess of the *moon in its negative aspect. The three faces portrayed in her depiction as Hecate Triformis corresponded to the three major phases of the *moon, the waxing *moon being her maiden aspect, the full *moon her mother aspect, and the waning *moon her *crone aspect. (Eliade, ER, vol. 6; Walker, *Crone*)

hermit: The hermit represents disengagement from life, yielding wisdom. He is often portrayed in picturesque fashion in Victorian literature, as in George William Russell's "The Hermit," and in William Wordsworth's (1770-1850) "Descriptive Sketches":

> But once I pierced the mazes of a wood
> In which a cabin undeserted stood;
> There an old man an olden measure scanned
> On a rude viol touched with withered hand.
> As lambs or fawns in April clustering lie
> Under a hoary oak's thin canopy,
> Stretched at his feet, with steadfast upward eye
> His children's children listened to the sound;
> --A Hermit with his family around!

The hermit's isolation from ordinary life often indicates his renunciation of the material world for the spiritual, as in the case of St. *Jerome. We see such an image of disengagement from material existence and immersion in the spiritual in Goethe's *Faust. The mountainous region to which angels carry *Faust's "immortal part" is populated by hermits residing in huts scattered at various heights. They symbolize, according to Thomas Davidson, "the various states of the soul after it has cast off the bonds of selfishness and partiality and begun to live with the life of the universe." (p. 147) Thus the hermit is here a symbol of disengagement from material existence and immersion in the spiritual. Davidson says, "They are examples of men who, unlike Faust, have discovered the secret of life before that last moment, and are now acting as a sort of medium between earth and heaven, apparently conscious of the life of both."

Iconography of the Middle Ages includes many images of hermits and anchorites, usually portrayed as very old, very thin men with long beards. (de Beauvoir) John Milton (1608-1674) presents an image of the old hermit in "Il Penseroso":

And may at last my weary age
Find out the peaceful hermitage
The Hairy Gown and Mossy Cell
Where I may sit and rightly spell
Of every star that Heaven doth shew,
And every Herb that sips the dew;
Till old experience do attain
To something like prophetic strain.

In *The Hermit (Il Solitario)* (1908), the American painter John Singer Sargent presents an image of disengagement. His aged hermit, lying barely clothed on the forest floor, appears literally to blend into his surroundings, withdrawing from the world of men into that of nature.

Hermit (Tarot): The Hermit figures prominently in the Tarot. He is depicted as an aged man with a *gray beard wearing a large *cloak. The *cloak figures symbolically in his depiction, its dark outside representing the material world and his detachment from it, and its blue inside representing heaven. He carries a *staff which takes various forms, sometimes straight, sometimes wavy, and sometimes entwined with *serpents. He carries a six-sided *lantern made of clay, symbolic of the feeble light of earthly knowledge, in his other hand. Some depictions show mountains, symbolic of elevation from the common earthly plane, in the background.

The Hermit signifies tradition, study, reserve, patient and profound work, the Eternal *Pilgrim, the Absolute Search, Absolute Wisdom, and Knowing the Way. His wisdom is reflected in the belief that, if he finds a *serpent (symbolic of instinct in this case) in his path, he doesn't attempt to destroy it, but rather charms it, coaxing it into twining around his *staff. (Cirlot) Other names of the Hermit are "Sage" and "Capuchin." (de Vries)

Hestia: Hestia, whose name literally means *"hearth," is the Greek goddess of the *hearth and home. (Graves, GM II, p. 395) As keeper of the homefire, she is associated with the traditional values of home, family, nurturance, and the continuity of generations. The following passage from the "Homeric Hymn to Hestia" alludes not only to her role as keeper of the home, but also to the high esteem in which she was held:

> Hestia,
> you who have received the highest honor,
> to have your seat forever
> in the enormous houses of all the gods
> and all the men who walk on the earth,

The traditional *circular *hearth and her attribute, the *hoop, link Hestia to the symbolism of the *circle--a symbol of completion, perfection, and eternity.
    Hestia is associated with aging in her function as the goddess entrusted with the perpetuation of tradition, the collective identity of her culture, and its continuity in succeeding generations. She is also associated with aging in her role as the archetypal *Old Maid. Pomeroy explains the necessity of Hestia's virginity to her role as perpetuator of collective identity: "Since a virgin belongs to no man, she can incarnate the collective, the city: she can belong to everyone." (p. 210) Hestia's Roman counterpart is *Vesta.

hind: The pursuit of the hind symbolizes the pursuit of wisdom and the search for immortality. A notable example is contained in the Classical myth of Hercules, whose pursuit of a hind led him to the *Hyperboreans, a group of people who lived in a land of perpetual springtime. These people enjoyed a life span of up to a thousand years. (de Vries; Zimmerman)

holly oak: The holly oak is a symbol of longevity in Pliny's *Natural History*, since some members of this species of tree found in Rome predated the city. (de Vries)
    The holly oak is the source of the golden bough which Aeneas carries into the underworld. The sibyl who accompanies Aeneas tells him that he cannot enter Hades without the golden bough, which must be offered to Persephone. (Wilstach)

hoop: As an attribute of *Hestia, the hoop shares in her symbolism as the propagator and keeper of traditional values and the continuity of generations.

As a form of the *circle, it functions similarly as a symbol of wholeness, and completion of a *cycle (as in old age).

The hoop is also related to magic and sorcery. In Shakespeare's The Tempest, the old *witch *Sycorax "with age and envy was grown into a hoop." Here Shakespeare employs the hoop as not only a symbol related to *witchcraft, but also as a form representative of the physical degeneration of old age. (Draper, "Shakespeare's Attitude...")

Horagalles: Horagalles was a Lapp god called "the *old man" to whom reindeer were sacrificed. Portrayed carrying two hammers, he was derived from the Old Norse god of thunder, Thor. (Lurker)

hourglass: The hourglass is a symbol of death and the passage of time. (Herder) The *sands flowing through the hourglass represent the incessant passage of time and the brevity of life. (Pierce) The hourglass became an attribute of *Father Time during the Middle Ages, serving as a reminder that, since life was short, one must proceed in performance of good deeds without delay. (Panofsky)

Because the hourglass must be reversed periodically, it represents the end and the beginning of *cycles, or alternating opposites. In its double meaning, it represents both the renewal of time, as in the beginning of a day, and *night (the inversion of day). Its aspect as a symbol of *night is found in the sailor's term for it: "nightglass." (de Vries)

The hourglass is a symbol of old age in Anne Bradstreet's (1612-1672) "Of the Four Ages of Man":

> Leaning upon his staff comes up Old Age:
> Under his arm a sheaf of wheat he bore,
> A harvest of the best, what needs he more?
> In's other hand a glass ev'n almost run,
> This writ about: "This out, then I am done."

In Pompeo Girolamo Batoni's painting, *Time Orders Old Age to Destroy Beauty* (1780), *Time appears as an old, bearded man with *wings holding an hourglass. He directs an *old woman to destroy the beauty of the allegorical figure of a young woman representing Truth. The *old woman reaches out to touch the face of the young one. (McKee and Kauppinen)

The Pre-Raphaelite painter Evelyn de Morgan presents an image of aging and the passage of time in *The Hour Glass* (1904-1905). The subject of the painting is Jane Morris, who, as a young woman, served as the model for numerous Pre-Raphaelite paintings. In de Morgan's piece, Jane is shown in her later years. She reaches out to turn an hourglass which sits upon a table, the base of which bears an image of a *sphinx. A figure allegorical of Eternal Life stands in a doorway behind her, and figures in medieval dress fill the tapestries on the wall behind her throne-like chair. The artist says of the work, "the seated woman is thinking only of the *Sands of Life running out in the Hour Glass at her side. The figures in the tapestry behind her are symbolic of the past joys of life." (Marsh, p. 132)

house: The house symbolizes the propagation and protection of the accumulated knowledge and tradition of a culture and of tradition as a form of wisdom (as in the case of *Hestia, the Greek goddess of *hearth and home). The house is also a symbol of the human body as the dwellingplace of the individual soul, the outside of the house representing the individual persona or mask which changes with time, as opposed to the inside which contains the eternal soul. (Cirlot)

In Ecclesiastes 12:3-4 we are presented with an allegory of old age, an old, ruined house serving as the symbol of the decrepit, aged body: "in the day when the keepers of the house tremble, and the strong men are bent, and the grinders cease because they are few, and those that look through the windows are dimmed, and the doors on the street are shut; when the sound of the grinding is low, and one rises up at the voice of a bird, and all the daughters of song are brought low."

In *The New Scofield Reference Bible*, the author explains one interpretation of this passage as a description of the aged body: "'The keepers of the house' may be likened to the hands; 'the strong men,' the teeth; 'those that look out of the windows,' the eyes; 'the doors,' the ears; 'the sound of the grinding,' the hum of conversation in the household." (Scofield, pp. 703-704)

T. S. Eliot employs the old house as a symbol of old age in *Four Quartets* (1943). Eliot uses the old house in "Gerontian," as well. In the following passage from this poem the narrator speaks of his aged body: "My house is a decayed house. . . . "

Both Samuel Taylor Coleridge (1772-1834) and Edmund Waller (1606-1687) employ the house as a symbol of old age:

This breathing house not built with hands,
This body that does me grievous wrong,
      (Coleridge, "Youth and Age")

The soul's dark cottage, battered and decayed,
Lets in new light through chinks that Time has made:
Stronger by weakness, wiser, men become
As they draw near to their eternal home.
Leaving the old, both worlds at once they view
That stand upon the threshold of the new.
      (Waller, "Of the Last Verses in the Book")

Huldra: Scandinavian folklore tells of a form of Wood Wife, the Huldra. She seemed to have a dual nature, since, by some accounts, she would sometimes appear as a beautiful young woman and at other times as an ugly old *crone. By other accounts, her dual nature consisted of a beautiful young body in front and a hollow and decrepit form behind. Often encountered in the forests singing a sad tune, she characteristically wore *gray and carried a milk pail. She could also be identifed by the tail which she took great pains to conceal. (Porteous)

Hyperboreans: The Hyperboreans of Classical mythology (cf. Aelian: *Varia Historia* 3, 18) symbolize the self-annihilative aspect of the desire for eternal youth. When *Silenus, Dionysus' aged companion, is captured by King *Midas' men and brought before *Midas, he entertains the king with a story about the land of the Hyperboreans "where splendid cities abound, peopled by gigantic, happy, and long-lived inhabitants, and enjoying a remarkable legal system." In this land are two streams which flow by a *whirlpool. Fruit on the *trees flanking the banks of the first stream cause "those who eat it to weep and groan and pine away." (Graves, GM I, p. 281) Fruit from the *trees on the banks of the other stream restore youth, causing those who eat it to go backwards in time until they disappear.

I

ivory: Ivory is a symbol of the positive value of aging, since it grows more beautiful and valuable with age. Karle Wilson Baker, in her poem "Let Me Grow Lovely," asks that she "grow lovely, growing old" as does ivory. (Lyell)

J

January: January is the old knight in Chaucer's *Canterbury Tales* (1387-1394) who uses his wealth to acquire a beautiful, young wife, May. However, he is cuckolded and made to appear an absurd old fool. (de Beauvoir)

Janus: The Roman god Janus is described by Virgil as "two-ways faced" (*Aeneid* 7, 182). He symbolizes wisdom as the product of both hindsight and foresight, since he sees both ways at once, perceiving both the future and the past. He is, further, a representation of wholeness through the joining of opposites. (de Vries)

Janus' name is identical to the name for the principal *door in a Roman house (*ianua*). There is uncertainty as to whether he was named after the *door or the *door was named after him; at any rate, Janus' name reflects his role as the *door god who presides over all states of transition. (Stapleton)

St. Jerome: St. Jerome, one of the four Latin Fathers of the Church, lived as a *hermit in the Holy Land. He settled in Bethlehem, where he translated the Bible until his death at the age of 80. A symbol of disengagement, he is often represented as a solitary aged scholar with a beard, at work in his study translating or holding a Bible in one hand. (cf. Reymerswaele's *St. Jerome in His Study*, 1541) Other depictions show him as an ascetic in the wilderness or with a *lion from whose paw he removed a thorn, thereby taming the animal. (cf. Lucas Cranach's woodcut, *St. Jerome*, 1509) He often wears a crimson cardinal's hat. (Pierce)

Jesse, Tree of: The Tree of Jesse, a popular visual art theme in the Middle Ages, symbolized the genealogy of Christ from David's father, Jesse. (Dahmus) It is described in Isaiah 11:1-2:

There shall come forth a shoot
    from the stump of Jesse,
and a branch shall grow out of his
    roots.
And the spirit of the LORD shall
    rest upon him,
the spirit of wisdom and
    understanding

This image consists of an *old man sleeping on the ground from whose navel a *tree grows. Each branch of the *tree holds a half-open *flower bearing the name of one of the ancestors of Christ. The figure of Mary holding the Christ child typically sits at the top of the *tree. (de Vries) A stained glass window in Chartres cathedral (12th-century French) bears a representation of the Tree of Jesse. In this image, Jesse lies at the bottom, the *tree of his descendants grows from his middle, and Jesus occupies the top.

journey: The journey typically represents *cyclic movement through space or time. It is a quest for self-knowledge through experience of the physical world. The *labyrinth is a vehicle for the archetypal Quest for the Center, a ritually expressed *journey into the dark, into the unconscious, and subsequent reemergence in a renewed, revitalized state. The *pilgrim's travel to the Holy Land is an expression of the archetypal *journey. (Cirlot; de Vries)

Jurojin: Jurojin, "Old Man of Long Life," is the Japanese god of longevity. (Lurker) Depicted riding a deer, he is surrounded by *cranes and *tortoises, symbols of longevity and contented old age. (cf. watercolor of Jurojin with a *stag in the Victoria and Albert Museum; in Pigott, pp. 112-113)

Jurojin is one of the seven gods that make up the "Seven Gods of Happiness" (*Shichi-fukujin). Usually portrayed in comical fashion, these *seven gods are often shown on a *boat, the "Treasure Ship" (Takarabune), which is filled to overflowing with precious objects. Pictures of this group of gods are often hung in commercial establishments in Japan, particularly around New Year's, to serve as good luck charms. (Grimal, *Larousse World Mythology*)

As explained by Pigott, Jurojin is often portrayed as a scholar: "He has a white beard and generally carries a shaku, a sacred staff or baton on to which is fastened a scroll containing the wisdom of the world." (cf. ink on paper *kakemono*, Museum für Völkerkund, Vienna, *Jurojin*; in Pigott, p. 105)

K

Kala: Kala is the personification of time as a "cosmogonic force" in India. He was both his own father and his own son. After 500 B.C., Yama, the god of death, is sometimes called Kala. (Lurker)

Kali: The East Indian goddess Kali takes the *crone as one of her forms. Because she represents both the dark void existing beyond the bounds of our universe and the darkness of the "unknown" existing before birth and after death, she is represented as *black and naked. Just as *black absorbs all colors, it is believed that she, at the "end of time," will absorb or devour all that exists on the temporal plane. (Walker, *Crone*, pp. 82-83)

kettle: The kettle, as a form of the *cauldron, symbolizes revitalization and restoration of lost youth. (see CAULDRON, MEDEA)

key: Keys are an attribute of *Saint Peter, who is one of the Christian saints associated with aging. He holds two keys, often crossed. The Key of Heaven, which is made of *gold, opens the gate to heaven. The Key of Earth, made of iron, closes the gate:

> . . . you are Peter, and on this rock I will build my church, and the powers of death shall not prevail against it. I will give you the keys of the kingdom of heaven, and whatever you loose on earth shall be loosed in heaven. (Matthew 16:18-19)

Keys are also an attribute of the old *crone, *Hecate, as the guardian of Hades; and they are a symbol of *Janus, who opens the *door of the sky. (de Vries)

Nicolaes Maes' painting, *An Old Woman Saying Grace* (1655), shows a solitary *old woman giving thanks for a simple meal. The shelf beside her table holds an *hourglass, a bell, and a *book. A pair of keys hang from the wall, possibly symbolic of the *old woman's nearness to "Heaven's *Gate" by virtue of advanced age.

king: The aged king represents the past, the collective consciousness of a culture and, in Jungian terms, the collective unconscious. Cirlot says the aged king (such as *Dhritarashtra of Vedic epics and Shakespeare's *King Lear) "is symbolic of the world-memory, or the collective unconscious in its widest and most all-embracing sense." (p. 168)

In depictions of the *Wheel of Life, popular in the Middle Ages, men are depicted at various stages of life, ascending and descending around the rim of a *wheel. The figure at the top of the *wheel, that representing midlife, is often depicted as a king wearing a *crown. (Sears)

King Lear: King Lear, the aged hero of the Shakespearean tragedy of the same name, experiences all of the indignities to which the aged are typically portrayed as subject: loss of social status, loss of property, loss of familial support, loss of mental faculties. However, he embodies not only the indignity of *old* age, but the limitations of the human condition at *all* ages. Through Lear, the experience of old age is presented as simply a magnification or dramatization of the general human state. In his madness and sense of betrayal, he serves as a truly tragic hero. The pessimistic view of life which Shakespeare presents in the character of Lear is similar to that exhibited in *Macbeth* when the title character describes his life's story as "a tale told by an idiot, full of sound and fury, signifying nothing." (act 5, sc. 5) (de Beauvoir)

De Beauvoir describes *King Lear* as an ancient legend with its source in Anglo-Saxon folklore: "Shakespeare took it from a chronicle play called *Leir* that was performed in 1594. He borrowed the parallel plot of Gloucester and his two sons from the story of the King of Paphlagonia in Sidney's *Arcadia*." (p. 165) Though the story's roots are much older, according to de Beauvoir, Lear's madness and old age combine to present a view of aging particular to the Middle Ages. In the Middle Ages, the insane were often believed closer to the divine than normal individuals and possessed of a certain degree of prophetic ability. Since the very old were often viewed as insane, they partook of this seemingly contradictory combination of insanity and divine intelligence, as well. Thus, Lear, in his role as both sage and lunatic, typifies this view.

In "The Witch of Atlas," Shelley (1792-1822) describes an aged character's dishevelment and foolish pride in terms of Lear:

> he, proud as dandy with his stays,
> Has hung upon his wiry limbs a dress

Like King Lear's "looped and windowed
raggedness."

Lear has served as the source for aged characters in numerous examples
from Western culture since Shakespeare's creation. He has served as the
subject, in modified form, for the work of two contemporary filmmakers. The
Japanese writer/director, Akira Kurosawa, based his film <u>Ran</u> on the story of
King Lear. In his version, the *king has three sons rather than daughters, and
the story takes place in feudal Japan. The Australian film *Traveling North* uses
King Lear as a primary source, as well.

King of the Forest: The King of the Forest from the Russian folktale, "The
False and True Nightingale," is, according to Jung, a "vegetation or *tree
numen who reigns in the woods and . . . also has connections with *water,
which clearly shows his relation to the unconscious since the latter is
frequently expressed through *wood and *water symbols." He is described in
the tale as "all wrinkled . . . and a green beard hung down to his knees."
(Jung, *Archetypes*, p. 222) He lived in a green hut in which everything was
green (all the objects, wife, children, food, etc.).

knives, three: Three knives left on the table at night are intended to appease
The *Fates and discourage them from using their own knives (to discourage
them from ending the life of anyone in the house). This custom is practiced
most often in the house of a newborn. (Walker, *Crone*)

knot: The "endless knot" represents longevity in Chinese Buddhism and is one
of the eight Emblems of Good Luck. (Cirlot)
      The Gordian knot of Western culture is a symbol of the *labyrinth. To
undo the Gordian knot is to find the *labyrinth's center, to solve the riddle or
dilemma of choice. As the symbol of psychological stasis, of an unchanging
situation, the knot is forbidden in the clothing of Moslems on *pilgrimage to
Mecca. (Cirlot)

Kronos (or Cronos): Kronos (or Cronos) is another name for the Roman god
*Saturn.

L

---

labyrinth: Journey through the labyrinth represents a life's course and the soul's *journey through life. Following the path of a mosaic labyrinth on the floor (commonly found in French and Italian cathedrals of the Middle Ages) was viewed as a substitute for *pilgrimage to the Holy Land. It was sometimes considered a penitential act, as well, since the *"pilgrimage" through the labyrinth is sometimes made on the knees. The labyrinth in Chartres cathedral is referred to as a mile (though it is much shorter) because it takes approximately an hour, at average speed, to traverse on one's knees. (de Vries) Some cross-shaped labyrinths, most notably *"Solomon's *Knot," have swastikas at their centers; thus, they share in the swastika's symbolism of change, flux, and the *cyclic nature of time. (Cirlot)

ladder: The ladder is a symbol of transcendence of the material world. Souls are thought to ascend a ladder at death. It is a symbol of the never-ending struggle of man, as seen in Jacob's Ladder, and the gradual accrual of knowledge and wisdom. (de Vries)

The ancient Egyptians believed that a ladder, up which the sould ascended at death to the barge of Re, was situated at every tomb site. The Pyramid Texts of 2350-2175 B.C. read: "The deceased ascends on the ladder that Re, his father, made for him." (Utterance 271:390a) "Every spirit, every god who shall open his arms to the deceased will be on the ladder of the god. United for him are his bones, assembled for him are his limbs; the deceased has sprung up to heaven on the fingers of the god, lord of the ladder." (478:980) (Campbell, MI, p. 185) This ladder is depicted in *The Ladder from Earth to Heaven* from the Papyrus of Ani, sheet 22 (16th-century B.C. Egyptian).

The Old Testament contains an image of a ladder reaching into the sky (Genesis 28:10-14, 18-19). In a dream, Jacob sees angels ascending and descending a ladder leading to heaven. The Lord, standing at the top, says to

Jacob: "the land on which you lie I will give to your and your descendants."
(Genesis 28:12-13) Jacob, upon awakending, declares the location upon which
he had his dream the gate of heaven. Jacob's Ladder is depicted in an Early
Christian wall painting in the catacombs under Via Latina, Rome. (Campbell,
MI, p. 184)

In Thomas Cole's *The Voyage of Life* (1839-1840), a series of paintings
depicting the *four stages of life, the panel titled "Old Age" shows an aged
man in a weathered *boat. He looks toward heaven, from which a brilliant
*light streams. Clouds form *stairs to heaven upon which angels descend,
welcoming the *boat's occupant to the afterlife.

In "I Fellowed Sleep," Dylan Thomas presents an image reflective of
Jacob's Ladder: "There grows the hours' ladder to the sun." His father's ghost
climbs the ladder.

Laimos: The Laimos are the Lithuanian version of the Three *Fates. (Lurker)

lake: The lake's surface serves as a *mirror and, thus, is related to self-
contemplation, revelation concerning the self, and man as a self-conscious
being (as in the Classical myth of Narcissus). As a form of the *mirror, it is
related to the life review common to aged characters.

Since the *sun rises from and sinks into the *water each day, the lake
symbolizes death and resurrection. The ancient Irish believed that the Land
of the Dead lay at the bottom of oceans and lakes. (Cirlot; de Vries)

lamp: The lamp is a symbol of wisdom and of the soul. (de Vries) It is often
employed as a symbol of reason which grows dim with age, as in Pierre Jean
de Beranger's "Fifty Years": "Then Reason's lamp grows faint and dim."
(Lyell)

It is used similarly in *Aegeon's description of his aged state in Shakespeare's *The Comedy of Errors*:

> Yet hath my night of Life some memory,
> My wasting lamps some fading glimmer left.

Shakespeare employs images of the "fading lamp," "wasting lamp," and "wasted
candle" often as symbols of fading vitality in old age. (Hankins) The following
are examples:

> These eyes, like lamps whose wasting oil is spent,
> Wax dim, as drawing to their exigent.
> > (*1 Henry VI*)

> My oil-dri'd lamp and time-bewasted light
> Shall be extinct with age and endless night;

My inch of taper will be burnt and done,
And blindfold Death not let me see my son.
                    (*Richard II*, act 1, sc. 3, 221-224)

Though now this grained face of mine be hid
In sap-consuming winter's drizzled snow,
And all the conduits of my blood froze up,
Yet hath my night of life some memory,
My wasting lamps some fading glimmer left,
My dull deaf ears a little use to hear.
                    (*The Comedy of Errors*, act 5, sc. 1, 311-316)

lantern: The lantern, an attribute of the *hermit, represents knowledge. It also symbolizes individual life as transitory, since it is regarded as only a fragment broken off from the greater whole of Eternal Light. (Cirlot; de Vries)

In the Bible, it is a symbol of breath as an expression of god-given life: "The lantern of the Lord is the breath of man." (Proverbs, 20:27) Consequently, in Biblical terms, the dying of the lantern's *light would indicate the waning of life.

lead: Lead is symbolic of the burden of material existence which increases with age, as in Shakespeare's description of old age as "leaden age" (*Venus and Adonis*, 34). It signifies inertia, heaviness, and oppression, as expressed in another passage from Shakespeare in which Juliet describes old people as "unwieldy, slow, heavy and pale as lead" (*Romeo and Juliet*). In *alchemy, lead is related to death as the opposite of *silver, which represents birth, and to *Saturn, portrayed as a decrepit *old man with a *scythe or as a dwarf. (Herder) The alchemist's idea that matter is the receptacle of the spirit is expressed in the image of a white dove contained in lead. (Cirlot)

leaf: The yellowed leaves of *autumn symbolize old age, as in the following passage from Shakespeare's *Macbeth* (act 5, sc. 3): "I have fallen 'into the sere, the yellow leaf.'" Falling leaves, as in Walter Savage Landor's (1775-1864) "Late Leaves," symbolize old age, as well: "The leaves are falling; so am I."

A solitary last leaf on a *tree is symbolic of an old person. In the case of Alexander Pushkin's (1799-1837) "Outlived Desire," "one shuddering leaf" hangs on the *tree in early *winter.

In "The Last Leaf" by Oliver Wendell Holmes (1841-1935), the solitary leaf has endured even the ravages of *winter, since the narrator survives as "the last leaf upon the tree."

light: As early as Sophocles, mental powers are equated with light, and old age is viewed as accompanied by a waning of this "light of reason": "When a man is old," says Sophocles, "the light of his reason goes out, action becomes useless and he has unmeaning cares." (de Beauvoir, p. 103) Later uses of waning light as representative of the fading of mental powers in old age include Shakespeare's "fading *lamp" and "wasting *lamp."

Light is symbolic of the spirit, as well, dying light signifying departure of the spirit from the material world in old age near death. (Herder) Numerous passages in the Bible refer to life as light or as a *candle, and to the belief that such light is extinguished in those who are ungodly (Hankins):

> The candle of the wicked shall be put out.
> (Proverbs 13:9)

> The candle of the ungodly shall be put out.
> (Proverbs 24:20)

> Yea, the light of the ungodly shall be put out, and the spark of
> his fire shall not shine. The light shall be dark in his dwelling,
> and his candle shall be put out with him.
> (Job 18:5-6)

Such images reflect the Judeo-Christian belief that longevity is a reward for virtue. This belief finds further expression in the image of the *candle and the common comparison of the face of an aged person to a *candle. The source of this comparison may be found in a passage from the Apocrypha (Ecclesiasticus 26, 22): "As the clear light upon holy candlesticks, so is the beauty of the face in ripe age."

lighthouse: The lighthouse symbolizes aging, yet retaining individual integrity throughout the passage of time. (de Vries) In *To the Lighthouse* (1927), Virginia Woolf employs the lighthouse as a symbol of the solitary and steadfast nature of the individual constantly impinged upon by the *sea's *waves, whose *cyclic action represents the passage of time.

linen thread: Linen thread, as the thread of The *Fates, is a symbol of the "slender thread" of life and the passage of time. Tradition states that shrouds must be made of linen. (de Vries)

lion: Since the lion commonly symbolizes the *sun, it shares in the *sun's symbolism. The young lion and the old lion correspond to the young *sun and old *sun. The *sun's course across the sky is often compared to the course of an individual life, the "old sun" nearing the horizon, its light growing dim, representing the "old man" nearing death. As a consequence of the "stand-in" relationship of the lion for the *sun, the old lion is representative of the old person.

In Mithraic form, *Aion is represented as a *winged figure with the head and *claws of a lion. These leonine characteristics may be an expression of a view of time as devouring and predatory. (de Vries) *Aion is the forerunner of *Chronos, the Greek personification of time as an all-consuming force.

The lion is a symbol of solitude and the life of the *hermit. It is an attribute of *St. Jerome, who is typically depicted as a *hermit in the wilderness. He is often accompanied by a lion which he tamed by removing a thorn from its paw. (cf. Lucas Cranach's woodcut *St. Jerome*, 1509). (Pierce) In a number of the tales of solitary Christian saints, such as St. Paul the Hermit and Mary of Egypt, lions appear upon their death and dig their graves. (de Vries)

lizard: In magical practice, the dried lizard is employed to restore youth. This use possibly springs from the belief that the lizard, in sloughing its skin, exhibits rejuvenating powers. (Leach, p. 637)

The lizard is a symbol of rejuvenation in old age since it is believed that, when it loses its sight with age, it crawls into a crevice which faces east and through the rays of the *sun is restored to sight. It is a further symbol of regeneration because, as mentioned above, it regularly sheds its skin. (de Vries) Because it seeks out *light, it is a symbol of the soul seeking the *light of the afterlife. (Herder)

loom: The loom is a symbol of time and a life's duration. It is symbolic of the joining of the diverse *threads of a life to form a continuous whole, as in the *weaving of a fabric. Through association with the *weavers, The *Fates, it symbolizes fortune and chance, as seen in Robert Southwell's (1561-1595) "Time Goes by Turns": "Her loom doth weave the fine and coarsest web."(de Vries)

Louhi: Louhi is the *crone of Pohja from the Finnish epic, the *Kalevala*, who engages with *Vainamoinen, the aged hero, in battles over possession of the Sampo, the world axis. She is described as the "old and gap-toothed dame of Pohja." (*Kalevala*, Runo 7, 169-170)

Louhi is depicted in *The Defense of the Sampo*, a painting by Akseli Gallen-Kallela (1896) in battle with *Vainamoinen for possession of the Sampo. (McKee and Kauppinen)

M

Magi: In medieval lore, the Three Magi, through folk belief not founded in Biblical scripture, were identified with the *Three Ages of Man. Literary and visual images from the Renaissance and Middle Ages show a man advanced in years carrying *gold, a man of middle age and a youth. (cf. Lucas Cranach's *The Adoration of the Magi*, 1514) In the *Collectanea* or *Excerptiones patrum*, an Irish text, the three are described as follows. *Melchior, the bearer of *gold, is an old man with long hair and beard. He wears a purple and green robe, purple and white shoes, and a Mithraic cap. Caspar, the youngest of the three, is red-haired and beardless. He is dressed in red and green clothing and purple shoes and carries frankincense. Balthassar has a full beard, red and white clothing, and green shoes. He carries a gift of myrrh. (Sears)

The Magi, who sought out the newborn Christ, are believed by some to be a later version of the Three *Fates of earlier pagan culture. (Walker, *Crone*) The Three *Fates are believed to always be present in the house of a newborn, as the Magi were present at Christ's birthplace. *Melchior, the oldest of the Three Magi, because of his advanced age, is believed to correspond to *Atropos, the *crone, the oldest of the Three *Fates. (de Vries; Sears)

Manda: Ruler of *Saturn in Indian culture, Manda is also called Sani. Described as old, unsightly, and crippled, he is said to ride on a *raven, blackbird, or *vulture, or to travel in a cart which is drawn by eight dappled horses. (Lurker)

Mathusala: Mathusala embodies the Christian concept of longevity as a reward for goodness and virtue. In the annals of generation in the Bible Mathusala is mentioned: "All the days of Mathusala were nine hundred and sixty-nine years, and he died" (Genesis 5:27). Mathusala's renowned longevity is the source of the phrase "as old as Mathusala." (Griffin)

Medea: Medea's *kettle, a form of the *witch's *cauldron, symbolizes the restoration of lost youth. Her name literally meaning "wisdom" or "cunning," Medea was known as a healer. Her function as healer is reflected in the fact that her name is the derivation of our word "medicine." (Graves, GM II, p. 399; Walker *Crone*, p. 101)

A *sorceress in Classical mythology who sometimes took the form of an old woman or *crone, Medea possessed the power to return mortals to youth. (cf. Ovid's *Metamorphoses*, book 8) Though she sometimes put this power to constructive use (such as when she restored the youth of Jason's aged father, *Aeson), she often used it as a tool of evil rather than good. In an effort to assist Jason in gaining control of Iolcos, she devised a plot against Pelias, Iolcos' existing *king. Medea entered Iolcos in the form of a wrinkled *crone, bringing with her an image of *Artemis. She informed Pelias that, as a reward for his piety, *Artemis wished to restore his youth. She convinced him of the supposed power of Artemis to restore youth by dropping the veil of illusion she had cast on herself, returning to her youthful form. Next, she cut an old ram to pieces and boiled the pieces in a *cauldron. A young lamb (which Medea had hidden in the hollow image of Artemis) emerged. This thoroughly convinced Pelias and two of his daughters, Evadne and Amphinome (the third daughter, Alcestis, was not convinced) of the *cauldron's capacity to restore youth. Evadne and Amphinome, as a result, consented to the *king's request that they dismember him, and they boiled his body in Medea's *cauldron. Medea's trick worked, causing Pelias to consent to and participate in his own murder.

Another version of the myth reflects an alternate view of Medea's powers. In this version, Medea's powers of rejuvenation are the result of *witchcraft with concrete results, not mere tricks of illusion. In this case, Medea is said to have added magic herbs to the *cauldron when boiling the ram, thereby actually restoring it to youth. When she wished to trick King Pelias, she merely neglected to add the herbs, thereby ensuring his death. At any rate, her actions resulted in elimination of King Pelias and control of Iolcos.

In another myth, Medea's *kettle, filled with mead, is the *kettle of poetic inspiration. When Odin stole it, spilling some of its contents on the ground, poets sprang up where the drops of mead had fallen. (Graves, GM; Stapleton; Zimmerman)

Shelley (1792-1822) alludes to Medea's powers in "Alastor; or, The Spirit of Solitude":

O, for Medea's wondrous alchemy,
Which wheresoe'er it fell made the earth gleam

In a painting by the Pre-Raphaelite Anthony Frederick Sandys, *Medea*, (1868) the sorceress mixes a potion in a flaming cauldron. Numerous other signs of *witchcraft occupy the picture, including a *crescent moon, a toad, and an Egyptian amulet. (Marsh, p. 119, Plate 100)

Melchior: Melchior, the eldest of the Three *Magi, brought gold as a gift to the infant Christ. When the *Magi are viewed as a later adaptation of the pagan concept of the Three *Fates, Melchior corresponds to *Atropos, the *crone. (de Vries)

Merlin: Merlin, the *sorcerer in the Celtic legend of King Arthur, is a form of the *Wise Old Man archetype. As an expression of this archetype, he can be both the incarnation of goodness and, conversely, wickedness personified. (Jung, ACU)

The first written reference to Merlin occurs in *Libellus Merlini* (*Little Book of Merlin*, ca. 1135), a Latin text by Geoffrey of Monmouth. It later became a part of Monmouth's *History of the Kings of Britain* (1137). Merlin was fully developed as a magician in Malory's *Morte d'Arthur* (ca. 1469). He also appears in Spenser's *Faerie Queene* (1590-1596), Tennyson's *Idylls of the King* (1859-1885), T. H. White's *The Once and Future King* (1958), and C. S. Lewis' *That Hideous Strength* (1945). (Benet)

Merlin advises King Arthur out of wisdom informed by the perception of the integration of opposites as the desired state of affairs. A view in accord with the natural world, it is a *cyclic view of man and of history, a view of life as, in Ralph Waldo Emerson's words in the poem "Merlin," a rhyme "sung by the sisters as they spin":

The rhyme of the poet
Modulates the king's affairs;
Balance-loving Nature
Made all things in pairs.

Thoughts come also hand in hand;
In equal couples mated,
Or else alternated;
Adding by their mutual gage,
One to other, health and age.

Subtle rhymes, with ruin rife,
Murmur in the house of life,
Sung by the Sisters as they spin;
In perfect time and measure they
build and unbuild our echoing clay.

Thus we see that, in Emerson's portrayal, Merlin is a character reflective of the archetype of the *Wise Old Man. Through experience of the world, he has developed a form of wisdom based on the integration of opposites and advises the *king from this viewpoint.

Figures from Arthurian legend were popular topics in the work of the British Pre-Raphaelites. Edward Burne-Jones' painting *The Beguiling of Merlin* (1874) is one example.

Midas: King Midas of Classical mythology exemplifies the folly of the *Old King. (cf. Ovid's *Metamorphoses*, book 11) Because he released Pan's aged companion, *Silenus, from captivity, he was rewarded by Pan with fulfillment of any wish he might have. In his greed, he chose the "golden touch" whereby everything he touched turned to *gold. He soon realized his folly, since even his food turned to *gold, thereby making nourishment impossible. He pleaded with Pan to reverse the charm and Pan told him to wash in the River Pactolus. Midas did as Pan advised, freeing himself of the golden touch.

In another tale, Midas deemed Pan the better musician in a contest between Pan and Apollo. Enraged, Apollo punished Midas with donkey's ears. Since Midas kept his head covered with a cloth, only his barber knew of his curse. However, the barber, unable to keep the secret of Midas' predicament as promised, dug a hole and told the earth. A clump of reeds grew over the hole and, when the south wind blew, the earth would reveal the secret to "anyone who knew how to listen." (Stapleton, pp. 139-140)

Nathaniel Hawthorne retells the story of King Midas in altered form in "The Golden Touch," one of the stories comprising *A Wonderbook for Girls and Boys* (1851), a collection of reformulations of Classical mythology.

midnight: As a form of the number *twelve and the completion of the day's *cycle, midnight signifies completion and the end of a *cycle, as in death at the end of a complete life. W. B. Yeats (1865-1939) uses midnight as a symbol of death in his poem "The Four Ages of Man": "At strike of midnight God shall win." (Lyell)

mill: The mill, through its *cyclic action, symbolizes time. (de Vries) Finnish mythology presents a cosmic mill, the Sampo, which generates the rotation of the heavens. It is represented as a *cauldron or mill located "nine fathoms deep" under the ground or the *sea, and is ruled over by the *Louhi, the *crone of *Pohja. (Walker, *Crone*, p. 105) The Sampo figures prominently in the Finnish epic the *Kalevala*, in episodes describing its creation and battles between *Vainamoinen and *Louhi over its possession. Akseli Gallen-Kallela's painting of 1896, *The Defense of the Sampo*, depicts this conflict. (McKee and Kauppinen)

The mill occurs as an image of time's passage in T. S. Eliot's "Journey of the Magi": "a running stream and a water-mill beating the darkness." In "The

Old Woman" Joseph Campbell describes the still thoughts of an aged woman as like the water "under a ruined mill."

Minerva: Minerva, the Roman goddess of wisdom, probably represented the *crone aspect of the earlier Capitoline Triad consisting of Juventas the Virgin, Juno the Mother, and Minerva the wise old *Crone. (Walker, *Crone*) Her animal familiar, the *owl, is evidence of her link to the *crone, since the *owl is typically the familiar of *witches and *crones (c.f. *Hecate). Romans used the same word for *"owl" and *"witch," linking the *owl to the *crone's stereotypic representation as a *witch. (Walker, WEMS)

mirror: The mirror is emblematic of self-reflection and life review. As the agent of life review it carries not only one's immediate physical reflection but also images of the past and the self stored in memory. It is thereby regarded as the carrier of the contents of one's inner life, as a reflector of one's inner self or the unconscious. In numerous tales, the mirror is portrayed as a magical object with the power to conjure up images and people from the past.

The mirror is symbolic of the soul through the belief that it holds an image of the soul. Marie-Louise von Franz explains how the mirror as a symbol of the soul operated in ancient Indian culture:

> In Old Indian, a mirror was thought of as a "self-seer" or as "seer of Doppelgangers." The mirror image was regarded as shadow or as Doppelganger, that is, as an image of the soul, and the mirror therefore possessed great magical significance; it was an instrument for becoming objectively conscious of one's soul by means of reflection, in the literal sense of the word.

The Old High German word for mirror, *scukar*, meant, literally, "shadow-holder" (from *skuwo*, "shadow", and *kar*, "vessel"). (von Franz, "Reflection," p. 34)

As an instrument of self-knowledge, the mirror is a particularly apt symbol of the life review common to old age. Kathleen Woodward in "The Mirror Stage of Old Age" in Woodward and Schwartz's *Memory and Desire* examines the mirror as a repeated motif in the literature of aging. She views it as an image specifically related to representations of the aging body. She sees it as having an inverse relationship to the myth of Narcissus: "The horror of the mirror image of the decrepit body can be understood as the inverse of the pleasures of the mirror image of the youthful Narcissus." (Woodward, p. 104) She sees it as related to the "psychological truth" that, as a person ages, the self image remains constant. The mirror image, thus, betrays the person's self-perception. She relates this betrayal of self-perception further to Simone de Beauvoir's discussion in *The Coming of Age* of perception of the aged self as the "Other," as an aged stranger within. She says: ". . . the recognition of our own old age comes to us from the Other, that is, from society. We study our own reflection in the body of the others, and as we reflect upon that reflection—reflection is of course a metaphor for thought—we ultimately are compelled to acknowledge the point of view of the Other which has, as it were, installed itself in our body." (pp. 104-105) This creates an inner conflict and serves as a source of anxiety in old age. A particularly relevant example from contemporary popular culture can be found in the film *On Golden Pond*. One of the film's aged main characters, Norman Thayer, engages in frequent mirror-gazing. He thereby betrays a strong sense of self-doubt and a crisis of identity in old age.

Traditionally, the mirror is related to the *moon, since it reflects images as the *moon reflects the *light of the *sun. (Cirlot) It is often viewed as a means of passage to "the other side," to the afterlife, as expressed by Lewis Carroll: "the door through which the soul frees itself by passing." Since it simultaneously stores images and people from the past and reflects images from current reality, it is sometimes an agent of realization of the continuity of generations, of the continuity of past and present. A ritual expressive of this function is described by James Fernandez:

> . . . a neophyte stares into a looking glass until the face of an ancestor appears and merges with his own. The identification between the ancestor behind the glass and the living descendant in front of it presents, literally, a picture of genealogical continuity between the living and the dead and allows the initiate to pass into a new state of being. In such instances the human body itself is a symbolic statement, presenting to the society and the individual the message that the group and its members are inseparable, that they are vehicles for each other and must coexist.

mistletoe: As an evergreen, mistletoe is a symbol of immortality. (de Vries) It is also a fertility symbol through vestigial associations of its use in ancient fertility rites. (Graves, GM) In *flower language, mistletoe signifies: "I surmount all obstacles." (de Vries) In Eudora Welty's "A Worn Path," mistletoe symbolizes triumph over the obstacles and hardships of impoverished old age.

In George Henry and E. A. Hornel's painting *The Druids: Bringing in the Mistletoe* (1890), we see an image carrying vestiges of the mistletoe's ancient role in fertility rites. A procession of Druids, including aged figures, returns from having harvested the mistletoe at the *winter solstice. The foremost figure carries a lunula which serves as a *scythe for cutting the mistletoe. A lunula serves, as well, as a *crown for the aged man in the procession, signifying his exalted status.

Moirai: The Moirai are the Greek version of the Three *Fates. They are Clotho the Spinner (Virgin), Lachesis the Measurer (Mother), and *Atropos the Cutter (*Crone). (Walker, *Crone*)

moon: The moon is known as the *"old man" in Germanic cultural tradition. (Herder) Because of its *cyclic nature, it is related to all things *cyclic and to the passage of time. Relation of the moon to time can be found in the reliance upon lunar rhythms as a measure of time prior to the present reliance upon solar rhythms. (Cirlot)

As an object which undergoes profound physical change throughout its *cycles, the moon has become associated with analogous processes in man, and is seen in its various phases to be symbolic of the stages of a person's life. In its three major phases, it is seen as representative of the Virgin (waxing moon), Mother (full moon), and *Crone (waning moon). (Walker, *Crone*)

Shelley (1792-1822) compares the waning moon to an aged woman in "The Waning Moon":

And like a dying lady, lean and pale,
Who totters forth, wrapped in a gauzy veil,
Out of her chamber, led by the insane
And feeble wanderings of her fading brain,
The moon arose up in the murky east,
A white and shapeless mass.

Two quarter-moons presented back to back, superimposed, symbolize a "decrepit, bony old man." (Cirlot, p. 217)

Morgan: Also known as the Celtic Triple *Morrigan or Cerridwen, Morgan was believed to live on *Avalon, an island paradise, where she led nine white-haired *sorceresses who were practiced in the arts of *alchemy, healing and flying. It was believed that they (like Morgan, who took various forms—sometimes a beautiful young maiden, sometimes a powerful old *crone) could change form, affect the weather, and foretell events. The word "glamorous" comes from Morgan-the-Crone, goddess of Glamorgan, through her abiilty to weave a veil of illusion and cast spells on men to trick and deceive them. This is related to our idea of the glamorous woman as "bewitching," "enchanting," "entrancing," and holding power over men as did the *crone. (Walker, *Crone*, p. 140)

Morgan Le Fay: Morgan Le Fay is the Celtic goddess also called "Morgan the Fate" who appears in Arthurian legend as the sister of King Arthur. (cf. Malory's *Morte d'Arthur* and *Sir Gawain and the Green Knight*) As a *sorceress, she tricks Arthur by taking on Guinevere's disguise, causing him to father her child. Mordred later kills Arthur in an attempt to usurp his power. As a manifestation of the *crone, Morgan Le Fay was all-powerful. (Walker, *Crone*)

Arthurian legend served as a fruitful source of subject matter for the 19th-century British Pre-Raphaelite painters. Anthony Frederick Sandys' *Morgan le Fay* (1862), in which we see the sorceress at her loom, is an example.

Morrigan: As a tripartite goddess, the Morrigan is a Celtic version of the Three *Fates (Virgin, Mother, *Crone). Her three forms correspond to the three phases of the *moon: waxing, full, and waning. Her name meaning "queen of the ghosts," she often took the form of a vengeful *crone, appearing on battlefields, relishing in the devastation and loss of life. (Lurker) At other times, she took the form of a *raven visible only to those near death in battle. (Stone, AMW)

Moses: The Judeo-Christian concept of longevity as a reward for a virtuous life can be seen in the Biblical figure Moses, who led the Jews out of Egypt and lived to be 120 in good health, his senses undiminished: "his eye was not dim nor his natural force abated." (Deuteronomy 34:7) Moses functions as the aged hero through his ascent of the *mountain and receipt of the tablets from Yahweh and as founder/foundation of culture through the tablets he brings back, his action forming the basis for a new culture. (Campbell, *Power of Myth*)

In Psalm 90, Moses speaks of old age:

> our years come to an end like a
>   sigh.
> The years of our life are threescore
>   and ten,
>   or even by reason of strength
>   fourscore;
> yet their span is but toil and
>   trouble;
>   they are soon gone and we fly
>   away.   (Psalm 90:9-10)

In a medieval manuscript illustration in the British Library, London (*Bible moralisée*), Moses, holding a book or tablet, appears to be teaching a group of five men representing the five *Ages of Man. (Sears, Plate 23) The implication is that his law applies to all ages. In another medieval manuscript, this one from the Oesterreichische Nationalbibliothek, Vienna (cod. 2739, fol. IIV), Moses and "senectus" are portrayed as corresponding to the ninth hour of the day. (Sears, Plate 28)

Moses was a popular subject in the art of the European Renaissance. Two notable examples of his portrayal are Lucas Van Leyden's (1494-1533) painting *Moses after Striking the Rock*, and Michelangelo's sculpture *Moses* from the tomb of Julius II (completed 1545) at S. Pietro in Vincoli, Rome. (Canaday, Plate 116)

Moss Women: Moss Women are a type of dwarf in folktales. Described as old and gray, they are believed to live in groups. Their name comes from their repulsive, hairy appearance, which results from the moss that covers them. The author of *The Fairy Family* describes the Moss Women (Porteous, p. 93):

> 'A moss-woman!' the hay-makers cry,
> And over the fields in terror they fly.
> She is loosely clad from neck to foot
> In a mantle of Moss from the Maple's root
> And like Lichen grey on its stem that grows
> Is the hair that over her mantle flows.
> Her skin, like the Maple-rind, is hard,
> Brown and ridgy, and furrowed and scarred.

Mother Goose: The origin of Mother Goose herself is uncertain. However, she is first mentioned in relationship to children's stories in Charles Perrault's collection of fairy tales, *Mother Goose* (*Contes de ma mère l'Oye*). This enormously popular collection, first published in France in 1697, included "Sleeping Beauty," "Little Red Riding Hood," "Bluebeard," "Puss in Boots," "The Fairies," "Cinderella," and "Tom Thumb." On the cover of the original edition, Mother Goose is portrayed as an *old woman around whom three children are gathered. In the first English-language edition of *Mother Goose*, the storyteller appears again, in an image forming the book's frontispiece, as an aged woman. This time, she spins *thread as she speaks to three people gathered around a *hearth. A placard above her head reads, "Mother Goose's Tales." This edition, translated by Robert Samber and published in England in 1729, bore the title *Histories, or Tales of Past Times, by M. Perrault*. (Opie, *The Classic Fairy Tales*, pp. 20-24)

It is unclear how Mother Goose, the aged storyteller came to assume the *witch's attributes; however, she is commonly portrayed in the traditional *witch's black cape and pointed hat. Her uncommon mode of transportation may find its basis in common regard during the Middle Ages of the *goose as the *witch's steed. (de Vries)

The following formed the first verse of an 1815 edition of Mother Goose, *Old Mother Goose, or The Golden Egg* (T. Batchelar):

> Old Mother Goose,
>   When she wanted to wander,

Would ride through the air
  On a very fine gander.
          (Opie, *Oxford Dictionary of Nursery Rhymes*)

Mother Hubbard: The nursery rhyme "Old Mother Hubbard," written by
Sarah Catherine Martin in 1804, was widely popular in 19th-century England.
The subject of the rhyme, an aged woman entirely devoted to her dog, is
believed to have been the housekeeper in the home of Ms. Martin's brother-
in-law. The first of fourteen verses goes as follows:

Old Mother Hubbard
  Went to the cupboard,
To fetch her poor dog a bone;
  But when she came there
  The cupboard was bare
And so the poor dog had none.

The rhyme bears a striking resemblance to an earlier British rhyme by T.
Evans, "Old Dame Trot, and Her Comical Cat" (1803). Its first verse was:

Old Dame Trot,
Some cold fish had got,
Which for pussy,
She kept in Store,
When she looked there was none
The cold fish had gone,
For puss had been there before.

The name "Mother Hubbard" derived from earlier sources, as well, including
a satire by Spenser, "Mother Hubbard's Tale," written in 1590. Spenser's work,
however, was dissimilar in content to the nursery rhyme. (Opie, *Oxford
Dictionary of Nursery Rhymes*, pp. 316-321)

mountain: As a place of *pilgrimage and solitude, the mountain is a symbol
of wisdom through disengagement. *Pilgrimages to sacred sites on mountains
have a long tradition in Chinese and Japanese religious practice. These sites
serve as places of disengagement from the material world for Buddhist monks
and other ascetics. (de Vries; Eliade)
    David Luke points out a "fascination with mountains and ruins as
enigmatic emblems of temporal processes of growth, endurance, and decay"
(p. 221) as characteristic of English Romantic poetry. This fascination can be
seen in the last passages of Wordsworth's "The Excursion" (1814):

> Rightly it is said
> That Man descends into the vale of years;
> Yet have I thought that we might also speak,
> And not presumptuously, I trust, of Age,
> As of a final eminence;
> . . .
> And may it not be hoped, that, placed by age
> In like removal, tranquil though severe,
> We are not so removed for utter loss;
> But for some favour, suited to our need?
> What more than that the severing should confer
> Fresh power to commune with the invisible world.

Luke further points out that Wordsworth extends his idealization of nature to another character common to Romantic poetry, the *"old man," a figure closer to the vicissitudes of nature by virtue of the hardship and poverty attendant upon old age. The mountain as a symbol of endurance comes to represent the endurance of the aged. Further, through its traditional function as an emblem of solitude and remove from the mundane in experience of its spiritual heights, the mountain comes to symbolize for Wordsworth such spiritual qualities as necessary elements of the life of the aged. Thus, aging, in Wordsworth's view, is romanticized as a time of spiritual elevation from the material world. Luke explains:

> Wordsworth instinctively describes the natural state of old age in negative terms and simultaneously interprets those terms as spiritual benefits. Thus, on one hand, he emphasizes old age as a state of "solitude" and "decay" and "loss," yet, on the other hand, he envisions old age as a "place of power" and a "privileged" state that is supposedly proximate to some transcendent "favour" from an "invisible world." (Luke, p. 229)

Luke warns that such romanticism of the state of the aged can all too easily become a justification for neglect of their physical well-being. If they are perceived as having "transcended" the physical, their physical needs can just as easily be perceived as consequently unimportant.

Mountain Woman: see YAMA-UBA.

mulberry: A symbol of wisdom, the mulberry was consulted as an oracle by the Biblical character David (2 Samuel 5:23 ff.). A slow-growing plant, the mulberry becomes hardier with age, flourishing late in its growth *cycle; consequently, it symbolizes old age as a time of fruition. (de Vries)

N

Naomi: The Biblical story of *Ruth and Naomi (The Book of Ruth) is an image of Christian virtue and respect for elders. Naomi, as an old, widowed woman, is rescued by her daughter-in-law, *Ruth, a young widow, from the common fate of such aged women in early Christian culture. The precarious fate of such women found its basis in the belief that women, in the sexual act, consumed a portion of their male partner's vitality. Consequently, a woman who outlived her husband was perceived as responsible for her widowhood and was left to suffer the consequences. (Walker, *Crone*)

Nemesis: Nemesis is the Greek counterpart of the Roman *Fortuna, who determines individual fate by the spin of her *wheel. She is thus associated with the life *cycle. Nemesis is depicted with an *apple branch in one hand and a *wheel in the other. She wears a scourge at her *girdle and a *silver *crown topped with *stags on her head. The daughter of *Oceanus, she was responsible for humiliating those who, favored by Tyche ("fortune") with riches from her horn of plenty, became boastful and failed to sacrifice a portion of them to the gods. Graves says: "That Nemesis's wheel was originally the solar year is suggested by the name of her Latin counterpart, Fortuna (from vortumna, 'she who turns the year around')." (Graves, GM I, p. 126)

Nereus: Nereus is the *"Old Man of the *Sea" of Classical mythology who possesses great wisdom, the gift of prophecy, and the power to change shape. (cf. Homer's *Iliad* 18, 36 ff.; Graves, GM I) He is portrayed as a bald old man wearing a wreath and a chiton, holding a wand in one hand and a *fish in the other. He is sometimes portrayed holding a dolphin or riding a seahorse while holding a trident. Other depictions show him as fish-tailed with three animals growing out of his body: a *lion, a *stag, and a viper. He fathered the Nereids, the mermaid-like sea deities who are regarded as personifications of the oceans' waves. His character is described in Hesiod's *Theogeny*: "And Sea begat Nerus, the eldest of his children, who is true and lies not: and men call him the Old Man because he is trusty and gentle and does not forget the laws of righteousness, but thinks just and kindly thoughts." (Evelyn-White; Graves, GM I; Pierce; Richardson; Stapleton)

Nestor: Nestor, whose name means "newly speaking," appears in both the *Iliad* and the *Odyssey* (book 3) as a wise, though somewhat pompous, old man. (Graves, GM II, p. 401) In Homer's *Iliad*, as a highly respected elder statesman, Nestor bores the troops with his endless counsel. He is listened to with patience, but his advice, based upon tales recounted from the past, is often perceived as useless and misplaced.

Nestor's brothers and sisters were killed by Apollo and *Artemis. As a form of restitution, Apollo afforded Nestor the right to live out the accumulated years of which his relatives had been deprived. His longevity allowed him a prominent role in the Trojan War. Living to a great age, Nestor ruled the city of Pylus for three generations. In old age, he led 90 ships into the Trojan War. (cf. *Pythian Odes* 6, 28-42; Grant and Hazel; Grimal, DCM; Spicker et al.; Tripp)

Simone de Beauvoir sees in Nestor the effects of a feudal society on the aged. Nestor is presented by Homer as an esteemed counselor; however, he has no real power. de Beauvoir points out that, although Nestor's experience and expertise prove valuable, he does not secure victory for the Greeks: ". . .

if property is not guaranteed by stable institutions but has to be earnt and defended by force of arms, the old are pushed back into the shadows: the system is based upon the young, and it is they who hold the reality of power." (p. 99)

night: Through the analogy of the *cycle of a day to the *cycle of an individual life, night symbolizes old age and/or death, the completion of a *cycle. (Herder) Shakespeare uses night as symbolic of the last years of a person's life in the following passages:

> Yet hath my night of life some memory.
> (*The Comedy of Errors*, act 5, sc. 1, 315)

> Where wasteful Time debateth with Decay
> To change your day of youth to sullied night;
> (Sonnet 15)

Norns: The Norns, whose name means "three," are the Norse equivalent of the Greek *Fates. (Graves, GM II, p. 402) In the *Volupsa*, these three old women are named Urd (past), Verdandi (present), and Skuld (future)—what has been, what is, and what will be. Like the Three *Fates, they were believed to determine even the fate of the gods, rendering all others powerless against the inevitable results of their actions. (Cavendish; Lurker)

Known as "Die Schreiberinnen" ("the writing women"), the Norns were given birth to by Mother *Night, who arose from chaos and gave birth to the *light of the world before the separation of heaven and earth. (Walker, *Crone*, p. 99) The Norns, regarded as Mother *Night's manifestation as ruler of past, present, and future, lived by a *spring beneath the roots of Yggdrasil, the world *tree. (Davidson)

north: In the *Ages of Man, the medieval artistic and literary convention which divides an individual's life into *ten stages, north (also connected with *winter and *Saturn) corresponds with old age. (de Vries)

Graves speculates that the north is generally associated with old age and death because the *sun never shines from the north and it is the source of cold winds. (Graves, WG)

O

oak: The oak is a symbol of longevity, endurance, and wisdom. (de Vries) Through such associations, it is commonly related to aging and the elderly.

In Nordic culture, oaks, as the dwelling place of departed elders, were considered the proper meeting-place for councils. (de Vries) Because it possesses hard, durable wood, the oak is a symbol of strength, masculinity, and steadfastness. (Cirlot; Herder)

The oak is a symbol of endurance in old age in Thomas Campion's (1567-1620) "Though You are Young":

The tender graft is easily broke,
But who shall shake the sturdy oak?

oar: The oar serves as the attribute of a number of figures in Classical mythology. It is a common attribute of old *river gods, including *Peneus (cf. Giovanni Battista Tiepolo's *Apollo and Daphne*, 1755) and *Tmolus. It is also an attribute of the Roman god *Saturn, who is the forerunner of *Father Time. Through such associations, stemming from its practical function, it seems to carry connotations of passage through life and of time's passage. That is, it appears to be emblematic of the temporal aspects of existence.

The oar figures prominently in the story of Odysseus, as well. In the *Odyssey*, *Tiresias prophesizes Odysseus' future when he visits Hades and consults the blind seer about his future. Tiresias tells Odysseus that, after his heroic exploits are over and he has returned home, his travels will not have ended. It will be necessary for him to take one last trip before he enjoys the comforts of old age. Though he will travel inland on this last trip, Tiresias tells Odysseus that he must carry an oar with him. He must keep traveling inland until he reaches a place where the inhabitants have never seen the sea. He will know this is the case when people mistakenly identify his oar as a harvesting tool. When he is approached by a stranger who asks him why he is carrying a winnowing fan, he must plant his oar upright in the ground and make a sacrifice to *Poseidon. Upon completion of this last *journey, Odysseus is promised an old age in which he will "sink under the comfortable burden of years," and death will come for him "gently, from the *sea." (*Odyssey*, book 23)

Helen Luke analyzes this episode in the *Odyssey* in her book *Old Age*. She views the oar as tied to Odysseus' youthful identity as a hero and traveler. In his middle age, the oar had become a burden. "Planting it" in a land where the intrigue and call of the *sea were not known symbolized for him a putting to rest of his youth. Luke explains the shift in significance of the oar, which has become a winnowing fan. She says the oar has become "a spirit of discriminating wisdom, separating moment by moment the wheat of life from the chaff," revealing "in both wheat and chaff their meaning and their value in the pattern of the universe." (p. 19)

Oceanos: Oceanos is *time in the form of a *river flowing around the edge of the earth, forming the boundary of the world. He controls change and constitutes *omega, the "round element," which in late antiquity represented various periods of time: a *year, a lifetime, eternity. He sometimes takes the form of an *ouroboros, a *serpent biting its own tail, surrounding the earth, forming the *sun's path and carrying the signs of the *zodiac on his back. (von Franz, *Time*, pp. 34-35)

In the story of the creation of the world in the *Metamorphoses* (book 1), Ovid says that, before the creation, when all was an undivided, formless mass called Chaos, no earth existed "nor Ocean's arms embraced the long far margin of the land." In Classical mythology, Oceanos was the oldest of the *twelve Titans, the offspring of Uranus and Gaea. Ovid describes him as "old Ocean, whom the gods greatly revere." (*Metamorphoses*, book 2) He was also called *Chronos (*Time) and later identified with *Kronos (Zeus's father) and *Aion. Oceanos is portrayed in *circular form with an *old man's face in a Roman relief, the *Bocca della Verità*, Santa Maria in Cosmedin, Rome. (von Franz, *Time*, Plate 2) Later, in Christian culture, Oceanos came to represent only the Ocean, father of *springs and streams. (Zimmerman)

Shelley (1792-1822) describes the ocean as aged in "The Witch of Atlas": "And Ocean with the brine on his grey locks."

Ocnus: Ocnus' name means "sloth"; however, he functions symbolically in Greek myth as an example of lack of accomplishment due not to laziness but, rather, to circumstances at odds with his industrious efforts. Ocnus is depicted as an aging, bald, and bearded man seated at the entrance to the underworld. (cf. tomb painting in the Villa Pamphili, Rome; and frieze from columbarium, Porta Latina, Rome) He plaits a rope which is devoured by a female donkey as quickly as it is formed. He was known as a hard-working man whose efforts were constantly subverted by his wife's extravagance and propensity for spending. As a figure associated with the underworld, he may more generally represent the futility of human effort and the accumulation of material wealth as a senseless human conceit, the ultimate futility of which is apparent when one is faced with death. (Howatson)

In *Myth, Religion and Mother Right*, J. J. Bachofen posits that Ocnus is a "nature symbol." (p. 59) He views Ocnus' rope plaiting as an activity akin to the *weaving of the Three *Fates and other goddesses whose *weaving and *spinning activity is an expression of the creative forces of nature expressed in human production. The donkey, on the other hand, represents nature in its destructive aspect. Bachofen, thus, sees the image as allegorical of human creativity as a positive force continually at odds with the negative, destructive forces of "animal nature": "Creation is an art; destruction is the work of brute force. Creation rests in the human hand; destruction is attributed to the demonic animal nature." (p. 56)

Ogmios: Ogmios is a Gallic god sometimes equated with Heracles. As his name indicates, he bears a relationship to the primary deity of the Irish pantheon, Ogma. Ogma was regarded as inventor of ogam (or ogham), the script used in ancient Irish texts. Ogmios, similarly, symbolizes "the power of speech." (Lurker, p. 264) He is portrayed as an aged figure, wrinkled and bald. He carries a bow or club, the club possibly constituting his identification with Heracles. Lurker speculates that an image found on early Irish coins consisting of a head with a chain of smaller human heads issuing from its mouth may be a representation of Ogmios, the chain of heads representative of human speech.

ogre: The ogre, a terrifying *old man who victimizes the weak and helpless, is a figure from folktales similar to *Saturn of Classical mythology. Like *Saturn, the ogre devours his own children, thereby expressing the idea central to the *Saturn myth—that, since it is of the natural, temporal world and is thereby necessarily *cyclic, creation inevitably involves the inverse process of destruction. As a personification of the devouring nature of time, the ogre is an expression of the archetype of the "Terrible Father." (Cirlot)

The word "ogre" is thought to have first been used by Charles Perrault in *Contes de ma mère l'Oye* (1697) as a derivation from Orcus, one of the various names of the lord of Hades of Classical mythology (also known as Pluto). (Benet, p. 712)

A number of Native American tribes, including the Crow, Hidatsa, and Gros Ventre, tell stories of an ogress named Pot Tilter. She is described as an old woman who carries a large boiling pot. The pot, when tilted toward someone, especially a very "bad" child, sucks him or her in. (Leach, p. 816)

Old Fortunatas: Thomas Dekker's allegorical comedy (1599) takes its title from its main character, Old Fortunatas, an aged beggar who is offered the choice of either health, beauty, long life, wisdom, strength, or riches. He chooses riches. The inexhaustible source of funds which *Fortuna puts at his disposal proves to be the cause of much folly and ultimate misfortune. (Benet)

Old Honest: Old Honest is an old *pilgrim encountered by the travelers in John Bunyan's *Pilgrim's Progress*. They find him asleep under an *oak tree and recognize him as a *pilgrim by his clothing, *staff and *girdle. Old Honest explains his name: "Not *honesty* in the *abstract*, but *Honest* is my name, and I wish that my *nature* shall agree to what I am called." (p. 295) By virtue of his honesty in life, his *journey to the other side of the *river (when he dies near the end of the *journey) is made easier by the assistance of Good Conscience. Old Honest is the "good" Christian, rewarded for his virtue by a long life in this world and eternal life in the next.

Old King: see FISHER KING.

Old Maid: The Old Maid represents the "spinster," the *old woman who has remained unmarried and is said to live a loveless, unfulfilled life. The popular card game, Old Maid, wherein one card, the queen of spades, is removed and pairs are formed throughout the course of the game until the queen of clubs is left unmatched (the person left with this card designated the old maid), reflects the Old Maid's definition as half of an unmatched pair, incomplete and unwanted. This negative view of the aged, never-married woman is reflected in *Barnham Downs II* by R. Bage: "Betake ourselves to chastity, cards, and scandal, the solid comforts of old-maidship." (OED, p. 1984)

In a more positive aspect in literature, the old maid or spinster, as the Outsider, is often portrayed as one who has the capacity to move freely in the world because she is unrestricted by the role of wife, mother, etc. Such freedom yields a degree of distance which affords objectivity and, thus, the capacity for astute perception. Agatha Christie's Miss Marple, a detective with acute powers of observation and reason, is such a character. (Haskell)

In Classical mythology, *Hestia is the archetypal old maid. Her refusal to marry allows intensification of her role as perpetuator of tradition and the continuity of generations. Pomeroy explains the necessity of Hestia's virginity to her role as perpetuator of collective identity: "Since a virgin belongs to no man, she can incarnate the collective, the city: she can belong to everyone." (p. 210)

old man: The *Wise Old Man is an archetype expressive of the age-old wisdom of humanity and, in Jungian terms, the collective unconscious. His various forms are the *Ancient of Days, the Creative Spirit, the Twenty-Four Elders of Revelations (Revelations, chapter 4), and *Coyote as Old Man in

Native American mythology. (de Vries) In stories and dreams, he represents the spiritual element in man (or in the individual) which, in times of hardship, appears and lends assistance in the form of advice (but never action). (Jung, ACU) In popular contemporary culture, Obi Wan Kanobe of George Lucas' *Star Wars* series functions as the *Wise Old Man, giving advice to the stories' hero, Luke Skywalker, yet never taking action himself. (Campbell, PM) In vegetation myths, he is the personification of the spirit of the Old Year, the state of dormancy. (de Vries) Similarly, in mining, an "old man" is a vein which has been exhausted and abandoned. (OED, p. 1984)

Old Man (Creator): In Plains Indian creation myths, the progenitor of man, the Creator who is born of the earth's womb is called "Old Man." A common facet of this creation myth is assistance by an "Earth Diver," an animal that dives down under the *water covering the entire world and brings back mud from which Old Man forms the earth and its people. The motif of the Earth Diver, according to Joseph Campbell, forms a link between Native American creation myths and those of Siberia. Numerous tales from both cultures recount Old Man's fashioning of features of the landscape after obtaining the necessary material from the diver. (Campbell, HAWM)

Old Man (Trickster): In Native American tales of Old Man as Creator, he is respected as one full of wisdom. On the other hand, when Old Man takes the role of Trickster, he becomes sly and often malicious and exhibits opposed qualities: wisdom and folly, strength and weakness. Consequently, he can never be trusted. He functions as an agent of disorder, disrupting the ordered harmonious pattern of life. He often appears as *Coyote, *Raven, or Hare, Trickster figures of various North American tribes. (Campbell, HAWM)

Old Man and Old Woman (Jicarilla Apache): In the tale of the Emergence, the Creation myth of the Jicarilla Apache of New Mexico, we find an explanation of the necessity of return to the underworld at death. When the first people emerged from the earth, one old couple were not able to emerge. Their failing eyesight caused them to fall behind the other humans and animals; consequently, when they reached the *ladder to emergence, it was worn out and they were unable to ascend. Their pleas for help were unanswered by those above because there was no means to help them. Angered at the turn of events, the Old Man and Old Woman declared that all those above would have to return one day. As a result, all people must return to the underworld at death. (Campbell, HAWM)

Old Man and Old Woman (Lakota): In Lakota cosmology, prior to earth's creation a number of gods populated an undifferentiated realm. Among these were Old Man and Old Woman, who gave birth to a daughter Ite ("face"). Ite married Wind and gave birth to four sons, the Four Winds.

The Lakota Trickster figure, Inktomi, the Spider Woman, devises a plot with Old Man and Old Woman to further their daughter Ite's status. They propagate an affair between Ite and the Sun, which is discovered by the Sun's wife, the Moon. A number of punishments by the god Takuskanskan ("something that moves") ensue, including the separation of the Sun and Moon into separate domains, resulting in the creation of Time. Ite is separated from Wind. Wind, the four sons of Ite and Wind (the Four Winds), and a child resulting from the affair of Ite and the Sun (the Fifth Wind) are joined to constitute Space. (Eliade, ER)

Old Man and the Sea: In Ernest Hemingway's "Old Man and the Sea" (1952), the aged protagonist's pursuit of his catch, a large marlin, is representative of the endless struggle of human existence, a struggle that does not diminish with age. The aged fisherman in this story, thus, serves as an image of courage and endurance in old age.

Old Man of Crete: In Dante's *Inferno*, in the seventh circle of hell is a wasteland devoid of plant life and covered by deep *sand. *Fire rains perpetually from the sky, burning the naked souls who populate the area. A *mountain, described as old, shrunken, withered or decayed (Dante uses the Latin word *vieta*, which can have any of these meanings, to describe the *mountain), is explained as the source of a red stream running through the area. This *mountain, named Ida, lies on the island of Crete. Within it stands an old man, the Old Man of Crete, who is described in the following (Canto 14, 106-110): "his head is fashioned of fine gold, his arms and breast are pure silver, then down to the fork he is of brass, and down from there is all of choice iron, except that the right foot is baked clay." (Singleton, pp. 147-149) Rivulets of tears stream from fissures in all areas of the *mountain, except for the area made of *gold. These streams coalesce to form the Acheron, Styx, and Phlegethon Rivers, finally coming together to form Cocytus, the *pool in Hell in which the damned souls bathe.

The old man within the *mountain is an image reflective of the *Ages of Man as described in Ovid's *Metamorphoses* (1, 89-93): "Golden was that first age, which, with no one to compel, without a law, of its own will, kept faith and did the right. There was no fear of punishment, no threatening words were to be read on brazen tablets; no suppliant throng gazed fearfully upon its judge's face, but without judges lived secure." After this first age, ruled by *Saturn, had passed, a new race of men, the *silver race came about: "After Saturn had been banished to the dark land of death, and the world was under the sway of Jove, the silver race came in, lower in the scale than gold, but of greater worth than yellow brass." (*Metamorphoses* 1, 113-115) Ovid goes on to describe the successive *stages of man, leading to greater moral decay with each stage, as corresponding to the succession of metals from the purest to the basest: from *gold to *silver to brass to iron. (Singleton)

The fact that the Old Man "gazes on Rome as on a mirror" is evidence that Dante intends him as a metaphor for the decline of civilization as reflected in Ovid's Ages of Man, the history of Rome being reflective of this progressive degradation. (Singleton)

The alleged discovery, described by Pliny, of a 69-foot skeleton of a man within a mountain in Crete, believed to be the remains of one of the members of the original *golden race, is further reflection of the belief in the progressive degeneration of the human race: "When a mountain in Crete was cleft by an earthquake a body 69 feet in height was found, which some people thought must be that of Orion and others of Otus." (Pliny, *Natural History*, book 7, chapter 16, 73) Just as the human body shrinks with age, so the whole of mankind was believed to have shrunken with age, becoming smaller with each successive stage: "with the entire human race the stature on the whole is becoming smaller daily."

Thus, we see in the Old Man of Crete an image of the world as grown old and decrepit, experiencing decay and corruption as the physical body undergoes in the process of aging. (Singleton)

Old Man of the River: The Old Man of the River is derived from the personification of *rivers in Greek mythology. They are typically represented as respectable old men with beards, long hair, and reed *crowns. The Old Man of the River is a symbol of old age and the passage of time through association of the *river with time. The river's movement through space is equated with movement through time. (von Franz, *Time*)

Giovanni Battista Tiepolo's painting *Apollo and Daphne* (1755) shows the old river god, *Peneus, protecting his daughter Daphne, from Apollo. (McKee and Kauppinen)

Old Man of the Sea: *Nereus is the Old Man of the Sea of Classical mythology (cf. Homer's *Iliad* 18, 36 ff.). He possesses great wisdom, the gift of prophecy, and the power to change shape. He is portrayed as a bald old man wearing a wreath and a chiton, holding a wand in one hand and a *fish in the other. He is sometimes portrayed holding a dolphin or riding a seahorse while holding a trident. Other depictions show him as fish-tailed with three animals growing out of his body: a *lion, a *stag, and a viper.

In "Sinbad the Sailor," one of the tales from the *Arabian Nights*, we find the source of the designation of something from which it is difficult to gain freedom as an "Old Man of the Sea." Sinbad frees himself of the Old Man of the Sea, who has climbed onto his back and refuses to release his hold, by plying his tormentor with liquor. (Brewer) Similarly, in modern psychological terms, the Old Man of the Sea is sometimes interpreted as the "burden of the subconscious." (de Vries) (also see GLAUKOS)

old nurse: According to Graves, old nurses in Greek legend, for example *Baubo, usually stand for the *Tripartite Goddess as *Crone. (Graves, GM I) In her search for her daughter, Persephone, *Demeter, the earth goddess of Classical mythology, takes on the guise of an *old woman. Consequently, when she comes to the home of Celeus and Metaneira (cf. "Homeric Hymn to Demeter"), she is offered the job of nurse, an occupation which the Greeks considered suitable for an old woman.

The 19th-century French painter Charles Gleyre, depicts such an old nurse in his work of 1866, *Saute-mouton*. Setting the scene in ancient Greece, Gleyre shows an old nurse tending a baby, while older children play around them. Shelley (1792-1822) in "Queen Mab" reveals the perpetuation of this tradition in 19th century England:

> Thousands shall deem it an old woman's tale,
> Such as the nurses frighten babes withal

old woman: "Old woman" has come to signify any person who is timid and fussy, as seen in Daniel DeFoe's *Journal of the Plague Year* (1722): "The Old Women, and the Phlegmatic Hypochondria Part of the other Sex, who I could almost call old Women too." (OED, p. 1984)

Old women in fairy tales, as aspects of the *crone, often function as symbols or agents of fertility. Illustrative examples are the tales of the "Old Woman Who Lived under a Hill," and "The Old Woman Who Lived in a Shoe," tales in which the dwellings of the old women augment their functions as fertility symbols. (de Vries) The nursery rhyme "The Old Woman Who Lived in a Shoe," as we commonly know it, goes as follows:

> There was an old woman who lived in a shoe,
> She had so many children she didn't know what to do;
> She gave them some broth without any bread;
> She whipped them all soundly and put them to bed.

An earlier version (from *Infant Institutes*, 1797) reads:

> There was a little old woman, and she liv'd in a shoe,
> She had so many children, she didn't know what to do.
> She crumm'd 'em some porridge without any bread;
> And she borrow'd a beetle, and she knocked 'em all o' the head.
> Then out went th' old woman to bespeak 'em a coffin,
> And when she came back, she found 'em all a'loffeing.

According to Opie: "The shoe has long been symbolic of what is personal to a woman until marriage. Casting a shoe after a bride when she goes off on her honeymoon, is possibly a relic of this, symbolizing the wish that the union shall be fruitful. This is consistent with the many children belonging to a woman who actually lived in a shoe." (*Oxford Dictionary of Nursery Rhymes*, pp. 434-435)

Old Woman (Australian): The Gunwinngu of northern Australia speak of a creator called Old Woman who takes the form of a rainbow *serpent, Ngalijod, and peoples the earth with the original humans which she carries within her body. (Campbell, HAWM)

Old Woman (Navajo): In a Navajo myth of the First People, the primordial twins (sons of Changing Woman, daughter of First Man and First Woman) travel beyond the known world to "the realm where death leads to rebirth" in search of their father, the *Sun. Here they encounter *Old Woman who warns them that they will die before they reach the *Sun. She warns them, as well, that they must not walk on her path. Forgetting her warning, they walk on the Old Woman's path; as a consequence, their steps shorten until they are unable to walk, even with the aid of sticks. Observing their mistake, Old Woman returns to rebuke them. She sings a song, naming the *four directions, exclaiming "old age!" after each name. She explains her actions to them: "I sang this song so that in the future everything should reach old age: people, animals, birds, insects, everything that grows. I mentioned the four directions, so that no matter how far the earth goes, there should always be old age." She performs a ritual, spitting into her hands, rubbing them in turn on her body and the twins' bodies, singing a song which includes old age. The twins are restored to youth and proceed on their *journey. (Campbell, HAWM)

omega: In late antiquity, omega constituted the "round element," which represented a lifetime, a period of time, and eternity. *Oceanos as *Time, in the form of a *river flowing around the edge of the earth, forming its boundary, is constituted of omega. (von Franz, *Time*)

ouroboros: The ouroboros, depicted as a *dragon, winged *snake or *serpent biting its own tail, symbolizes time, eternity, the continuity of life and the natural world in its *cyclic aspect. (de Vries) Primarily a Gnostic symbol, it unites the *serpent (an earthbound creature) and the *bird (a creature of the heavens), creating a union of opposites. It is often portrayed half light and half dark, similar to a yin-yang symbol, constituting evidence of its function as a symbol of alternating *cycles. The ouroboros' devouring of its own tail is interpreted as representative of both self-fecundation (as in nature) and self-destruction (through ingestion of its own poison) to effect rebirth. (Cirlot) It is thus a symbol of the devouring nature of time. In Renaissance imagery, Father Time often carries an ouroboros. In *The Triumph of Time*, a woodcut from Petrarch by Gregorio de Gregorii, 1508, Time, personified as an *old man, holds a *scythe in one hand and an ouroboros in the other. (Panofsky, Plate 53)

In his later poetry, William Carlos Williams (1883-1963) uses the ouroboros as an image reflective of the union of opposites and the *cyclic nature of existence, the awareness of which develops in old age. He describes self-direction, individual orientation, as changed at this point, as a *serpent with "its tail in its mouth." (*Paterson V*, I, iii, 1959)

owl: In the *Ten Ages of Man, the medieval artistic and literary convention which divides an individual's life into *ten stages, an owl is a woman of 70 to 80. The owl is a common symbol of wisdom, since its acute vision allows it to penetrate the darkness and its countenance is serious and pensive. (Herder) The owl is also a symbol of retired life. (de Vries)

It functions as the totem of *Minerva, the Roman goddess of wisdom who probably represents the *crone aspect of the earlier Capitoline Triad consisting of Juventas the Virgin, Juno the Mother, and Minerva the wise old *crone. Romans used the same word for owl and *witch, *strix*, linking the owl to the *crone in her stereotypic portrayal as a *witch. (Walker, WEMS) Lilith, Adam's first consort in the Old Testament, became the prototype of the witch. Another name for Lilith was "scritch owl." This correlation of the *witch and the owl is seen in many images related to the contemporary observance of Halloween.

A common motif in fairytales reflects the belief that sages could understand the owl's speech after their ears were licked by the serpents of the Wise Goddess. (Walker, *Crone*)

The owl's popular conception as a symbol of the wisdom of age is seen in the following rhyme (of unknown origin) quoted by John D. Rockefeller in 1915:

A wise old owl lived in an oak
The more he saw the less he spoke;
The less he spoke the more he heard.
Why can't we all be like that wise old bird?
(Opie, *Oxford Dictionary of Nursery Rhymes*, p. 340)

P

Pallas (Athene): In Ovid's *Metamporphoses*, book 6, Pallas (Athene) appears as an old woman in the tale of her contest with Arachne. The young weaver, Arachne, was renowned in her craft. Her skill was of such a high order that others declared she must have been taught by Pallas herself. Denying this, Arachne proclaimed that she would confidently compete with Pallas in a test of skill. Hearing of the challenge, Pallas disguises herself as an old woman and attempts to give Arachne one last chance to back down. Tottering feebly, supported by a stick, and wearing a wig of gray hair, she visits Arachne:

> "Not everything
> That old age brings," she said, "we'd wish to avoid.
> With riper years we gain experience.
> Heed my advice. Among the world of men
> Seek for your wool-craft all the fame you will,
> But yield the goddess place, and humbly ask
> Pardon for those rash words of yours; she'll give
> You pardon if you ask."

Incensed, Arachne answers:

> "You're too old, your brain has gone.
> You've lived too long, your years have done for you.
> Talk to your daughters, talk to your sons' wives!
> My own advice is all I need. Don't think
> Your words have any weight. My mind's unchanged."

Asking why Pallas has not come herself, Arachne is answered when Pallas throws off her crone's disguise and says, "She's come!"

The competition ensues. The results, showing Arachne in fact to be the superior weaver, anger Pallas, and she attacks Arachne in a rage. Arachne, despondent, tries to hang herself; however, Pallas takes pity on her and allows her to live, though in a transformed state. Pallas sprinkles Arachne with a potion, turning her into a spider. She thus is still able to practice her craft, though on a scale less competitive with the goddess. (trans. Melville)

palm: The palm is a symbol of self-renewal and rejuvenation. The Greek name for the palm, *phoenix*, reflects its relationship to the myth of the *phoenix, the bird that is symbolic of eternal life and resurrection. The *phoenix periodically destroyed itself by fire and was subsequently reborn out of its own *ashes. The legend according to Tacitus states that it was born and reborn in the branches of a palm tree, living 1,461 years in each *cycle.

The palm is often referred to as the *Tree of Life, because it does not periodically lose its *leaves like other trees; and it continues to bear *fruit until the end of its life *cycle. It is a symbol of *pilgrimage, as evidenced by the fact that one who has made a *pilgrimage to the Holy Land is called a "palmer." (de Vries; Herder)

Pantaloon: One of the two *old man stock characters from the commedia dell'arte (the other being the *Doctor), Pantaloon is portrayed as an amorous, repulsive, old fool, who attempts to seduce young women by means of his money. He is typically depicted as a tall, thin, sickly old man with a beard and an absurdly large, erect phallus. Attempting to appear all-knowing and wise, he is actually regarded as foolish and irritating. In fact, he is so bothersome that others repeatedly beat him to keep him quiet.

Pantaloon was known by different names in various parts of Italy: Pancrace, Cassandre, or Zanobio. In France, he was known as Gaultier-Garguille or Jacquemin-Jadot. Examples of the amorous old man occur frequently in the plays of the Italian Angelo Beolco, known as Ruzzante, particularly in *Aconitaire* and *Deuxième dialogue rustique* and in the character of Tura in *Piovana*. (de Beauvoir)

de Beauvoir explains the 16th-century portrayal of the aged in the character of Pantaloon as a reaction against the nouveau riche, whose wealth was perceived by those younger with envy and suspicion. Their newly acquired riches were seen as resulting from avarice and greed.

By the close of the 17th century, Pantaloon had changed considerably. He becomes a family man and is no longer miserly, only thrifty. de Beauvoir cites the work of the Venetian playwright Goldoni as exemplary of the change in the stock character Pantaloon. His early work presents Pantaloon in standard commedia dell'arte fashion as a miserly, disagreeable old man; however, Goldoni's later work shows a marked change in Pantaloon's character, a change reflecting a new perception of the Venetian merchant class. Because the economy of Venice had become dependent upon a mercantile class, the merchant had become "the incarnation of common sense and straightforward honesty." According to de Beauvoir, "The ideal man was the honest, sparing, industrious merchant." (p. 188) Pantaloon, as a merchant, came to take on the characteristics of the ideal merchant. He became a sensible family man and was no longer portrayed as aged.

The man described by Jacques as representative of the Sixth Age of Man in Shakespeare's *As You Like It* is based upon the stock character, Pantaloon. He is described as "a lean and slippered pantaloon."

Parcae: Their name derived from the Latin word *parere* ("to bear, give birth"), the Parcae were originally two Roman birth goddesses, Decuma and Nona. Later, when they became a version of the Greek *Moirai (or Three *Fates), a third goddess was added, Morta (goddess of death), and they became forces determining fate. (Lurker, p. 275)

patorra: As a figure symbolic of Lent which was burned on Easter day in the Middle Ages, the patorra took the form of an old woman with seven feet representing the seven weeks of Lent. Simone de Beauvoir regards the patorra as expressive of the misogyny and ageism prevalent in the Middle Ages: "it was the old women who were symbolically expelled or killed in the small towns and the countryside to rid society of old age." (p. 136)

Peneus: Peneus is an old river god from Classical mythology. In Ovid's *Metamorphoses*, book 1, he protects his daughter, Daphne, from the advances of Apollo. Nearly exhausted by Apollo's chase, Daphne sees her father, "the river, swift Peneus," and cries out to him for help. In response, Peneus turn her into a tree, and she escapes Apollo.

Giovanni Battista Tiepolo's *Apollo and Daphne* (1755) shows Peneus protecting Daphne. Cupid, who initiated Apollo's pursuit by shooting him with a golden arrow and thus causing him to fall in love with Daphne, hides behind Daphne and Peneus. (McKee and Kauppinen)

St. Peter: St. Peter's name, meaning "rock," forms the origin of his designation as the foundation of the Church: "Thou art Peter, and upon this rock I will build my church." (Matthew 16:18). St. Peter is portrayed as a stolid, robust old man, sometimes balding, with a square face and a short, curly beard. As the keeper of the *keys to heaven (given to him by Christ), he can be identified by the one or two large *keys which he carries. (cf. "The Apostle Peter" from the woodcut series *Christ and the 12 Apostles with St. Paul*, by Lucas Cranach the Elder, ca. 1515) He is sometimes shown on a cross upside down because, since he felt unworthy of a crucifixion identical to Christ's, he requested that he be crucified in an inverted position. (Pierce)

Philemon and Baucis: In the tale of Philemon and Baucis from Classical mythology (Ovid's *Metamorphoses*, 8, 618-724), Zeus and Hermes planned to release a worldwide flood. Before doing so, however, they traveled the countryside together with the aim of testing mortals to determine if any worth saving remained. Passing through the Phrygian countryside disguised as mortals, Zeus and Hermes came upon the cottage of the old peasant couple, Philemon and Baucis. Unlike their neighbors, who had repeatedly turned Zeus and Hermes away, the couple offered the travelers refuge. Hospitably entertaining their guests despite their humble means, Philemon and Baucis noticed that the wine bowl at their dinner table kept miraculously refilling itself. Prompted by what they perceived as evidence of the presence of company worthy of great veneration, the couple made preparations to kill their only *goose and serve it to their guests. Zeus and Hermes stopped them, revealing their true identities. They revealed to them, as well, that the surrounding area had been devastated and turned into a lake. They had been saved and their home had been turned into a temple as reward for their goodness. As further reward, Zeus and Hermes offered to grant any wish Philemon and Baucis might have. The old couple asked that they be allowed to remain together as keepers of the temple and that they die together. Their wish was granted, and when they died they were transformed into an *oak and a linden (or, according to some accounts, an *oak and a lime), standing side by side in front of the temple. (de Beauvoir; Grant and Hazel; Grimal, DCM; Tripp)

In Rubens' painting of 1630, *Philemon and Baucis*, Zeus reaches out to stop Baucis, who is trying to catch the *goose to prepare it for their meal. (McKee and Kauppinen)

Phineus: Phineus, a character from Classical mythology, was cursed with "lingering old age" as a punishment for having revealed the prophecies of Zeus. (Richardson, p. 49)

phoenix: The phoenix symbolizes longevity, immortality, eternal youth, and self-regeneration. It is representative of the culmination of a process or *cycle since, when in advanced age it sees its death approaching, it effects its own destruction through self-immolation and is reborn out of its own *ashes. Various accounts give differing maximum ages for the phoenix, ranging from 500 to 12,154 years. Tacitus gave its age as 1,461 years, reflecting its nature as a calendar beast, since Egyptian culture had no leap year and subsequently lost one year in every 1,460 years. (Cirlot; de Vries)

Ovid describes the phoenix in *Metamorphoses* 15 as a bird which "renews and re-begets itself" (Melville trans.):

This bird, when five long centuries of life
Have passed, with claws and beak unsullied, builds

A nest high on a lofty swaying palm;
And lines the nest with cassia and spikenard
And golden myrrh and shreds of cinnamon,
And settles there at ease and, so embowered
In spicy perfumes, ends his life's long span.
Then from his father's body is reborn
A little Phoenix, so they say, to live
The same long years. When time has built his strength
With power to raise the weight, he lifts the nest--
The nest his cradle and his father's tomb--
As love and duty prompt, from that tall palm
And carries it across the sky to reach
The Sun's great city, and before the doors
Of the Sun's holy temple lays it down.

The aged main character in Eudora Welty's "A Worn Path" is named Phoenix, reflecting her longevity and endurance of hardship as based in her capacity for self-renewal.

Phorcys: Phorcys, whose name means "boar," as a wise *Old Man of the Sea in Classical mythology, possessed prophetic wisdom (cf. Virgil's *Aeneid* 5). (Graves, GM II, p. 405) He was also a god of death, being the masculine form of Phorcis, "the goddess or sow who devours corpses." (Graves, GM I, p. 129)

pig: The goddess as *crone sometimes takes the form of a white sow (the Southeast Asian Diamond, the Syrian Astarte, and the Greek *Demeter-Persephone).

Pigs in Indo-European mythology are typically related to (as attributes or as metamorphosed forms of) the death goddess or *crone. Graves speculates that the common colors of the pig (white, red, and black) are at least a partial basis of this relationship, because they are the colors of the *Triple Goddess, as well. Further, he views the crescent-shaped tusks of the boar as reminiscent of the *crescent *moon (which is symbolic of the *crone or *witch) as further basis for this relationship. The pig is related to the Three *Fates through its relationship to the *Graiae. They were known as the "daughters of Phorcus." Phorcus "became a synonym for the Underworld; it is the same word as porcus, a pig, the beast sacred to the Death-goddess, and perhaps as *Parcae, a title of the Three *Fates, usually called *Moirae, 'the distributors.'" (Graves, WG, pp. 229-230)

pilgrim: The pilgrim represents the *journey through life, through material existence. This is expressed in Shelley's (1792-1822) "Queen Mab":

The mountain-paths of virtue, which no more
Were stained with blood from many a pilgrim's feet.

He can be identified in traditional imagery by his attributes: shell, crook or *staff, *girdle, *well of the *water of salvation which he finds in his path, road, and *cloak. (Cirlot; Herder) The pilgrim is shown with his traditional attributes in a 17th century painting from the Italian School, *Old Man Holding a Pilgrim Bottle*. (McKee and Kauppinen)

In John Bunyan's *Pilgrim's Progress*, when the travelers come across *Old Honest asleep under an *oak, they identify him as a pilgrim by his clothes, *staff, and *girdle: "Now a little before them stood an oak, and under it when they came to it, they found an old Pilgrim fast asleep; they knew that he was a Pilgrim by his Clothes, and his Staff, and his Girdle." (Bunyan, p. 293)

The pilgrim is thematically related to the *labyrinth, since passage through the *labyrinth commonly found in medieval churches is a ritual symbolic of the pilgrimage. The pilgrim is traditionally a metaphor for the aged Christian, since the Christian properly perceives the material hardships of life as the opportunity for spiritual growth. Whitehead in *Aging and the Elderly* explains how the open attitude to growth and change necessary to the pilgrim relates to acceptance of the process of aging: "The acceptance of life as a process, the appreciation of the open-endedness of both personal and social development, the identification of oneself as a pilgrim-on-the-way--these realizations suggest that one's experience of *change* in aging can be interpreted as an invitation from God to continue the process of growth toward full human maturity." (Spicker, et al., p. 44)

The pilgrim on his *journey becomes a liminal figure, one no longer bound by the constraints of social structure. He thus confronts himself, possibly for the first time, without structure. Consequently, as pointed out by Victor Turner in "Pilgrimages as Social Processes," the pilgrim becomes a fitting symbol for the aged of contemporary society, who are often confronted with an unstructured existence. Such a situation of change resulting in loss of an established identity causes the aged person to confront life as a process of growth, as a pilgrimage.

The role of pilgrim is one traditionally associated in Christianity with honor and respect, as reflected in the fact that the old pilgrim in *Pilgrim's Progress* (described in the passage above), is named *Old Honest. As well, the pilgrim in W. Collins' "Ode Written in the Year 1746" is named Honour:

There Honour comes, a pilgrim grey,
To bless the turf that wraps their clay.

Pilgrimage is a wide religious practice in Tibet. The Tibetan word for any living creature is *gro-ba*, which means "one who goes," reflecting a view that the defining condition of life is movement and growth. This idea, combined with the fact that extensive travel is a necessary result of the geographic and economic conditions of Tibet, and that all actions are perceived as religious in nature, causes the travel which is a necessary condition of everyday life to become a form of religious pilgrimage.

Circumambulation is an important aspect of Tibetan pilgrimage, the entire pilgrimage being perceived as one large circumambulation composed of smaller circuits. This circumambulation is accompanied by recitation of a mantra, the mantra being a means to effect a favorable rebirth; consequently, the pilgrimage is linked to the longer *journey of a soul's progression to the next life. The greater the difficulty of the *journey, the more religious merit accrues; consequently, as much hardship as possible is sought out, sometimes accomplished by means of prostration and other ascetic practices. (Eliade, ER)

The pilgrim as a Jungian archetype signifies renunciation, transcendence, release, and the decisive steps in life which must be taken without assistance. (de Vries) Such transendence and renunciation are reflected in Shelley's (1792-1822) description of the "mountain paths of virtue" as those traveled by the pilgrim in "Queen Mab":

> the remembrance
> With which the happy spirit contemplates
> Its well-spent pilgrimage on earth,
> Shall never pass away.

The completed circuit of the pilgrim's journey symbolizes the completion of a life in old age in Wordsworth's "Resolution and Independence" (1802/1807) (D. Luke):

> Such seemed this Man, not all alive or dead,
> Nor all asleep--in his extreme old age:
> His body was bent double, feet and head
> Coming together in life's pilgrimage.

We see another image of the aged pilgrim in Benjamin West's (1738-1820) painting *The Pilgrim Mourning his Dead Ass* (a scene from Laurence Stern's *Sentimental Journey*).

pine: As an evergreen, the pine tree is a symbol of immortality and longevity. (de Vries; Herder) It is often found in Chinese and Japanese art with a *stag and a *stork or *crane as a cluster of images which signifies longevity. In a print by the Japanese artist Shunsen, *Spirits of the Pine Tree*, an *old man and *old woman sweep the needles which have fallen from two pine trees which rise above them. Pigott says that the old couple, Jo and Uba, represent the spirits of the pine trees. They are, as well, personifications of old age and marital fidelity. Like the two pine trees, they have stood side by side for many years. The scene contains *tortoises and storks, common symbols of old age and longevity.

In Christian symbolism, the pine forms the *crown of the *Tree of Life, possibly relating it to the Christian concept of old age as "the *crown of life." (Herder) It is also a symbol of the individual personality or spirit which maintains its integrity throughout the hardships of life, thereby becoming an apt symbol for the aged person. In Eudora Welty's "A Worn Path," the main character, Phoenix, encounters pine trees on the path up the hillside. They become a symbol of this aged character's endurance of hardship.

plane tree: see SYCAMORE.

Plutus (or Plutos): As son of *Demeter and Iasion (the "first sower of seed"), Plutus is "the benefactor who gave mankind the boon of farming." (Lurker, p. 284) He originally was the child or young man carrying a horn of plenty who accompanied *Demeter and Persephone in their processional rite in enactment of the Eleusinian mysteries. Representing "plenty" in this ritual context, he was later separated from his identification with *Demeter and came to personify wealth in terms of material goods. He appears in this later capacity in Aristophanes' comedy and last play, *Plutus*, as an old man who distributes gifts without discretion. In this context, he is depicted as *blind because, according to Aristophanes, Zeus blinded him so that he could not distinguish the virtuous from the wicked and wealth would thereby be bestowed indiscriminately through his visitation upon both. (Grimal, DCM)

Polonius: Polonius, an aged character from Shakespeare's *Hamlet*, exemplifies one who has not gained wisdom through benefit of years of experience, but rather has become almost a caricature of the amoral, conniving scoundrel which he had always been. (Freedman)

pool: The pool symbolizes wisdom and self-knowledge. (cf. the Classical myth of Narcissus) As a form of the *mirror, the pool functions as an instrument of self-reflection in life review. In Theodore Roethke's (1908-1963) "Infirmity," the aged narrator stares into a "deepening pool" and tells himself, "my image cannot die." (de Vries)

poplar: The poplar is a symbol of old age and *Time. It signifies the letter "e" in the *tree alphabet of the Celts, which corresponds to the *autumnal equinox. (Graves, WG) The poplar is related to *Saturn, who symbolizes the devouring nature of time, and to the underworld, since in Classical mythology it grew at the entrance to Hades. (de Vries)

Poseidon: Poseidon, Roman god of the *sea, appeared as an *old man to Agamemnon when he was preparing to depart for the Trojan War.

Pot, broken (or broken vessel): Since the pot symbolizes the vessel of life (the human body), a broken pot is symbolic of a body which, through physical decay, can no longer contain the life force (like an aging body). An ancient burial custom among Native Americans involved covering the face of a dead person with a pot broken so that the spirit could be released from the body.

In John Bunyan's *Pilgrim's Progress*, the broken pitcher is a symbol by which Mr. Valiant-for-Truth realizes that death is upon him: "Mr. Valiant-for-Truth was taken with a summons . . . and had this for a token that the summons was true, that his pitcher was broken at the fountain." (pp. 375-376) The image of the broken pitcher found here echoes an image from the parable of old age in Ecclesiastes 12:6-7, symbolizing the failure of the aged body to contain the life force: "Or ever the silver cord be loosed, or the golden bowl be broken, or the pitcher be broken at the fountain, or the wheel broken at the cistern. Then shall the dust return to the earth as it was: and the spirit shall return unto God who gave it."

Pot Tilter: The Crow Indians, the Hidatsa, and the Gros Ventre "coerce" children by threatening that, if they are not "good," they will end up in Pot Tilter's boiling pot. Pot Tilter is an old *ogress who carries a boiling pot which sucks in those toward whom she tilts it. (Leach, p. 816)

Prakriti: Prakriti is the Sanskrit name of *Kali, meaning "nature." Kali controls the *gunas*, the "white, red, and black *threads of Creation, Preservation, and Destruction." As a form of the *Triple Goddess, her tripartite manifestation corresponds to past/present/future, earth/sea/sky, and youth/maturity/old age. (Walker, WEMS)

prison: Like the *cage, the prison symbolizes the restriction of old age, as in Matthew Arnold's (1822-1888) "Growing Old":

> It is to spend long days
> And not once feel that we were ever young;
> It is to add, immured
> In the hot prison of the present, month
> To month with weary pain.

Proteus: Proteus, the wise old prophet of the *sea, is sometimes confused with *Nereus, the *Old Man of the Sea. Though he probably was the model upon which *Nereus' behavior was based, Proteus is a character distinct from *Nereus in Classical mythology.

Proteus' name means "first man." As the possessor of great wisdom and prophetic knowledge, he is often sought by Classical heroes. However, he is not fond of dispensing his knowledge and assumes numerous shapes so as to avoid doing so, giving advice only after being seized and held for a length of time and assuming his original form. In the *Odyssey*, when captured by Menelaus on his journey home from Troy, Proteus' changes of form mark the movement through the *seasons and progression from birth through death of the Sacred *King. The animals corresponding to the five *seasons, whose shapes Proteus progressively assumes, are: *lion, *goat, horse, *serpent, and bull-calf. Proteus shape-shifting capacity is also described in Ovid's *Metamorphoses* 8. (Graves, GM; Stapleton)

Q

quaternary: The tetradic division of the human lifespan reflects a view of the individual as a microcosm of the macrocosm, the human body correspondingly possessing *four directions and the lifespan possessing *four *seasons. Cosmograms consisting of a *circle divided into *four quadrants with a human at the center, common during the Middle Ages, reflect this view. In such schema, *winter and *north correspond to old age.

A crypt in the Cathedral at Anagni holds one such diagram. A lone figure appears at the core of a *circle at the intersection of a cross marking the *four quadrants. Each quadrant bears a bust of a man of one of the *four ages. (Sears, Plate 5)

The division of the *seasons, the elements, the *stages of life, and the stages of the day's and the month's cycles into *four, corresponding to the *four directions (the "quaternary"), are as follows (Cirlot, p. 269):

East: "spring, air, infancy, dawn, crescent moon"
South: "summer, fire, youth, midday, full moon"
West: "autumn, water, middle age, evening, waning moon"
North: "winter, earth, old age, night, new moon"

R

Ra (Re): Ra is the *sun god and the lord of time in ancient Egypt. He marks the *sun's passage as he sails in his barge across the day sky (the upper world) and the *night sky (the underworld); cf. the boat of Ra, scene from the *Book of Gates*, papyrus. Each hour is marked by his transformation into a different animal, thereby causing the passage of time to be identified with a succession of *cyclically changing archetypes expressed in varied animal form. Ra rises as a scarab and descends as a *crocodile. The *crocodile is thereby identified with the end of a *cycle, as in old age. (von Franz, *Time*) The final chapter of the Egyptian Book of the Dead is titled "Chapter of Sailing in the Great Sun-Boat of Re." (Budge)

rack: The rack symbolizes the hardships of life which take their toll in their cumulative effect in old age, as seen in John Banister Tabb's (1845-1909) "Childhood":

> And yet I would not call thee back,
> Dear Childhood, lest the sight of me,
> Thine old companion, on the rack
> Of Age, should sadden even thee.

raven: The raven is a symbol of longevity, since, by some accounts, it lives three times longer than a human. Hesiod asserts that it lives 108 times longer than man: "A chattering crow lives out nine generations of aged men, but a stag's life is four times a crow's, and a raven's life makes three stags old, while the phoenix outlives nine ravens." (Evelyn-White, p. 75)

Shakespeare employs the raven as a symbol of the benefits of old age in *The Tempest*: "ravens feed on the dew of heaven, when they have 'no blade feathers by benefit of age.'" (de Vries)

reaping: Reaping, as a form of *harvest, is a symbol of the devouring nature of time, as in "ripe old age." Reaping, as time's ravaging, is an activity of *Kronos, *Saturn, and *Time (the Grim Reaper).

relic: The relic symbolizes the aged as a diminished version, a remnant, of what they were in youth, their current diminished value a consequence of their previous state (cf. the film *Love Among the Ruins*).

ring: As a closed *circle, having no beginning or end, the ring symbolizes continuity and repeated *cycles, as in the passage of time. The ring may take the form of the *ouroboros, a symbol of time and eternally repeated *cycles. A ring of *flames surrounds the dancing Shiva, the East Indian god, signifying both the *cycle of the universe and the individual life *cycle, "the circular dance of nature in eternal process of creation and destruction." (Cirlot, p. 274)

Rip Van Winkle: Rip Van Winkle, a character from early American literature created by Washington Irving, serves as an allegorical figure instructive of the price of laziness and of the proverb "you shall reap what you sow."

On a stroll through the woods with his dog, Rip comes upon an old man carrying a keg of liquor. Rip helps him carry the keg to a hollow where a group of old men are playing ninepins. The old men ask Rip to serve the liquor to them. He does, and serves himself as well, falling into a deep sleep lasting twenty years. When he awakens, Rip returns to town, only to find everything changed. He has aged twenty years, as well, having grown old and stooped with a beard a foot long. His former house has fallen to ruin, his wife has died, and—worst of all—his son has become a virtual copy of himself at the same age. Rip's dismay at the way things have changed during his 20 years' sleep signifies each person's dismay at the swiftness with which time escapes. (Irving)

John Quidor's painting *The Return of Rip Van Winkle* (1829), shows Rip returning to his village as an old, bearded man. (McKee and Kauppinen)

river: The children of *Oceanos (*Time) and Tethys (a sea goddess), rivers are personified in Greek mythology as *old men with long hair, beards, and reed *crowns. (de Vries) (see OLD MAN OF THE RIVER, PENEUS, TMOLUS) The conception of time as a river is widespread, the river's movement in space correlated to movement in time and its incessant flow representative of the nature of time. Early Western devices for measuring time were based on the flow of a substance (liquid in water and mercury *clocks, or *sand in *hourglasses), reflecting the original image or concept of time as a river. (von Franz, *Time*)

The river as a symbol is often ambiguous, being both benevolent (as the agent of fertility) and malevolent (as the agent of loss through the irreversible passage of time). This ambiguity is exemplified in "The Old Demon" by Pearl S. Buck (1892-1973).

Other literary examples of usage of the river as a symbol of time are found in T. S. Eliot's *The Wasteland* (1922): "at the source of the longest river" and Benjamin Franklin Taylor's (1819-1887) "The Isle of Long Ago":

> Oh, a wonderful stream is the River Time, . . .
> And a broader sweep and a surge sublime
>   As it blends with the ocean of Years.

road: The road, as a symbol of life traversed by the individual, is often found in imagery related to aging. Since old age is often a time of contemplation of one's life, the road's prominence in imagery reflective of the experience of aging can be explained by the fact that understanding or knowledge of the road (or life itself) has become not merely a means to a goal but the goal itself. It thus becomes not merely a background element but an element of great prominence and importance (see PILGRIM). The road as a symbol of a life's course can be seen in Robert Frost's (1874-1963) "The Road Not Taken."

rod: The rod, like the *staff and the *cane, is a symbol of the physical support necessary in old age. It is also an attribute of the *pilgrim and is related to the *Tree of *Jesse (Isaiah 11:1). (de Vries) The flowering rod, seen in Biblical images of the aged, symbolizes fertility at an advanced age as a reward for Christian virtue. Such an image is presented in a painting by an artist from the circle of the Spanish painter, Jusepe de Ribera (1588-1652), *St. Joseph with a Flowering Rod*.

rosary: The rosary, as an object originally used to mark the passage of time and as an object circular in form, symbolizes the *cyclic nature of time and its inexorable passage. In his "Essay on Man," Pope calls *beads (which make up a rosary) and prayer books the "toys of age." (de Vries)

In Matthias Stomer's painting *Old Woman Praying* (Dutch, 17th century), an *old woman, her face illuminated by a nearly concealed *flame, sits fingering her rosary in prayer.

In Guariento's depiction of the *Seven Ages of Life, from the Church of the Eremitani in Padua, the sixth age is personified as Jupiter. He is flanked by a man and a woman representing early old age. The woman, holding a rosary, sits in meditation. (Sears)

rose: The rose is a symbol of completion and perfection, as in a completed life. The seven-petalled rose is related to the septenary division of the *Ages of Man, the *seven days, the *seven planets, and so on. (Cirlot)

In medieval symbolism, the rose functioned as a symbol of the individual, mirroring man's state, as in the following passage attributed to Alan of Lille (from Edgar de Bruyne, *Etudes d'esthétique Médiévale*):

Every creature of this earth
is like a picture or a book:
it is a mirror of ourselves.
It is a faithful mark
of our life and of our death,
of our state and of our fate.
The rose is a picture,
a fitting image of our state,
a lesson on our life;
for it flowers in early morning,
and the fading flower flowers
in the evening of age.

The guelder rose is a symbol of age, of *winter, and of the state of being "young" though physically old. (de Vries)

The rose is used in A. Mary Robinson's "Temple Garlands" as symbolic of positive memories that do not fade with age:

. . . garlands that forever last,
That gathered once are always sweet;
    The roses of the Past!

Round of Existence: The Buddhist Round of Existence or *Wheel of Becoming symbolizes the totality and *cyclic nature of phenomenal existence. It is diagrammatic of all phases of life from birth to death, the outer circle containing *twelve divisions (similar to the *zodiac). The eleventh of the twelve images is an aged blind woman, representing "the absence of knowledge, the blindness of ignorance leading to death." The last image shows a man transporting a corpse, signifying "death and suffering, leading to rebirth." (Cooper, p. 142)

rowing: Rowing symbolizes memory and travel through life in reverie, as in Yuan Mei's "Seven Poems on Aging," I: "To row me on, plenty of hands at the oars." (Lyell)

Rowing is a symbol for one's passage through life, through its relationship to the *boat, which is the vessel which symbolically carries the soul through physical existence. The *boat serves as a substitute for the body at death, carrying the soul to the next world after the earthly body falls away. The *oar is an attribute of many *river gods in Classical mythology, who are personifications of time. *Peneus is depicted with his *oar in Giovanni Battista

Tiepolo's painting *Apollo and Daphne* (1755). The *oar also figures in the story of Odysseus' final journey in the *Odyssey*.

In *Traveling North*, a contemporary Australian film, rowing becomes symbolic of the main character's struggle with his own physical decay with age. As age increases his infirmity, it becomes necessary for his mate to row him across the lake which has been his daily haunt. His inability to row himself is expressive of his increasing dependence on others with age.

ruins: Ruins, as objects imbued with the past and evocative of the deterioration caused by time's passage, are often employed as symbols of the process of aging (cf. the film, *Love Among the Ruins*). (Cirlot) However, as Poe's imagery expresses, ruins are viewed in a positive aspect, as well. They are seen as rich repositories of history and not merely diminished versions of the original. In "The Coliseum," Poe presents a ruin of Roman culture as a symbol of aging and time's passage:

> Rich reliquary
> Of lofty contemplation left to Time
> . . .
> Vastness! and Age! and Memories of Eld!

Ruth and Naomi: Ruth and Naomi figure prominently in the Book of Ruth of Hebrew scripture. Ruth's story comprises four chapters.

In the first chapter, Naomi's husband and two sons die. Naomi and her daughter-in-law, Ruth, come together in mutual support, both widows in a "man's world," and travel to Bethlehem. In chapter 2, Ruth finds protection as the maidservant of Boaz, and in chapter 3, she asks Boaz to allow her to be his handmaid and provide for Naomi, as well. Boaz asks instead that Ruth marry him. In chapter 4, they marry and Boaz agrees to provide for Naomi. Ruth later bears Boaz a son, who fathers Jesse, who fathers David.

Ruth thus becomes a heroine, since she succeeds in remedying her own situation of dependent widowhood while honoring and protecting her former mother-in-law, Naomi, as well. Ruth is thereby a Biblical image of virtue and of respect for elders. (Eliade, ER; Scofield)

The story of Ruth and Boaz is the subject of the French painter Charles Gleyre's *Ruth et Boaz* (1853-1854).

Ryujin: Ryujin, Japanese *dragon *king of the *sea, is portrayed as an aged, emaciated *old man carrying the "Tide Jewel." (cf. *Ryujin, the Dragon King of the Sea*, a sculpture in the Victoria and Albert Museum) The fierce expression he wears reflects the belief that his anger causes turbulent seas. (Pigott)

S

salmon: The salmon is found in numerous tales as a symbol of wisdom. (see FISH) It is also found as a symbol of endurance and rebirth, as in Theodore Roethke's (1908-1963) "Meditations of an Old Woman," in which the poet describes a salmon moving upstream as the spirit's *journey.

sand: The grains of sand in an *hourglass represent fragments of time, as in Poe's "Al Aaraaf": "The sands of Time grow thinner as they run." Sand running through an *hourglass represents the passage of time, as in the following from Shakespeare: "for ere the glass, that now begins to run, Finish the process of his sandy hour. . . ." (*1 Henry VI*, act 4, sc. 2) Sand is a symbol of endurance and courage since it withstands the constant action of *water on beaches and on the ocean's floor. (de Vries) Sand is found in the Apocrypha as a symbol of time:

> Like a drop of water in the sea or a grain of sand,
> So are [man's] years in eternal time.
> (Ecclesiasticus 18:10)

In the tale of the *Sibyl of Cumae from Classical mythology, the sibyl is granted by Apollo as many years of life as she can hold grains of sand in one hand. She thereby lives 1,000 years.

sap: Shakespeare often relates the human body to vegetative life. Since sap constitutes the tangible evidence of the life force coursing through the plant, the sapless vine or *tree symbolizes the aged person whose life force is depleted. The following passage from *The Comedy of Errors* (act 5, sc. 1, 311-313) exemplifies Shakespeare's use of the image of sap:

Though now this grained face of mine be hid
In sap-consuming winter's drizzled snow,
And all the conduits of my blood froze up. . . .

Just as *winter stops the flow of sap through the *tree, so old age restricts the flow of what was in Shakespeare's time referred to as "radical humor" through the human body. Another example can be found in *Henry VI*:

. . . pithless arms, like to a withered vine
That droops his sapless branches to the ground.
(*1 Henry VI*, act 2, sc. 5, 11-12)

Sarah: The Biblical figure Sarah, who bore Isaac in old age, symbolizes, like her husband *Abraham, the Judeo-Christian concept of longevity and fertility as rewards for a virtuous life (Genesis 21:2-7).

Saturn: The central idea of the Saturn myth from Classical mythology is that, since creation takes place in time and is thereby *cyclic, it inevitably involves the inverse process of destruction. The devouring nature of time in its destructive aspect is symbolized by Saturn devouring his own children. (cf. Francisco Goya's *Saturn Devouring One of His Children*, 1819-1823)

As the ruler of the planet Saturn, the Greek and Roman God Saturn embodied characteristics associated with that planet—slow motion and gloominess--and became associated with malevolent forces—natural disasters, famine, old age, poverty, and death. In astrological imagery, Saturn is a sickly, gloomy *old man carrying a *sickle or *scythe or sometimes a spade which he uses as support in his decrepit state. Originally a god of agriculture (reflected in his early attribute of the *sickle, *scythe, or spade), he later became confused with *Chronos, the Greek personification of time, and became representative of old age and death in the form of *Father Time. (Panofsky)

Saturn's later traditional attributes reflect his relationship to time. He carries an *oar, indicative of the equation of movement through space with movement through time, an *hourglass emblematic of the passage of time, and a *scythe symbolic of reaping. (Cirlot; de Vries) Because he is depicted with four eyes, two looking behind and two looking forward, de Vries notes that Saturn shares in the dualism of *Janus "representing the moment in and out of time." Guariento executed a series of paintings in the early 1360's in the Church of the Eremitani in Padua depicting each of the Seven Ages as corresponding to the *moon and planets. In the painting depicting the seventh age, old age, we see Saturn flanked by elderly figures. Old and bearded, he leans upon a *scythe as he sits upon a *tree stump throne. The reclining figures on each side of him, an *old man and an *old woman, attempt to warm themselves over the embers of dying fires. (Sears, Plates 45-48)

Much later representations of Saturn reflect the late 15th-century shift in Saturn's conception. He becomes the god of philosophical and religious thought, his gloomy appearance a result of his immersion in profound questions of great import. (Panofsky)

In one of a number of Elizabethan schemes of old age, Henry Cuffe depicts Jupiter and Saturn as ruling the last two stages of life: ages 50 to 60 are under the influence of Jupiter, and over 65 ("decrepit old age") is under the influence of Saturn--a melancholy and unlucky influence. This agrees with the schemes of Bartholomaeus and Lemnius. (Draper, "Shakespeare's Attitude Towards Old Age," p. 123)

Cirlot describes Saturn as "a symbol of the law of limitation which gives shape to life, or the localized expression in time and space of the universal life." (Cirlot, p. 279)

Saturnus Africanus: A god of Roman North Africa derived from the Roman *Saturn, Saturnus Africanus is the divinity of time and agriculture and is considered the ruler of heaven. His attributes are a *sickle, honeycomb or fir-comb, and a *lion. (Lurker)

scarecrow: The scarecrow is a symbol of old age and the soul. (de Vries; Herder) In "Sailing to Byzantium," W. B. Yeats (1865-1939) uses the scarecrow as a symbol of an aged man, describing him as "a tattered coat upon a stick."

scissors: Scissors are an attribute specifically of *Atropos, the *crone, who cuts the thread of life. They are associated with the Three *Fates as a group, as well, symbolizing the power of the *Fates to terminate life at any time. They are, thereby, a symbol of the precarious quality of human life.

In Dylan Thomas' "When, Like a Running Grave," the poet presents an image of time as a predator who tracks one "like a scissors stalking."

Scrooge: Ebenezer Scrooge, the main character of Charles Dickens' *A Christmas Carol* (1843), is a miserly, unhappy old man who undergoes a process of self-examination resulting in a profound personality change. A thoroughly unpleasant character, Scrooge is described by Dickens as carrying "his own low temperature always about with him." (p. 32) Unconcerned with the chilling effect of his selfish, miserly personality on others, and completely oblivious to the needs of those about him, he leads an isolated existence. Haunted by *ghosts of the past and visited by an unpleasant specter of the future, he comes to reevaluate his past actions. Through this process, he comes to see himself as those around him see him and, not liking what he sees, changes dramatically.

Scrooge's experience can be viewed as exemplary of the process of life review in old age. Such a process of reviewing one's past has been observed as typical of a final stage of human development. Often involving great anxiety and personal crisis, this stage, if successfully passed through, can lead to a reintegration of the personality and a positive adaptation to the limitations of age. (Butler)

scythe: The scythe is an attribute of *Saturn, who has become the personification of old age, through his role as god of agriculture and his consequent association with *harvest. It is a symbol of *autumn as the time of *harvest and death of the *year's *cycle. The scythe became an attribute of time by way of the confusion through the similarity of names of *Kronos (or *Saturn), god of agriculture, with *Chronos, god of time. (de Vries; Panofsky)
    Shelley (1792-1822) employs the scythe as *Time in its destructive aspect in "Queen Mab":

> Youth springs, age moulders . . .
> They rise, they fall; one generation comes
> Yielding its harvest to destruction's scythe.

Alternatively, Jean Detroy presents *Time with his scythe as revealor of truth in *Time Unveiling Truth*, a painting from 1732. (McKee and Kauppinen)
    The 19th-century American painter Eastman Johnson presents an image contrasting age and youth in *Scythe Sharpening* (1862). A young boy watches and assists as an *old man sharpens a scythe.

sea: Through its rhythmic, *cyclic action, the sea is a symbol of the *cyclic, never-ending passage of time. (de Vries)

seasons: The *four phases of the *sun's orbit constituting the seasons are related to the *four stages, or "seasons" of human life. (Cirlot) The Greeks represented the Seasons as four women:

> Spring (infancy and childhood): depicted with a crown of flowers beside a blooming shrub.
> Summer (young adulthood): depicted with a crown made of ears of corn, a sickle in one hand and a sheaf in the other.
> Autumn (adulthood and middle age): depicted carrying grapes and a basket of fruit.
> Winter (old age): depicted bare-headed next to trees that are leafless.

The Greeks also depicted the seasons as *four animals: a sheep (Spring); a *dragon (Summer); a hare (*Autumn); and a salamander (*Winter). (Cirlot)
    Aristotle explains the relationship of the *ages of man's life to the seasons: "The seasons of the year are the turning-points of their lives, rather than their age, so that when these seasons change they change with them by growing and

losing feathers, hairs, or leaves respectively. But the winter and summer, spring and autumn of man are defined by his age." (Aristotle, *De generatione animalium* 5,3)

In ancient Greece, the view of the ages of man as having a basis in the seasons was associated with Pythagorean theory, as seen in the following passage from Diodorus Siculus' *Bibliotheca Historica* 10, 9,5: "The Pythagoreans divided the life of mankind into four ages, that of a child, a lad, a young man, and an old man; and they said that each one of these had its parallel in the changes which take place in the seasons in the year's course, assigning the spring to the child, the autumn to the man, the winter to the old man, and the summer to the lad." (Sears)

serpent (or snake): The serpent is a symbol found in numerous cultures with widely divergent meaning; however, a number of common meanings are relevant to the process of aging.

A number of its meanings relate to processes of rejuvenation and/or rebirth. First of all, because the serpent is long-lived and sheds its skin yearly (sheds its age), it is symbolic of longevity and self-rejuvenation. Second, portrayed in *circular form, it becomes an image of the self-devouring *ouroboros and represents the *cyclic and destructive/regenerative nature of time. In *circular form, it is connected with birth and rebirth and is thus related to the *cyclic *Wheel of Life.

In psychological terms, the serpent's poisonous nature and its habit of locomotion cause it to be symbolic of the "stealthily creeping nature of time, consuming our bodies." (de Vries, p. 414)

Twin snakes symbolize death and the conjunction of opposites (male/female, heaven/earth, life/death, etc.) In the Classical myth of *Tiresias, the wise old seer of Thebes who struck mating snakes with his *staff and was thereby turned into a woman, mating snakes become a symbol of the perception of opposing viewpoints as a prerequisite of wisdom. Joseph Campbell explains:

> In this tale the mating serpents, like those of the caduceus, are the sign of the world-generating force that plays through all pairs of opposites, male and female, birth and death. Into their mystery Tiresias blundered as he wandered in the green wood of the secrets of the ever-living goddess Earth. His impulsive stroke placed him between the two, like the middle staff (*axis mundi*); and he was thereupon flashed to the other side for seven years--a week of years, a little life--the side of which he formerly had had no knowledge. Whence, with intent, he again touched the living symbol of the two that are in nature one, and, returning to his proper form, was thereafter the one who was in knowledge both: in wisdom greater than either Zeus, the god who was merely

male, or his goddess, who was merely female. (Campbell, MG, p. 26)

*Tiresias' experience as both male and female yields the integrative understanding necessary to his role as the wise elder. His wisdom and power of prophecy were so great that he provided advice to the gods from Hades even after death. Erich Neumann views integrative understanding as a cognitive style typical of old age. He believes that three different forms of "mysticism," or cognitive styles, accompany three major stages of psychological development. The last stage, accompanying old age, is characterized by "mature mysticism" where "the self emerges: opposites are reconciled, and harmony is achieved between the conscious and unconscious aspects of the mind." (Woodward, *Memory and Desire*, p. 19)

Philo of Alexander theorized that, since the snake could both kill with its poison and cure through self-regeneration, it was symbolic of both the positive and negative forces shaping the world. Hence, its conflicting meanings in various cultures (male/female, birth/death, etc.).

seven: Seven symbolizes perfection, fulfillment, and completion of a *cycle. A number of *cyclic systems consist of seven phases: the seven *Ages of Man, seven days of the week, Plato's Seven Heavenly Spheres, etc. (de Vries) *Tiresias, the blind aged seer of Thebes who obtained wisdom through experience of both sexes, was a woman for seven years and lived seven generations. Shakespeare employs the *Seven Ages of Man in *As You Like It* (act 2, sc. 7).

The number seven was a number of great importance in early Western culture (Graeco-Roman). Not only were there *Seven Ages of Man, but there were also "7 planets, 7 stars in the Pleiades and the Great Bear, as well as 7 vowels in Greek, 7 strings on the lyre, and 7 movements (up, down, forward, back, right, left, in a circle)." And the body had 7 parts: "the head with 7 openings, the neck, torso, two legs, and two arms" and had "7 visceral organs (the stomach, heart, lungs, liver, spleen, and two kidneys)." (Sears, pp. 39, 40) In Graeco-Roman culture, seven was of great significance in systems of periodization of time. The 28-day lunar month was divided into four seven-day periods, the *moon's monthly *cycle was believed to pass through seven phases, and the equinoxes and solstices succeeded one another in *cycles of seven months. Consequently, in a view the human as a microcosm of the macrocosm, such sevenfold divisions of natural phenomena formed a strong basis for a view of human life as composed of seven ages.

Seven Ages of Man: The course of an individual human life is often divided into seven ages, as seen in Shakespeare's *As You Like It* (act 2, sc. 7):

All the world's a stage,

And all the men and women merely players.
They have their exits and their entrances,
And one man in his time plays many parts,
His acts being seven ages.

John Winter Jones presents an image from the 15th century of a *wheel divided into the Seven Ages of Man, starting from the earth (the point of origin labeled "Generacio") and returning to the earth (labeled "Corrupcio"). A man's body is spread across the *wheel which carries the following seven divisions: Infans, Puericia, Adolescencia, Juventus, Virilitas, Senectus, and Decrepitus. (Hankins)

*Seven as related to the life *cycle has traditionally taken two major forms: (1) the division of life into seven-year *cycles or seven-year intervals ending with 7, 14, 21, 28, 35, 42, 49, 56, 63, and 70; and (2) the division of the human lifespan into seven periods. In some systems, each period had a corresponding planet and the length of that period was determined by that planet. Sometimes each *cycle (corresponding with the first system of division) was of *seven years, and sometimes the length of each *cycle was unspecified. The correspondence of the *seven planets to the Seven Ages of Man was most widespread and influential in the Middle Ages, progressing from the *moon (ruling infancy), through Mercury, Venus, the *sun, Mars, Jupiter, and *Saturn.

In the *Tetrabiblos*, Ptolemy explains that each of the seven ages are influenced by and develop in accordance with the qualities seen to correspond to each of the planets. The *moon influnces infancy (the body in its moist, rapidly growing, unstable state). Mercury influences childhood and the developing, rational mind, influencing and catalyzing learning and bringing forth individual traits of personality. Venus influences young adulthood, stimulating development of sexual drive and passion. The sun influences development of self-control and stimulates maturity and desire for social standing in adulthood. Mars promulgates an awareness of having passed one's prime and thereby stimulates a desire for achievement. Jupiter brings about a sense of freedom from the hard work of youth and the opportunity to enjoy the fruits on one's earlier labors. It brings, as well, the respect and honor that have accrued from such achievements. Saturn, influencing old age, diminishes vitality and satisfaction and propagates feebleness and decrepitude.

According to medieval thought, each of the seven planets ruled the ages of man for a period of years based upon the duration of its own *cyclic movement as observed from earth:

*Moon: 4 years (possibly related to its quarters)
Mercury: 10 years (1/2 of its 20 year cycle)
Venus: 8 years
*Sun: 19 years

Mars: 15 years
Jupiter: 12 years
*Saturn: 30 years until death (Sears, p. 49-50)

Such correspondences are evidence of the medieval perception of the individual as a microcosm of the macrocosm, as mirroring the heavenly *cycles of the planets in the *cycles of human life.

shadow: In the Bible, old age is represented as a declining shadow: "My days are like a shadow that declineth." (Psalms 102:11)

shears: Shears are an attribute and symbol of the Three *Fates, especially *Atropos (the *crone) who cuts the *thread of life. They thus become a symbol of destiny or fate, as in Shakespeare's *King John*, act 4: "Think you I bear the shears of destiny?" In "To Age" Walter Savage Landor (1775-1864) makes reference to the *Fates' shears:

The Fates have laid aside their shears
Perhaps for some few more.

shepherd: The shepherd is a symbol of wisdom as the guardian of ancient knowledge and lore, especially regarding nature. (de Vries) The shepherd is often employed, especially in Victorian poetry, as a *Wise Old Man. (cf. "Michael, A Pastoral Poem" by William Wordsworth)

Shichi-fukujin: Shichi-fukujin is the complex of deities comprising the Japanese Seven Gods of Happiness: Benten (goddess of eloquence and music); Hotei (the friend of children); *Jurojin (Old Man of Long Life); *Fukuro Kuju (Happiness--Emoluments--Longevity); Bishamon (missionary zeal), Daikoku (riches); and Ebisu (patron of fishermen). Usually portrayed in a comical fashion, these *seven gods are often shown together on a *boat, the "Treasure Ship" (Takarabune), which is filled to overflowing with precious objects. (cf. depiction of the Seven Gods of Luck in a boat with Mt. Fuji on the horizon, in the Victoria and Albert Museum; Pigott, pp. 58-59) Pictures of this group are often hung in commercial establishments in Japan, particularly around New Year's, to serve as good luck charms. Two of the gods making up this complex, *Fukuro Kuju and *Jurojin, are commonly associated with aging and longevity. (Grimal, LWM; Lurker; Pigott)

ship: The ship is a symbol of the human body as vessel of the soul; therefore, an aged, decrepit ship is symbolic of an aged person. (de Vries)
In *The Stages of Life* (1835), Kaspar David Friedrich presents an image of ships at *sea corresponding to figures of a youth, a middle-aged man, and an *old man on the shore. The only figure of this group looking out to *sea

contemplating the ships is the figure of the *old man, supposedly a self-portrait.

Shou Lao (Shou Xing Lao Tou-zi): Also called Nan-ji Xian-weng ("the ancient of the South Pole"), Shou Lao, the Chinese god of longevity, presides over and administers the human lifespan. He is accompanied by a white *crane, symbolizing longevity, and carries a peach. (Lurker)

Shozu-ga no Baba: The Japanese deity Shozu-ga no Baba guards the *crossroads through which each soul must pass on its *journey of transmigration. Tribute must be paid to this aged *crone who sits at the beginning of the threefold path to the Buddhist afterlife. (cf. *The Genji of the World Beyond* by Kukuchi Yosai, 1788-1878, Museum of Fine Arts, Boston; Anesaki, Plate XII) Her relationship to the afterlife, her relationship to *crossroads, and her *crone-like aspect point to a similarity to *Hecate of Classical mythology.

shuttle: The shuttle is used as a symbol of the passage of time in an individual life by Shakespeare in *Merry Wives of Windsor* (act 5, sc. 1, 23-24) in the words of Falstaff: "I fear not Goliath with a weaver's beam; because I know also life is a shuttle." A similar use of the image of the shuttle, possibly the source of Shakespeare's image, occurs in the Book of Job in the Bible:

> My flesh is clothed with worms and *dust of the earth*. . . . My days pass over more speedily than a *weaver's shuttle*, and are spent without hope. . . . (Job 7:5-21). (Hankins)

A modern use of the shuttle as a symbol of time's passage is found in T. S. Eliot's "Gerontian" (1920): "vacant shuttles weave the wind."

Sibyl of Cumae: Sibyls were priestesses in Classical mythology who possessed the power of prophecy through the inspiration of Apollo. (cf. Ovid's *Metamorphoses* 14) The original sibyl, Sibylla, who lived at Marpessus near Troy, gained such renown that her name became the term to designate a prophetess. (Walker, *Crone*)

Varro, a Roman writer, listed ten sibyls occupying three continents, the most famous of them being the Cumaean Sibyl (known variously as Amalthea, Demophile, Herophile, or Deiphobe) who pronounced oracles from a *cave at Cumae in Campania. Some accounts maintain that she was the same sibyl as the Sibyl of Erythrae, since both sibyls lived to an age of approximately 1,000 years.

The Sibyl of Erythrae had been granted by Apollo as many years of life as grains of *sand could be contained in one of her hands, provided she never returned to Erythrae. To honor her end of the bargain, she came to reside in Cumae, living for 990 years.

Alternately, in the myth of the Sibyl of Cumae, Apollo offered to grant the sibyl any wish if she would become his lover. Accepting, she asked that she be granted as many years of life as grains of *dust contained in a pile of sweepings. Her wish was granted, and she lived for 1,000 years.

From this point on, the myths of the Sibyl of Cumae and the Sibyl of Erythrae converge and become identical. In both stories, the sibyl had forgotten to ask Apollo to grant her perpetual youth as an accompaniment to great longevity. As a result, she was cursed with prolonged decrepitude, becoming smaller and more wizened until she resembled a *cicada. She was then enclosed in a *cage or bottle hanging from the ceiling of her *cave. When children visiting her *cave asked her what she desired, she answered, "I want to die."

The Sibyl of Cumae figures prominently in Virgil's *Aeneid*, serving as Aeneas' guide as he descends into the underworld, instructing Aeneas on how to utilize the Golden Bough in his passage.

The Cumaean Sibyl also played a prominent role in later Roman religion and history, providing the Sibylline books which contained instructions for various rites and actions appropriate in the unforeseen occurrence of extraordinary events. These books, housed in the temple of Capitoline Jupiter, were entrusted to the care of special magistrates who preserved and consulted them when necessary. They were lost in 83 B.C. in a fire which destroyed the whole temple.

Michelangelo's Sistine Chapel frescoes contain a representation of the Sibyl of Cumae with an open *book in her lap. (Grant and Hazel; Grimal, DCM; Tripp)

The title character of Shelley's (1792-1822) "Witch of Atlas" bears strong resemblance to the Sibyl of Cumae:

All day the wizard lady sate aloof,
    Spelling out scrolls of dread antiquity,
Under the cavern's fountain-lighted roof;
    Or broidering the pictured poesy
Of some high tale upon her growing woof

In an example from modern poetry, in the first line of Robert Frost's (1874-1963) "Our Doom to Bloom," the narrator asks the "Cumaean Sibyl, charming Ogress" for advice. To answer him, the sibyl consults "the Surviving Book."

Sibyl of Erythrae: see SIBYL OF CUMAE.

sickle: Like the *scythe, the sickle symbolizes *harvest. As an emblem of *Kronos-*Saturn, the sickle is a tool of castration and, through confusion with *Chronos (*Time), became symbolic of the destructive, devouring nature of time. An example is Shakespeare's Sonnet 116: "Love's not Time's fool, though rosy lips and cheeks Within his bending sickle's compass come." (de Vries)

Silenus: Silenus, an elderly companion of Dionysus in his revels, is portrayed as a satyr-like creature, bald and potbellied, with a snub-nose, the tails and ears of a horse, and riding a *donkey from which he is always in danger of falling because of his perpetual inebriation. (cf. Ovid's *Metamorphoses* 2, 89-101) He was noted for his wisdom, his prophetic powers, and his propensity to tell long and engaging tales and to dispense prophecy when captured.

Because of his age, Silenus had trouble keeping pace with Dionysus and his other companions in their revelry. Consequently, peasants captured him, tied him up with garlands and took him to King *Midas (the mythical *king of Phrygia) who was a devotee of Dionysus. Because he was a follower of Dionysus himself, King *Midas treated Silenus with honor and returned him to Dionysus. As a reward for his return, Dionysus granted *Midas a gift of his choice. *Midas chose the "golden touch" whereby everything he touched turned to *gold—a choice that proved unwise. (Cavendish; Crowel; Graves, GM; Grimal, DCM; Stapleton)

In an alternate version of the tale of Silenus and King *Midas, *Midas trapped Silenus in an attempt to obtain his wisdom. When he was brought before the *king, Silenus revealed to him the secret of human life: "that the best thing for man is not to be born at all, and the next best thing is to die as early as possible." (Grant and Hazel)

Silenus is the chief comic character of the satyr plays. Known for his musical ability, he is depicted in the frescoes from the Villa of the Mysteries at Pompeii (1st century B.C.) playing a lyre while a young Pan plays the flute. This is an example of the association of a stringed instrument with old age (symbolic of integrative understanding and the ability to produce harmony out of diverse, conflicting elements) (see VIOLIN) and a wind instrument with youth, which is found as an attribute of numerous youthful figures. (Cavendish)

In another scene from the Pompeiian frescoes, Silenus is shown holding a *silver wine cup or bowl into which he and a satyr gaze, possibly practicing a form of prophecy whereby the future is foretold by gazing into a vessel filled with liquid. (Pierce)

Silenus appears in Shelley's "Witch of Atlas" 8:

And old Silenus, shaking a green stick
    Of lilies, and the wood-gods in a crew.

Rubens presents an image of Silenus in his revels in *Drunken Silenus Supported by Satyrs* (1618). (McKee and Kauppinen)

silk: Silk is a symbol of longevity and the positive value of age, since old silks are valued. Karle Wilson Baker, in "Let Me Grow Lovely," uses silk in this symbolic sense, asking that she "grow lovely, growing old," like fine silks, which need not necessarily be new. (Lyell)

Silvanus: Silvanus is the Roman divinity of the *woods. Because he was portrayed as an *old man possessing the strength of youth and was the god of uncultivated land, he became identified with the Greek satyrs and sileni and with Pan, the Greek god of nature. Residing in the *woods outside the bounds of the village, he was regarded as somewhat foreign and dangerous. He was worshipped by *shepherds as the god of flocks. (Grimal, DCM; Hammond; Tripp)

silver: Silver is a symbol of wisdom and old age. (de Vries) In "The Paradox of Time" Austin Dobson (1840-1921) describes his hair, which once "had shamed the crow," and his companion's, which once was curly and golden, as signifying attainment of "the silver age."

In Timothy Cole's (1852-1931) "The Year's End," "silvered days of vistas gold and green" form part of an image of old age filled with serenity and contentment.

Six Ages of Man: No particular schema for the *Ages of Man is supplied in the Bible. However, various explications through interpretation of Biblical parable exist. One of the most influential systems thus developed originated with Augustine. He based his series of six ages upon the six days required by God for creation of the world. Church doctrine, basing its view of the course of human life (the microcosm) as corresponding to the historical course of salvation (the macrocosm), divided the human lifespan into six ages. This six-age schema of the course of an individual's life was often paired with a corresponding six-stage division of world history.

Influenced by Manichean thought, Augustine rejected a literal interpretation of the Biblical creation of the world. He viewed an interpretation which presented God as requiring rest on the seventh day of his labors as demeaning and as not befitting the image of a divine creator. Augustine interpreted the seven-stage creation of the world, rather, as a representation of the history of the world as progressing through seven stages: "It reveals that man must toil for six epochs but that in the seventh he will enjoy eternal repose in God." (Sears, p. 55)

Augustine further related this sevenfold division of world history to a six-fold division of individual life followed by a seventh stage of afterlife. Augustine's ideas are described in detail in *On Genesis against the Manichees* (A.D. 388-390). Our present age, the sixth age which began with Christ's preachings, corresponds to old age.

In *Eighty-three Different Questions* (A.D. 388-396), Augustine described his system of thought. Saying that the present, or sixth, age was "the old age of an old man," he described the six ages as corresponding to the six ages of an individual: "*infantia, pueritia, adolescentia, iuventus, gravitas,* and *senectus.*" (Sears, p. 58) The first age extended from Adam until Noah; the second age from Noah to *Abraham; the third age from *Abraham to David; the fourth was from David through "the Babylonian exile"; and the fifth extended to the Second Coming. The sixth age would last until the world's end. During this age, the "outer man," or "old man . . . is corrupted by old age, as it were, and the inner man is renewed from day to day. Then comes the eternal rest which is signified by the Sabbath." (Sears, p. 58)

The influence that this conception of the ages of man had upon the Middle Ages is reflected by a number of writings from the 11th and 12th centuries. (de Beauvoir) The concept of the congruence of the six ages of individual life and the six ages of humankind is expressed in the following from the 11th-century *Vie de saint Alexis*:

The world was good; it will never be as good again.
It is old and feeble; everything is going down,
Getting worse, and good is no longer done in our time.

And, in the 12th century, Otho of Frersing in his *Chronicle* expresses a similar view: "We see the world failing and, as it were, breathing out the last sigh of extreme old age."

Numerous depictions of the Six Ages of Man occur in visual art of the Middle Ages, as well. A depiction of the Six Ages of Man occurs on the Portal of the Virgin (ca. 1210-1220) on the façade of Notre Dame Cathedral in Paris. Six images, beginning with a boy on the bottom, and progressing to an aged figure leaning on a *stick at the top, occupy the right side of the portal. They are balanced on the left side by images of the *seasons extended from *four to six to serve as a symmetrical presentation.

skull: The skull symbolizes man's mortality and the transitory nature of life. In Elizabethan times rings of skulls were worn as *memento mori*. (de Vries)

sleep: As the provider of prophetic dreams, sleep is often presented as the source of wisdom. Shakespeare employs sleep as an image of aging in *Measure for Measure* (Draper, "Shakespeare's Attitude Towards Old Age"):

. . . Thou hast nor youth
   nor age,
But, as it were, an after-dinner's sleep,
Dreaming on both; for all the blessed youth

Becomes as aged, and doth beg the alms
Of palsied eld; . . .

In a tale from the Selk'nam Indians of South America, a culture hero, Kenos, and three ancestors, having reached old age, attempt to fall into a deep sleep, effecting death. They succeed in falling into a long sleep, but do not die. To their frustration, when they wake, they are still old. They travel *north "wearily dragging themselves along, speaking feebly, in the way of the old, mortally tired." (Campbell, HAWM, pp. 254-255) Upon reaching the *north, ancestors lay them in the ground where they remain for several days, awakening young again. Thereafter, all ancestors experienced the same transformational sleep: "These people would rise again and again, lie down to sleep and rise again, until, no longer wishing to come back, one would be transformed into a mountain, a bird, or a wind, a sea animal, rock or land animal. Others, following Kenos to the sky, became stars or clouds." (Campbell, HAWM, pp. 254-55)

snake: see SERPENT.

snow: Snow is related to aging by its explanation as an aged woman plucking a *goose (e.g., *Mother Carey*). (de Vries) Gray hair is often described as snow-like, as in Shelley's "The Witch of Atlas": "and there lay calm/Old age with snow-bright hair and folded palm." As a characteristic of *winter (symbol of old age), snow is further related to aging.

Solomon: As a Biblical hero (10th-century B.C. *king of Israel) who bestowed law and order but was guilty of the sin of arrogance, Solomon represents both human wisdom and human folly. He is the solar hero exhibiting the *cyclic nature (sometimes strong, sometimes weak) of the *sun. (de Vries)
    Solomon is commonly regarded (though this is definitely disputed) as the author of Ecclesiastes, the book of the Bible regarded as the advice, culled from long experience, of an aged *king handed down to his successor. Ecclesiastes contains an allegory of old age (12:1-6) employing an image of a ruined *house as representative of the decrepit, aged body.

Sophia: The Old Testament character Sophia is regarded as the personification of the wisdom of the universe. (de Vries)
    Early Christianity, or Gnosticism, featured a *crone figure who constituted part of the complex forming the forerunner of the Holy Trinity. She is described in the following passage from the *Trimorphic Protennoia*: "the one born first of all beings, the one who has three names and yet exists alone, as one. She dwells at all levels of the universe; she is the revealer who awakens those that sleep, who utters a call to remember, who saves." (Walker, WEMS, p. 588)

Early Christian personifications of the *crone were Sophia (personification of wisdom), the Pneuma or Holy Spirit, and the Grandmother of God. (Walker, *Crone*) Her name meaning "wisdom," Sophia is described in the following from the apocryphal text *The Wisdom of Solomon*: "emanation of God's glory, the Holy Spirit, the immaculate mirror of his energy." (Septuagint 8:3)

Sophia, named the Mother of God in the Apocryphon of John, a Gnostic text from the 8th century A.D., infused God with creativity and wisdom. The Book of the Secrets of Enoch, another Gnostic text, stated that Sophia created man from the *seven "consistencies": His flesh was made of earth; his blood came from dew; his eyes were of sunlight; his bones found their source in stone; his intelligence came from the clouds; his hair and veins were from the grass; and his soul came from the wind. This gave him "seven natures." (Walker, *Crone*, p. 61)

Viewed as the "feminine embodiment of Wisdom," Sophia was but one manifestation of the belief widespread in Indo-European religions that a god was dependent upon such an element for his power. This is further reflected in the Gnostic belief that, if man is to become like man before the Fall, if he is to be restored to innocence, he must unite with his "inner Sophia." (Eliade, ER, vol. 13, p. 416-17)

sorcerer: The sorcerer personifies the archetype of the Terrible Father who, like *Saturn, in his destructive aspect represents the devouring nature of time. Conversely, in his positive aspect he is the *Wise Old Man, bestower of wisdom and advice. He is often portrayed as an *old man with a long white beard, white hair, and *claw-like hands, as in the figure from Arthurian legend, *Merlin the Magician. (Cirlot; de Vries)

sorceress: The female sorceress, like the male *sorcerer, exhibits both positive and negative qualities. Like *Medea, the sorcerer of Classical mythology, she is capable of performing good through her power (as in *Medea's restoration to youth of Jason's aged father, *Aeson) as well as evil (as in her murder of King Pelias). The sorceress, as a form of the *crone, often takes the guise of an *old woman as one of her many forms. The sorceress is often a split characterization portrayed in both of her aspects in folktales and legends, as in *The Wizard of Oz*, where she takes the form of both the Good *Witch (Glenda) and the Bad *Witch (the Wicked *Witch of the *West).

sphere: The sphere represents the *Wheel of Life and is thus a symbol of perfection and completion, as in completion of the life *cycle. (de Vries) *Fortuna's Greek forerunner, Tyche, juggles a *ball, the course of which, sometimes up and sometimes down, is indicative of individual fate. (Graves, GM I)

In Neoplatonic philosophy, the soul is represented as a sphere. The soul's substance is deposited as "quintessence" around the four elements, which lie in concentric spheres beneath it. In Plato's *Timaeus*, primordial man is described similarly. (Cirlot)

Sphinx: The answer to the riddle of the Sphinx of Classical mythology involves a representation of the Three Ages of Man. The Sphinx, a hybrid creature with a woman's head, a *winged *lion's body and a *serpent's tail, was sent by Hera to punish the Thebans. She questioned travelers as they passed over the mountainous route leading to and from the city, killing and devouring those who could not answer her riddle. Given to her by the three muses, the riddle was: "What being, with only one voice, has sometimes two feet, sometimes three, sometimes four, and is weakest when it has most?" No one but Oedipus was able to provide the answer: "Man . . . because he crawls on all fours as an infant, stands firmly on his two feet in his youth, and leans upon a staff in his old age." Vanquished, the Sphinx threw herself on the rocks below and died. As a consequence of his heroic act, Oedipus was proclaimed *king of Thebes. (Graves, GM II, p. 10)

Spider Grandmother: Both the Kiowa and Pueblo have accounts of a mythical ancestress, Spider Grandmother. In Kiowa legend, she brings *fire and *light to the world. Wishing to end the state of eternal darkness within which inhabitants of the New World were forced to exist, the council of animals met to find a solution. Even the cleverest and most powerful animals, including Fox, Rabbit, *Eagle, and Woodpecker, could not devise an effective plan. Old and feeble, Spider Grandmother suggests that she may be able to resolve the dilemma. Though she is ridiculed by the other animals, she quietly and patiently proceeds with her plan. She sets out on a long *journey to the Eastern land of the Sun People. Coming on a bed of moist clay, she forms a bowl which she carries with her. After walking for many days, she reaches her destination. Resting as close as possible to the blazing *fire lighting the land, she inches closer and closer to the source as the evening passes. Stealthily she reaches out and plucks a piece of *flame from the *sun and drops in into her bowl. She returns to her people, following the *thread which she spun and laid across her course on the *journey out. As the days of her long *journey go by, the *fire which she carries grows steadily brighter and more immense. It finally grows so strong that she desperately flings the flaming sphere into the air, where it becomes the *sun. However, she retains one small piece. This piece she carries back home in her bowl, thus providing her people with *fire for cooking, warmth, and clay-fired vessels. (Stone)

spindle: Like the *distaff, the spindle symbolizes life and its temporal quality. Like the *moon, it represents the *cyclic and transitory nature of existence as an object that undergoes physical transformation through its *cyclic phases, similar to the aging process. Deities associated with the *moon usually possess the spindle or *distaff as an attribute. (Cirlot) As a tool of *weaving, the spindle is an attribute of one of the Three *Fates, Clotho. All three of the *Moirai (or *Fates) are described in the *Lycophron* (584 ff.) as possessing "brazen" spindles. (de Vries)

spinning: Spinning is an activity of the Three *Fates, especially Clotho, who spins the *thread of life. Through this association, spinning is symbolic of the passage of time in an individual life. (de Vries; Tripp)

Aged women are often portrayed spinning or with spinning wheels. In Nicholas Maes' *Old Woman Peeling an Apple*, an old woman sits by a window peeling apples. The *light from the window illuminates her face, hands, and upper body, as well as several objects in the room: an open *book (symbolic of an individual life); a seashell (attribute of the *pilgrim); a jug; and, most priminently, a spinning *wheel.

spring: A spring symbolizes the eternal life force running through the individual which transcends the vicissitudes of aging and temporal existence. (see FOUNTAIN OF YOUTH)

In Eudora Welty's "A Worn Path," a spring flowing through a hollow log functions as a symbol of the undiminished vitality of the aged main character, *Phoenix.

staff: The staff is a symbol of old age, blindness and infirmity through its function as the physical support often necessary to such states. It is also an attribute of the *pilgrim, signifying his faith through endurance of hardship on the pilgrimage. (de Vries) The staff, in an ancient Egyptian ritual described by Sir James Frazer, becomes the support of the aged *Sun after the *autumn solstice. This ritual, which was performed during the festival called the "Nativity of the Sun-Stick," was based upon the belief that the *sun needed support as the days grew shorter. (Cirlot)

Anne Bradstreet (1612-1672) in "The Four Ages of Man" employs the staff as a symbol of the support necessitated by old age:

> And last of all to act upon this stage,
> Leaning upon his staff comes up Old Age.

Wordsworth (1770-1850) presents a similar image in "The Old Cumberland Beggar":

>   Poor Traveller!
> His staff trails with him; scarcely do his
>   feet
> Disturb the summer dust

The flowering staff found in Christian imagery symbolizes fertility and signifies God's favor, as in the case of Joseph's staff as an indication of God's favor in selecting him as Mary's husband. (cf. *St. Joseph with Flowering Rod*, from the circle of the Spanish painter, Jusepe de Ribera, 1588-1652) (de Vries)

stag: The stag is symbolic of *cyclic rejuvenation and self-regeneration since it sheds its age yearly, growing new antlers. It is also a symbol of longevity because, according to Hesiod, "it lives four times as long as a crow, which lives nine times as long as man." It is associated with the *Tree of Life through the visual correlation of its antlers to the branches of a *tree. In Greek and Roman culture its function as a symbol of regeneration was manifested in its association with the power of healing, since it was believed that the stag could recognize medicinal plants. (Cirlot; de Vries)

The stag serves as a symbol of longevity in Japanese art as the companion of the god of longevity, *Jurojin.

stage: Shakespeare's *Seven Ages of Man are played out on the stage of life as seven acts in *As You Like It* (act 2, sc. 7, 136-143):

> All the world's a stage,
> And all the men and women merely players.
> They have their exits and their entrances,
> And one man in his time plays many parts,
> His acts being seven ages.

Shakespeare describes the final scene, old age:

> Last scene of all,
> That ends this strange eventful history,
> Is second childishness and mere oblivion,
> Sans teeth, sans eyes, sans taste, sans everything.

Another Shakespearean character, *King Lear, calls life "this great stage of fools." (*King Lear* act 4, sc. 6, 182-187) (Hankins)

stairs: Stairs are symbolic of the gradual development of the self, each step representing a new phase. (de Vries) Some depictions of the *Ages of Man show the successive ages as separate steps in a pyramidal form, midlife forming the zenith, infancy and old age forming the two ends. (cf. *Steps of Life*, 1540, by Jorg Breu the Younger in the British Museum, London) In some depictions of the *Seven Ages of Man, a gradually descending succession of steps is portrayed, each step corresponding to one of the *seven planets and consisting of one of the *seven metals. The bottom-most step in this depiction is *lead, corresponding to *Saturn and old age. (Sears)

Steps of Life: The Steps of Life were a visual image of a pyramid of steps, found beginning in the 16th century, used to portray the stages of life. In an engraving by Jorg Breu the Younger from 1540, *ten steps corresponding to *ten stages of life are shown, an infant at the left, a middle-aged man at the top, and an old man at the right. Animals corresponding to each of the ages occupy niches below each of the steps. In a print from 1482 the correspondences, which varied from one representation to another and were entirely different for women, are: 10, kid; 20, calf; 30, bull; 40, *lion; 50, fox; 60, *wolf; 70, hound; 80, *cat; 90, *ass; 100, *goose. (Sears, pp. 153-54)

Depictions of the Steps of Life, originating in late medieval times, are found in European and American art into the 20th century. In *The Coming of Age,* Simone de Beauvoir comments upon the peculiar nature of this image. Noting that then, as now, it was very unusual for an individual to live to the age of 100, she says that these depictions "were not in fact concerned with human life as it was in its contingent reality but with establishing a kind of archetype." (p. 160) She finds the source of this pessimistic imagery in Christianity, which urges the individual, "doomed to a sad decline," to "above all look to his salvation, even in the time of his prosperity." (p. 160)

In "A Lament," Shelley (1792-1822) presents an image of the aged person as occupying the "last steps" of life:

> Oh, world! oh, life! oh, time!
> On whose last steps I climb
>   Trembling at that where I had stood before;
> When will return the glory of your prime?
>   No more—O, never more!

stick: Like the *staff, the stick is a symbol of old age and the physical support often necessary in old age. In fertility rites, sticks, as symbols of old age or the finished *cycle, are pounded on the ground in an attempt to awaken the dead ancestors who will unleash the fertility within the earth. (de Vries)

The stick is also a symbol of wisdom. According to Cirlot, a burnt stick symbolizes death and wisdom.

storyteller: Storytellers are often depicted as aged, reflecting a view of the elderly as repositories of knowledge and perpetuators of tradition. Nathaniel Hawthorne's short stories "Old Esther Dudley" and "An Old Woman's Tale" contain aged female storytellers as central characters. The narrator of Joel Chandler Harris' *Uncle Remus, His Songs and His Sayings* (1880) is an aged black ex-slave. Uncle Remus' humorous stories are told to a young white boy. As the aged storyteller, the old slave passes along to the young the values of antebellum Southern culture. In an example from visual art, E. Blumen-schein's painting *The Old Story Teller* (1934) shows an aged Native American storyteller with a young child as her audience. (McKee and Kauppinen)

Strigae: Striga means "she who screeches." Bird-like demons in Roman culture who were believed to be *old women transformed into *birds, the Strigae carried children away. (Lurker)

Struldbruggs: Gulliver, the hero of Jonathan Swift's *Gulliver's Travels*, encounters in his travels the Struldbruggs or Immortals. When he first learns of the existence of a group of people who are immortal, he conjectures that they must certainly be wise through benefit of their years and free of anxiety and depression through lack of apprehension of death. However, he finds that the Struldbruggs, rather than exemplifying all that is possible in life and serving as a source of inspiration to others, serve as a negative example, thereby decreasing the enthusiasm for life and generating malaise in Luggnagg, the island they inhabit along with mortals. Since the Struldbruggs' immortality was not accompanied by eternal youth, it caused them to experience the physical and mental disadvantages of old age to a greater degree and of longer duration than mortals.

In what must surely be one of the most negative portrayals of old age in literature, Gulliver describes the Struldbruggs:

> . . . they commonly acted like Mortals, till about Thirty Years old, after which by Degrees they grew melancholy and dejected, increasing in both till they came to Fourscore. . . . When they came to Fourscore Years, which is reckoned the Extremity of living in this Country, they had not only all the Follies and Infirmities of other old Men, but many more which arose from the dreadful Prospect of never dying. They were not only opinionative, peevish, covetous, morose, vain, talkative; but uncapable of Friendship, and dead to all natural Affection, which never descended below their Grand-children. Envy and impotent Desires, are their prevailing Passions.

> At Ninety they lose their Teeth and Hair; they have at that Age no Distinction of Taste, but eat and drink whatever they can get, without Relish or Appetite. The Diseases they were subject to still continue without encreasing or diminishing. In talking they forget the common Appellation of Things, and the Names of Persons, even of those who are their nearest Friends and Relations.

He further describes them as "the most mortifying Sight I ever beheld; and the Women more horrible than the Men. Besides the usual Deformities in extreme old Age, they acquired an additional Ghastliness in Proportion to their Number of Years, which is not to be described." (Swift in Asimov, pp. 197-199) He then goes on to explain that, after they have reached the age of 80 years, the Struldbruggs are considered "dead in Law." He perceives this action as justified, since "as Avarice is the necessary Consequent of old Age, those Immortals would in time become Proprietors of the whole Nation, and engross the Civil Power; which, for want of Abilities to manage, must end in the Ruin of the Publick." (p. 200) Gulliver's perception of avarice as "the necessary Consequent of old Age" is explained in Isaac Asimov's annotated version of *Gulliver's Travels*:

> What makes vices attractive is the pleasure they give the senses.
> In old age, however, the senses dull and there is nothing left but
> the joy of material possession. The connection of age and avarice
> was mentioned as long ago as 160 B.C. by the Roman playwright,
> Terence (190?-159 B.C.). In *Don Juan*, Lord Byron (1788-1824)
> said sardonically, "So for a good old-gentlemanly vice/I think I
> must take up with avarice." (p. 203)

sun: The sun's course across the sky is a common symbol of the process of aging, the setting sun representing the aged individual, as in Robert Herrick's (1591-1674) "To the Virgins, To Make Much of Time"):

> The glorious lamp of heaven, the sun,
>   The higher he's a-getting,
> The sooner will his race be run,
>   And nearer he's to setting.

Carl Jung uses the sun's course across the sky as symbolic of the withdrawal into the self which he perceives as necessary in old age:

> I must take for comparison the daily course of the sun--but a sun
> that is endowed with human feeling and man's limited conscious-
> ness. In the morning it rises from the nocturnal sea of uncon-
> sciousness and looks upon the wide, bright world which lies
> before it in an expanse that steadily widens the higher it climbs
> in the firmament. In this extension of its field of action caused by
> its own rising, the sun will discover its significance; it will see the
> attainment of the greatest possible height, and the widest possible
> dissemination of its blessings, as its goal. . . . At the stroke of
> noon the descent begins. And the descent means the reversal of
> all the ideals and values that were cherished in the morning. The

sun falls into contradiction with itself. It is as though it should
draw in its rays instead of emitting them. Light and warmth
decline and are at last extinguished. . . . Aging people should
know that their lives are not expanding, but that an inexorable
inner process enforces the contraction of life. For a young person
it is almost a sin, or at least a danger, to be preoccupied with
himself; but for the aging person it is a duty and a necessity to
devote serious attention to himself. After having lavished its light
upon the world, the sun withdraws its rays in order to illuminate
itself. (Carl Jung, "The Stages of Life," pp. 397, 399)

Martianus Capella in his 5th century allegory *On the Marriage of Philology
and Mercury* bases a system of three ages of man upon the cyclic movement
of the sun. Sol, joining the gods, is described entering with a glowing
countenance like a young boy, progressing to a condition of breathlessness and
the appearance of a young man, and ending as an aged man in a state of
decline. (Sears)

The winter sun's "spent radiance" is an image of old age in Joseph
Campbell's "The Old Woman." And the setting sun symbolizes old age in
Lydia Maria Child's (1802-1880) "The World I am Passing Through":

When I approach the setting sun,
And feel my journey nearly done,
May earth be veiled in genial light,
And her last smile to me seem bright!
Help me till then to kindly view
The world that I am passing through!

The sun is also a symbol of the solar hero or *king who, when aged, is often
portrayed as a setting sun.

Susannah and the Elders: The story of Susannah and the Elders from the
Book of Daniel 13 (167-164 B.C.) is a parable of vice and abuse of respected
position in old age. Two elders were enamored of Susannah. They hid and
watched her bathing. When they left their hidingplace and approached
Susannah, she refused their advances. The two elders sought revenge, claiming
that they had observed Susannah committing adultery with a young man.
Susannah was sentenced to death; however, she was proved innocent by
Daniel, who obtained conflicting stories from the two elders through separate
questioning. This resulted instead in the execution of the elders.

This story, though excluded from the Protestant Bible, was highly popular.
Its exclusion reflected, according to de Beauvoir, the high degree of respect
afforded *old men by the Puritans. Its popularity, on the other hand, resulted
from a resentment against church elders who abused positions of power.

Susannah and the Elders was a popular subject among Italian painters of the early 17th century. The parable was the subject and title of paintings by Artemisia Gentileschi (1610), Guido Reni (1632), and Lodovico Carracci (1555-1619).

The story of Susannah and the Elders provides the basis for Wallace Stevens' (1879-1955) musings on desire, beauty, and memory in his poem, "Peter Quince at the Clavier": "The body dies; the body's beauty lives."

swan: In Nordic mythology, the *Norns (the Nordic equivalent of the Three *Fates) sometimes take the form of swans. As symbols of time and the transitory nature of life, swans swim in the waters of *Time surrounding and nourishing Yggdrasil, the world tree. Swans are related to a similar trio from Classical mythology, the *Graiae or "the gray ones," who are considered the personification of age. The *Graiae were variously described as "swan-like" or as actually taking the form of swans. (Graves, WG, p. 229) Swans often function as psychopomps and are thereby associated with death and the underworld. Traditionally, the horse pulls the *sun god's chariot across the day sky and the *swan pulls his bark across the *night sky. (Cirlot; de Vries)

swastika: The swastika, commonly identified since World War II with Nazism, has numerous meanings beyond those appropriated to fascist ends. The swastika represents the *cyclical nature of the natural world and flux and change as constants of experience. Its *four-armed form represents the *four cardinal points, the *four quarters of the moon, the *four winds and the *four *seasons. Similarly, it is viewed by some as a representation of the *four stages of life, its arms' hooked ends signifying the *"ships of life." (Cirlot)

Other sources describe the swastika as symbolic of the revolution of the *Wheel of Life, and of the Buddhist *Round of Existence or *Wheel of Becoming. The two forms of the swastika, one turning clockwise and the other counterclockwise, symbolize opposing principles: *sun and *moon; masculine and feminine; yin and yang; celestial and chthonic powers; and the rising, vernal *sun and the descending, *autumnal *sun. The swastika turning in a counterclockwise direction is related to Clotho, one of the Three *Fates, who spins in the same counterclockwise direction, a direction perceived as destructive of life.

In Chinese imagery, the swastika symbolizes perfection and longevity and as a border element it represents the *Wan tzu*, "the Ten Thousand Things or Continuities, i.e. infinite duration without beginning or end, infinite renewal of life, perpetuity." (Cooper, p. 166)

Sweet Hope: In Plato's *Republic*, Socrates converses with the aged Cephalus. Cephalus describes how, in old age, one develops a different awareness because of the nearness of death. He says that after he felt he had settled matters, Sweet Hope (Pindar called her the *nurse of old age) cared for him. (Boyle and Morriss)

sycamore: The sycamore, or plane tree, is a symbol of wisdom and a place of rest for the *pilgrim. (de Vries) The sycamore was, as seen in Wordsworth's "Inscription for a Fountain on a Heath" (1802), the tent of the Patriarchs:

> This Sycamore, oft musical with bees,--
> Such tents the Patriarchs loved! O long unharmed
> May all its aged boughs o'er-encanopy
> The small round basin, which this jutting stone
> Keeps pure from falling leaves!

The Greek philosopher Socrates, the elderly sage, sits beneath a sycamore in a pastoral setting outside the walls of the city as he dispenses wisdom to his student, Phaedrus, in Plato's *Phaedrus*. This may be the source of Wordsworth's reference to "the Patriarchs."

Sycorax: In Shakespeare's *The Tempest*, the aged *witch Sycorax occupied Prospero's island prior to his arrival. Shakespeare describes her as having grown into the shape of a *hoop through the process of aging. Thus, he here employs the *hoop in its relationship both to aging and *witchcraft. (Benet; Draper, "Shakespeare's Attitude Towards Old Age")

T

---

tailor: Dylan Thomas (1914-1953) describes Time as "tailor age" which fashions "time's jacket" in his poem "When, Like a Running Grave." Such an image reflects concepts of time and human destiny as woven by some force, such as the Three *Fates or *Moirai, which is beyond human control.

ten: The number ten is a symbol of completion, totality, and perfection. Along with six, it is related to common divisions of time: 60 minutes, 60 seconds, and so on. (de Vries)

Ten Ages of Man: In German culture as far back as the 13th century, depictions of the Ten Ages of Man are found. In this system of division, later variations of which are found in the *Steps of Life consisting of ten stages, each of the ten ages lasts ten years. (cf. Jorg Breu the Younger's *Steps of Life*, 1540; Sears)

In the 15th century, the Ages of Man became a widespread literary and artistic convention, lasting well into the 20th century and occuring in imagery from Germany, France, Italy, Spain, England, and the United States. Animals were added, a different one corresponding to each of the ten ages. A set with corresponding animals for women was devised, as well. (see AGES OF MAN)

thread: Thread is a symbol of the continuity of a lifespan and individual destiny. The three goddesses (the Greek *Moirai, the Roman *Fates or *Parcae, and the Norse *Norns) prepare the thread of an individual human life, *spin it, and cut it off at the time of death. As described in the *Odyssey* (1,34), they control "the thread that fate spins for every man," thereby determining the fate of each individual.

The Triple Goddess is symbolized in numerous contexts by the colors white, red, and black, corresponding to past, present, and future or birth, life,

and death. Her weaving of threads of these colors is believed to form the
*"web of time." Known in India as the *gunas* or "strands" of the Creatress,
Kali-Maya, the white thread belongs to the Virgin, the red to the Mother, and
the black to the Crone. Together, the three weave the *web of temporal
existence. In Western literature, the white, red, and black threads of life are
found in the writings of Horace, Ovid, and Theocritus. (Walker, *Crone*)
Shelley's (1792-1822) "Witch of Atlas" similarly spins three threads:

> she took her
>   spindle
> And twined three threads of fleecy mist
>   . . .
> And with these threads a subtle veil she wove.

In a depiction of the *Four Ages of Life, a *Tractatus de quaternio* by an
anonymous 12th-century Anglo Saxon author, we see a depiction of the thread
of life. The third of four female figures represented holds a spool onto which
she winds the thread. The fourth figure spins the thread with a *distaff and
spindle. (Sears, p. 24, Plate 6)

Three Ages of Man: The Pythagoreans felt that three represented a totality
because it possessed a beginning, a middle, and an end. Aristotle, basing his
ideas on this, described life as divided into three ages.

This division of an individual life *cycle into three stages is seen in the
riddle of the *Sphinx from Classical mythology, which was solved by Oedipus:
"What is that which has one voice and yet becomes four-footed and two-footed
and three-footed?" The answer: a man in the three phases of life, crawling on
four feet, walking on two feet, and supporting himself in old age with a cane
or stick forming a third "leg." (Sears, p. 90)

A number of complex images from Western culture embody the Three
Ages of Man, including the Three *Magi and the Three *Fates.

In *Allegory of Prudence*, Titian, the 16th-century Venetian painter,
presents an image of the Three Ages of Man. He painted it in his eighties or
nineties (he lived, by various accounts, into his nineties or beyond), ten years
before his death. He joins three busts so as to form a sort of three-faced
image. Three animals' heads lie below the busts, constituting a similar
corresponding three-faced beast. The left-hand image, an *old man with a
long, white beard, is a self-portrait. The portrait in the middle is of Titian's
son, Orazio, and the right-hand image is of his adopted grandson, Marco. The
animals corresponding to each of the three portraits are a *wolf on the left,
a *lion in the middle, and a *dog on the right.

threshold: The threshold is related to the symbolism of both the two-faced
god, *Janus, whose form is representative of past and future and the three-

headed goddess, *Hecate, whose form represents past, present, and future. The threshold represents the point of transition between these temporal states. Edmund Waller (1606-1687) describes in his poem "Of the Last Verses in the Book" how age illuminates and brings together the past and the present:

> The soul's dark cottage, battered and decayed,
> Lets in new light through chinks that Time has made:
> Stronger by weakness, wiser, men become
> As they draw near to their eternal home.
> Leaving the old, both worlds at once they view
> That stand upon the threshold of the new.

Shelley (1792-1822) presents a similar image of the threshold of the afterlife in "An Allegory":

> A portal as of shadowy adamant
>   Stands yawning on the highway of the life
> Which we all tread, a cavern huge and gaunt.

Theodore Roethke (1908-1963), in "Meditations of an Old Woman," further relates a form of consciousness characteristic of old age to experience of the threshold. Here the body delights in thresholds and "rocks in and out of itself."

The 17th-century Dutch artist Gerrit Dou did a number of paintings in which solitary figures, often aged, occupy thresholds. In *Old Woman in a Window* (1699), the artist places an *asphodel, symbolic of the afterlife, just outside the window through which an old woman leans.

thrush: The thrush is a symbol of age, as in Chaucer's (ca. 1343-1400) "The Parliament of Fowles" (p. 364): "the throstel [song-thrush] olde." It is also a symbol of the solitary existence of the *hermit, as seen in these lines from Walt Whitman's (1819-1892) "When Lilacs Last in the Dooryard Bloomed":

> Solitary the thrush,
> The hermit withdrawn to himself,
>   avoiding the settlement,
> Sings by himself a song. (de Vries)

Time: see AION, CHRONOS, FATHER TIME, KRONOS, SATURN.

Tiresias: Tiresias means, literally, "he who delights in signs." (Graves, GM II, p. 409) Tiresias was the ancient seer of Thebes from Classical mythology. He can be identified by his attribute, the *cornel *staff, made from the divinatory *cornel tree. (de Vries) Though he was blind as a result of an incident in his youth, he lived to a great age, advising the gods even after his death. The incident leading to his blindness and the compensatory gift of the "inner eye" of prophecy takes the form of two different tales.

The first tale states that, as a youth, Tiresias happened upon Athena bathing, and as a result of exposure to the beauty and power of the unveiled goddess, he was immediately struck blind. (cf. Callimachus, *The Bathing of Pallas*) But, by way of compensation, Athena bestowed upon him the gift of inner vision. (Graves, GM)

In the second story, Tiresias comes upon a pair of mating *snakes in the road. Various accounts describe his reaction as either striking and killing the female *snake, separating the two *snakes, or wounding them. At any rate, as a result of his action, Tiresias was changed into a woman. *Seven years later, he again encountered two *snakes mating in the road, repeated his previous action, and consequently became a man again. This renowned experience resulted in Tiresias' being called upon to settle a dispute between Zeus and Hera as to whether women or men had more "enjoyments." (cf. Ovid's *Metamorphoses* 3) Since Tiresias had experienced both sexes, he was considered the perfect one to consult. In agreement with Zeus, he declared that women had more pleasures. This angered Hera, who blinded Tiresias. But Zeus, in turn, gave Tiresias the gift of prophecy and long life. As a result, Tiresias lived *seven generations, advising the gods and goddesses on numerous matters throughout his long life and, even after death, speaking to them from Hades.

The first person ever to consult Tiresias was Leiriope, mother of Narcissus. Tiresias advised her that Narcissus would live to a ripe old age as long as he never knew himself. However, Leiriope was not able to prevent her son's self-knowledge, since the young Narcissus, fulfilling Tiresias' prophecy, fell in love with his own reflection in a *pool and was changed into a *flower (the narcissus or daffodil). This tale is perhaps instructive of the folly of too great a degree of self-involvement and self-knowledge in youth, a danger perceived by Tiresias from the vantage point of old age.

Tiresias plays the role of prophet in the *Odyssey*, as well. Odysseus travels to Hades and consults the aged seer about his future. Tiresias tells him that, before he settles into a comfortable old age after returning from his heroic exploits, he will take one last *journey inland. (see OAR)

As Joseph Campbell explains, Tiresias' wisdom was a product of integrative understanding resulting from perception of both sides (masculine and feminine) of matters:

> Those who, like Tiresias, have seen and come into touch with the mystery of the two serpents and, in some sense at least, have been themselves both male and female, know the reality from both sides that each sex experiences shadowlike from its own side; and to that extent they have assimilated what is substantial of life. (Campbell, MG, p. 171)

As a consequence of this experience, Tiresias possessed greater wisdom than even Zeus (who was only male) or Hera (who was only female). (Grant and Hazel; Graves, GM; Grimal, DCM; Tripp)

Erich Neumann, known for his studies of human development, says that three different forms of mysticism accompany three major stages of psychological development. The last stage, old age, is characterized by "mature mysticism" where "the self emerges: opposites are reconciled, and harmony is achieved between the conscious and unconscious aspects of the mind." (Woodward, *Memory and Desire*, p. 19) The form of integrative understanding exhibited by Tiresias, the *Wise Old Man, can be viewed as an example of Neumann's "mature mysticism."

Tiresias figures prominently in T. S. Eliot's *The Wasteland* (1922): "I Tiresias, though blind, throbbing between two lives." Eliot says: "Tiresias, although a mere spectator and not indeed a 'character,' is yet the most important personage in the poem, uniting all the rest." Reflecting his role in the Classical myth, Tiresias in Eliot's poem is the point where all the male characters (who Eliot says are all one) and all the female characters (as Eliot says, all the women in the poem "are one woman") meet: "the two sexes meet in Tiresias. What Tiresias sees, in fact, is the substance of the poem." (Eliot, p. 50)

The Hindu equivalent of Tiresias is *Trisiras, whose magical powers came from his ability to change sex. (Walker, WEMS)

Tithonus: Tithonus, connected with the Trojan cycle of Classical mythology, is a symbol of the folly of the human desire for immortality. (cf. "Homeric Hymn to Aphrodite," 5, 218-238; Homer's *Iliad*, 20, 236-237; Euripides' *The Trojan Women* 853-858; Hesiod's *Theogeny* 984-985) Eos (Dawn) fell in love with Tithonus, an extremely handsome young man, and abducted him. She subsequently asked Zeus to make Tithonus immortal like herself, but forgot to ask that he be given eternal youth. As a result, Zeus' granting of her wish was a mixed blessing. Sometime later, Eos noticed that Tithonus was noticeably aging, his hair graying and his skin wrinkling. She realized her error and asked that Zeus grant Tithonus eternal youth, as well; however, Zeus would not comply.   At this point, the myth diverges into two conflicting versions. The first states that Eos grew bored with Tithonus as he aged and locked him in a room so she would not have to listen to his incessant babbling. According to the second version, Eos turned Tithonus into a *cicada (or a *cricket or *grasshopper, depending upon the source), placing him in a basket that she carried with her, so that she might listen to his pleasant chirping. His form as a *cicada allowed him to shed his aged skin once a year, thereby subverting some of the effects of aging.

Ovid's depiction of Tithonus in the *Metamorphoses* (9, 421) as symbolic of the waxing and waning day (or *year), deserted by the youthful Eos (dawn) and imprisoned in darkness from where he cries out, is based upon the first version of the story. Alternately, Homer and Virgil following the second story line, speak of the never-ending love of the pair, Eos (dawn) rising from Tithonus' couch each morning. ("Homeric Hymn to Aphrodite," *Iliad*; de Vries; Grant and Hazel; Graves, GM; Grimal, DCM; Tripp)

In *The Coming of Age*, Simone de Beauvoir says that Tithonus demonstrates the ancient Greek view of the physical decay which accompanies very old age, "a curse worse than death itself." (de Beauvoir, p. 98)

In Tennyson's (1809-1892) "Tithonus," the subject of the poem laments his state:

> The woods decay, the woods decay and fall,
> The vapours weep their burthen to the ground,
> Man comes and tills the field and lies beneath,
> And after many a summer dies the swan.
> Me only cruel immortality
> Consumes. . . .

Tmolus: Described variously as an old *river god and an old *mountain in Classical mythology, Tmolus judges the musical contest between Apollo and Marsyas in Ovid's *Metamorphoses* 11. Midas objects to Tmolus awarding the prize to Apollo and is punished for his dissension by Apollo's bestowal of ass's ears.

Tmolus' metamorphosis into a *mountain is described in another story (Apollodorus, book 2, part 6, 3). Tmolus fell in love with the huntress Arrhippe and pursued her relentlessly. An attendant of Artemis, Arrhippe went to her goddess' temple to elude Tmolus. After Tmolus found her and raped her on Artemis' couch, Arrhippe hanged herself. To avenge Arrhippe's death, Artemis loosed a mad bull upon Tmolus, causing a painful demise. Tmolus' son buried him at the place of his death, calling the *mountain Tmolus. (Graves, GM)

Ovid describes "old Tmolus" as a "craggy, sacred mountain" in his description of the contest between Apollo and Marsyas:

> On his mountain top
> The judge was seated; from his ears he freed
> The forest trees; only a wreath of oak
> Fringed his green locks, with acorns dangling round
> His hollow temples.

In Shelley's (1792-1822) "Hymn of Pan," old Tmolus serves as Pan's musical audience:

> The wind in the reeds and the rushes,
>   The bees on the bells of thyme

The birds on the myrtle bushes,
The cicale above in the lime,
And the lizards below in the grass,
Were as silent as ever old Tmolus, was
        Listening to my sweet pipings.

torch: The "passing of the torch" signifies the continuity of generations, the passage of tradition, knowledge, etc. from the older to the younger generation. Consequently, it may be related to *Hestia, the goddess of Classical mythology who was responsible for both perpetuation of the *hearth fire and the perpetuation of tradition in succeeding generations. The torch is also a symbol of development of the spiritual through illumination and guidance. (de Vries)

tortoise: The tortoise is a symbol of longevity and endurance in a meager environment, because it is believed to survive on dew in an environment not conducive to other animals. (de Vries) As a symbol of longevity, it accompanies *Fukuro Kuju, Japanese god of good luck, and *Jorujin, Japanese god of longevity.

tree: The tree symbolizes the endurance of the individual, as in Edna St. Vincent Millay's (1892-1950) "What Lips My Lips Have Kissed": "Thus in the winter stands the lonely tree." (Lyell)
    In Theodore Roethke's (1908-1963) "Infirmity," the aging tree symbolizes the aging person who conforms to "divinity by dying inward, like an aging tree."

Tree of Life: Trees of Life from the Middle Ages are often variations of the *Wheel of Life. In trees of the Ages of Life, figures of men at various stages of life are depicted on a tree's branches, ascending up one side and descending down the other in a manner similar to that depicted in *Wheels of Life, in which the depictions occur upon a *wheel. (cf. Ulrich of Lilienfeld, *Concordantia caritatis*; Sears, Plates 93-96)
    Trees of Life occur in numerous myths. Yggdrasil, the Tree of Life from Nordic mythology, forms the world axis. The Nordic version of the Three *Fates, the *Norns, live at its base.

Tree of Wisdom: In the Middle Ages, an image representative of man's progression toward greater wisdom by passage through the *seven ages and the *seven liberal arts found expression in the *Arbor sapientiae*, the Tree of Wisdom. (cf. MS. 9220, fol. 16r, Bibliothèque Nationale, Paris; Sears, Plate 84) At the top is *Sancta Trinitas* (divine wisdom) with the inscription: "I order, I create, I bestow all things." At the root is the inscription: "I wish it, I command it, I effect it according to my law." At the branch ends on the left the *seven *ages, under the heading *Natura*, progress upwards from *infans* through *decrepitus*. On the right, under the heading *Philosophia*, the *seven liberal arts are found at the ends of the branches, from grammar to astrology. Lines of verse are written on lines connecting each of the ages with each of the arts. This depiction reflects a view that the path to wisdom is a *seven-step process and that nature (growing old) and philosophy (study) are the paths toward the goal. Trees of Wisdom often function as such didactic diagrams. (Sears, pp. 140-141)

triform: "Triform" is another name for *Hecate, the *Crone, reflecting her function as one aspect of the *Triple Goddess complex of Virgin/Mother/-Crone.

Triple Goddess: The Triple Goddess is the threefold manifestation of the Great Goddess found in numerous ancient cultures. Barbara Walker states: "From the earliest ages, the concept of the Great Goddess was a trinity and the model for all subsequent trinities, female, male, or mixed." (Walker, WEMS, p. 1018) The Triple Goddess is the Virgin/Mother/*Crone complex which takes the form of the Three *Fates of Roman mythology, the *Norns of Nordic mythology and the *Morrigan of Ireland. (Walker, WEMS) The Triple Goddess is symbolized in numerous contexts by the colors white, red, and *black, corresponding to past, present, and future or birth, life, and death. Her weaving of *threads of these colors is believed to form the *"web of time." Known in India as the *gunas* or "strands" of the Creatress, *Kali-Maya, white, red, and *black represented, respectively: "(1) radiant, pure tranquillity; (2) blazing energy and passion; and (3) weight and darkness, the silent night of the tomb." (Walker, *Crone*, and WEMS, p. 1018) The white *threads belonged to the Virgin, the red to the Mother, and the black to the *Crone. Together, the three weave the web of temporal existence.

   In Western literature, the white, red, and *black *threads of life are found in the writings of Horace, Ovid, and Theocritus. (Walker, *Crone*)

   A product of matriarchal culture, the Triple Goddess did not survive intact in later culture. The Virgin and Mother aspects of the complex were assimilated to Christianity; but the *Crone, as a threatening and powerful image of death, was rejected and repressed. Separated from the complex, she took satanic form, becoming wholly malevolent in the form of the *witch. (Walker, *Crone*)

Trisiras: The Hindu equivalent of *Tiresias from Classical mythology, Trisiras possessed magical abilities which derived from his capacity to change sex. (Walker, WEMS)

turtle: The turtle is a symbol of longevity and of material, as opposed to spiritual, existence. It is related to natural evolution (which is slow like the turtle), as opposed to spiritual evolution (which is believed rapid). (Cirlot; de Vries)

twelve: The number twelve signifies perfection and completion. As the number of houses of the *zodiac, the number of months of the *year, and the number of hours of day and of *night, twelve is related to the division of time into repeated, *cyclical units. (de Vries) As the last number in each of these *cycles, twelve, like the *circle, represents completion, the end of the *cycle, as in old age.

Twelve Ages of Man: Based upon the widely accepted concept of the *Four Ages of Man, in the late Middle Ages a conception of the Twelve Ages of Man became prominent. This found its basis in the *twelve months of the *year, reflecting a view of man as a microcosm of the greater macrocosm.

*Trees of the Twelve Ages of Life were a popular subject of medieval manuscripts. (cf. Ulrich of Lilienfeld's *Concordantia caritatis*, cod. 151, fol. 257v, Stiftsbibliothek, Lilienfeld; Sears, Plates 93, 94) They typically consisted of a *tree at the base of which are seated God and Christ ("Pater" and "Filius"). Branches on both sides extend out and curl back upon themselves, the interior space of the curve forming leafy frames for depictions of twelve successive *ages of man. Six ascend up the left side, starting with an infant at the tree's base and descending on the right to old age. (Sears)

twilight: Twilight signifies the end of a *cycle. (Cirlot; de Vries) In this view, a day's *cycle is analogous to an individual life *cycle; consequently, twilight corresponds to old age. Twilight symbolizes old age in the following passage from Shakespeare (Sonnet 74):

> In me thou see'st the twilight of such day
> As after sunset fadeth in the West,
> Which by and by black night doth take away.

U

Ukko: Ukko is the Finnish god of thunder, also known as Isainen ("granddad"), whose name means "old man." His attributes include a blue cape, a flaming animal pelt, a hammer, an axe, and a sword. He is the source of thunder and lightning. Lightning is created when the hooves of the horses that power his wagon create sparks on a stony path. Thunder occurs when Ukko grinds corn or rolls boulders around the heavens. (Lurker)

Uncle Remus: An aged, black ex-slave is the title character of Joel Chandler Harris' *Uncle Remus, His Songs and His Sayings* (1880). Uncle Remus' humorous stories, told to a young white boy, center upon the exploits of a variety of animals (Brer Rabbit, Brer Fox, etc.) exhibiting human characteristics.

As the aged *storyteller, Uncle Remus allegorizes and passes along to the young the values of his particular cultural milieu (in this case, antebellum Southern culture). Harris, who calls Uncle Remus' tales "plantation legends," states that the old storyteller "has nothing but pleasant memories of the discipline of slavery." (pp. xvii-xviii)

Urd: Urd is the personification of *Fate in Old Norse literature. Her name's relationship to the Latin *vertere* ("to turn") may stem from the fact that she sits under the world *tree or world axis, Yggdrasil. (Walker, *Crone*)

Urme: In Poland, Russia, and Siberia, the Three *Fates are called "Urme."

V

Vainamoinen: Unlike most heroic figures from mythology, Vainamoinen of Finnish cosmology is advanced in age. He appears in the *Kalevala*, the Finnish epic named after the mysterious ancestor, Kaleva, who is Vainamoinen's father. Kaleva himself does not appear in the tale.

Vainamoinen's name comes from the word *vaina*, which means "a strait or a wide, slowly flowing river." (Eliade, ER, v. 16, 166-67). Often referred to as "the old one" and "the everlasting wise man" and described as "old since birth," he is the creator of the primeval sea and is builder of the primeval *boat. (Eliade, ER) Through his magical song, he acts as "midwife" to nature, causing her to produce various forms of animals and trees. (Santillana) His accomplished musicianship makes joy and song possible.

Vainamoinen figures prominently in the creation myth describing the origin of the Sampo, the cosmic *mill, the *axis mundi*, or world pole. *Louhi, the *Crone of Pohja, asks him to create the Sampo, but this task being beyond his powers, he coerces his brother Ilmarinen, the primeval smith, into forging the pole with a "many-colored cover." (Santillana) The *crone carries the Sampo into the Mount of Copper where she secures it behind nine locks. Here it forms a deep tap root into Mother Earth.

Other tales revolve around Vainamoinen's battles with *Louhi over possession of the Sampo, possibly forming allegorical battles of *Fate as personified by *Louhi, the *crone, and *Time as personified by "the old one," Vainamoinen. He displays great strength, vitality, and sometimes shamanistic powers in these battles. In a final story, Vainamoinen leaves the world in an iron-bottomed *boat. (Eliade, ER)

After leaving this world, Vainamoinen is believed to have taken residence in the heavens, where the constellation Orion forms his *scythe and the Pleiades his shoes. It is believed that he will return at some point in the future. (Lurker)

Akseli Gallen-Kallela's painting *The Defense of the Sampo* (1896) shows Vainamoinen and Louhi fighting for possession of the Sampo. (McKee and Kauppinen)

Vertumnus: Vertumnus, Roman god of the changing seasons, appears as an *old woman in Ovid's *Metamorphoses*. He dons the disguise of a *crone in order to win the confidence and trust of Pomona, goddess of fruit trees.

The beautiful young Pomona, wholly involved in cultivation of her gardens and orchards, is the object of attraction for numerous would-be suitors. However, she has no interest in such matters as love and courtship, and to stave off any further advances, she walls off her orchard. Vertumnus, undeterred, dresses as an old woman and gains admittance to her garden. Gaining her favor by praising her skill as a gardener and admiring her beauty, he steals a kiss. In order to further his cause, he gives her grandmotherly advice in the form of a parable. Admiring an elm tree and the healthy grape vines growing out of it, he tells her (*Metamorphoses* 14):

> "But had the tree," he said, "not wed the vine,
> Its only value now would be its leaves.
> So too this clinging vine that rests at ease
> Upon the elm, had it remained unwed,
> Would struggle prostrate, sprawling on the ground.
> But you, unmoved by this tree's lesson, shun
> A husband, and will link your life with none.

Vertumnus tells Pomona that, if she were only willing, she would have more suitors than Helen of Troy, and if she were really wise, she would heed the old woman's sage advice and return the affections of the most worthy of her potential suitors, the graceful, skillful, devoted Vertumnus.

He goes on to warn her that, if she remains cold-hearted, she may invoke the wrath of Nemesis. In order that she may further benefit from the wisdom of the old woman's years, Vertumnus goes on to relate the story of Iphis' unrequited love for Lady Anaxarete. Repeatedly spurned by the beautiful Anaxarete, Iphis hangs himself. At the sight of Iphis' corpse, the cold-hearted Anaxarete is turned to stone.

Upon finishing his story, Vertumnus sheds his disguise. Moved by his youth and beauty, Pomona succumbs to his seduction. (Grimal, DCM)

Vesta: Vesta is the Roman counterpart of *Hestia, the Greek goddess of the *hearth.

violin: As a stringed instrument, the violin, often seen in depictions of aged men, symbolizes the balance of conflicting elements. The violin possesses a number of strings tuned so as to work together to produce harmony;

consequently, it can be viewed as a symbol of integrative understanding, the cognitive style often cited as typical of old age, which draws diverse elements into harmonious relationship.

In "Descriptive Sketches," Wordsworth (1770-1850) presents a picturesque depiction of the old musician:

> But once I pierced the mazes of a wood
> In which a cabin undeserted stood;
> There an old man an olden measure scanned
> On a rude viol touched with withered hand.

The old musician serves as the subject of Edouard Manet's *The Old Musician* (1862) and Nicolai Fechin's *Old Violinist* (1936). (McKee and Kauppinen)

vulture: In the Ages of Man, the medieval artistic and literary convention dividing an individual's life *cycle into *ten stages, the vulture is a woman of 70 with a *distaff. (de Vries)

W

wallet: In Shakespeare's *Troilus and Cressida* (act 3, sc. 3), the wallet, as a symbol of memory, serves as an attribute of time (de Vries):

> Time hath, my lord, a wallet at his back
> Wherein he puts alms for oblivion.

water: Because of its reflective quality, water shares in the symbolism of the *mirror and thus becomes a medium of self-reflection in life review. As a symbol of the unconscious, it also symbolizes the storehouse of memory and experience contained in the individual unconscious. Water also signifies transition between phases of existence--between worlds, between life and death. (de Vries)

Water bears a symbolic relationship to the *pilgrim, through the *well of the water of salvation which he finds in his path. Here water is a symbol of the redemptive function of acceptance of Christ as savior. *Pilgrims are often depicted with a water bottle or jug, which serves as a symbol of salvation and redemption. (cf. *Old Man Holding A Pilgrim Bottle*, 17th century, Italian School; McKee and Kauppinen)

In *Faust*, Goethe uses water, which is constantly transforming, as a symbol of man's life, which is constantly changing also. He particularly stresses the *cyclic nature of water as an image of the neo-Platonic concept of the world soul "which similarly emanates into matter and then returns to itself." (Dieckmann, p. 16)

water-mill: Because of its *cyclic action, and because it functions through the force of two symbols of time and time's passage (the *river or stream and the *wheel), the water-mill signifies the *cyclic nature of time. T. S. Eliot uses the water-mill as a symbol of time in "Journey of the Magi" (1927): "a water-mill beating the darkness." (de Vries)

wave: The wave is a symbol of regeneration and the *cyclic (involutive/evolutive) passage of time, as in Virginia Woolf's *To the Lighthouse* (1927). (de Vries) (see LIGHTHOUSE)

weaving: Weaving is linked with *fate or destiny in numerous mythologies. The Latin term *destino* (destiny) means that which is *woven, or fixed with cords and *threads. (Walker, WEMS, p. 302) The *Triple Goddess in her numerous forms (*Fates or *Parcae of Classical mythology, *Norns of Nordic mythology, *Weird Sisters of the Celts, *Zorya of the Slavs, *Morrigan of the Irish, and Triple Guinivere or *Brigit of the Britons) is almost always engaged in *weaving as a manifestation of her determination of the *fate of individuals. (Walker, WEMS)

A similar figure, *Kala (meaning "time", "destiny"), is found in East India in the epic *The Mahabharata*. She is represented as the cosmic *weaver, composing the fabric of life of each individual and of the whole universe from the *weaving of white *threads (symbolic of *light and life) and *black *threads (symbolic of death and darkness). (Eliade, ER, p. 367)

In Goethe's *Faust*, the Earth Spirit (Goethe's own invention) appears to *Faust in a vision, describing himself:

> I soar up and down
> I weave back and forth.

And, further describing himself, the Earth Spirit says that he *weaves "on the rushing loom of time the godhead's living garment." (Dieckmann, pp. 49-50)

web: As a cognate of *weaving, the web symbolizes the unfolding of an individual's life. As an instrument of entrapment, it also symbolizes the limitations of the human condition and individual fortune. (Eliade, ER)

Shelley (1792-1822) presents an image of the individual life as woven on "nature's vast frame" in "Alastor; Or, The Spirit of Solitude":

> Nature's vast frame, the web of human things,
> Birth and the grave, that are not as they were.

Weird Sisters: The three *witches in *Macbeth*, the Weird Sisters, are a form of the Three *Fates. Joseph Campbell explains: "Weird was a Saxon name of the death-goddess or *Crone, who often stood for the whole trinity. Her name was variously given as Wyrd, or Wurd, or Urd, meaning both "Earth" and the Word of *Fate's immutable law." (MG, p. 485)

Reference to Wyrd as *fate is made in *Beowulf*: "Every man in this life will go lay him down on the bed where Wyrd has decided to nail him." Wyrd is further described in *Beowulf* as "writing the fate of every man in her book of life." (Walker, *Crone*, p. 99)

Barbara Walker notes in *The Crone* that the Weird Sisters in Tudor England were the *Fairy Godmothers who visited each child at birth to determine its future.

well: The well of the *water of salvation which the *pilgrim finds in his path is symbolic of the redemptive power of Christ. It is, further, a symbol of truth and the wisdom of the deep as an object into which one looks in contemplation. The well is a symbol of time in Germanic tradition, because the Well of Time nourishes the World *Tree, the ash. (de Vries)

West: As the direction in which the *sun sets, West symbolizes completion and the end of a *cycle, as in old age. In most religions the land of afterlife is in the West or *North. (Cirlot; de Vries)

In "Stepping Westward" by William Wordsworth (1770-1850), moving westward symbolizes advancing age:

The dewy ground was dark and cold;
Behind, all gloomy to behold;
And stepping westward seemed to be
A kind of heavenly destiny

West Wind: The West Wind is related to *autumn and, thus, to middle or old age, as in Shelley's "Ode to the West Wind" (1820): "O Wild West Wind, thou Breath of Autumn's being." (de Vries)

wheel: As a form of the *circle, the wheel represents a totality, a closed circuit, as in a completed life. (de Vries) Numerous variants of the wheel, such as the *Wheel of Fortune, the *Wheel of Life, and the broken wheel, symbolize the passage of time and a life's course, as seen below. The wheel is the symbol of a life's course in Shakespeare's *King Lear* (act 5, sc. 3, 174): "The wheel is come full circle." (Hankins) Division of a wheel into *twelve segments symbolizes time as manifested in the *year's *cycle of *twelve months and in the day's division into two *twelve-hour *cycles. (de Vries)

In "Rabbi Ben Ezra" Robert Browning (1812-1889) uses the potter's wheel as symbolic of the *cyclic and transforming nature of *time, shaping human clay through its repeated revolution:

This, I was worth to God, whose wheel the pitcher shaped.
    Ay, note that Potter's wheel,
    That metaphor! and feel

Why time spins fast, why passive lies our clay.--

. . .

Time's wheel runs back or stops: Potter and clay endure.

wheel, broken: The broken wheel, as in the case of the broken wheel at the cistern in *Pilgrim's Progress*, symbolizes death: "Then there came forth a summons for *Mr. Steadfast. . . . The contents whereof were, That he must prepare for a change of life, for his master was not willing that he should be far from him any longer.* The messenger said: *'Thy wheel is broken at the cistern.'*" (Bunyan, p. 376)

The image of the broken wheel echoes an image from the parable of old age in Ecclesiastes 12 from the Bible symbolizing the failure of the aged body to contain the life force:

> Or ever the silver cord be loosed, or the golden bowl be
>   broken,
> Or the pitcher be broken at the fountain, or the wheel
>   broken at the cistern.
> Then shall the dust return to the earth as it was: and
>   the spirit shall return unto God who gave it. (Scofield)

Wheel of Fire: see FIRE, WHEEL OF.

Wheel of Fortune: The Wheel of Fortune was emblematic of the *cyclic nature of luck in the Middle Ages. Boethius, the 5th-6th century author of *Consolation of Philosophy*, described *Fortuna, who turns the Wheel of Fortune, as two-faced, blind, and deaf. Man is afixed to her *wheel, powerless to affect its turning. According to Boethius, *Fortuna represents the temporal world which is distinct from and subordinate to divine providence, which "employs the seemingly random acts of Fortune to a purpose." (Sears, p. 144)

Many depictions of the Wheel of Fortune show *four men along the rim; one ascending; one on top (often wearing a *crown); one descending, falling; one lying at the bottom. These *four are not differentiated as to age. (cf. "Wheel of Fortune" from MS. of John Lydgate's *Troy Book and Story of Thebes*, England, ca. 1455-1462; Von Franz, *Time*, Plate 13) The later variant of the Wheel of Fortune, the *Wheel of Life, presents the *four at different ages, representing the *Four Ages of Man. (Sears; von Franz, *Time*)

Wheel of Fortune (Vanitas) (1977-1978) by Audrey Flack provides a contemporary example of the Wheel of Fortune. In this still-life painting, the artist presents a complex of objects symbolic of chance, fortune, and time's passage. This *memento mori* consists of the Wheel of Fortune card from a Tarot deck, a *candle nearly burned down, a skull reflected in a *mirror, an *hourglass, and a photograph of the artist's young daughter.

Wheel of Life: The Wheel of Life is a variation of the earlier *Wheel of Fortune. *Fortuna is portrayed as turning a *wheel to which are afixed figures of men representing the *Four Ages of Man, Youth ascending, Adulthood on top, Middle Age descending, and Old Age at the bottom. In a *wheel from 1240 by the English artist William de Brailes, figures at the *four cardinal points of a spoked *wheel hold scrolls inscribed with the following: "I am borne again to the stars" (held by a young man); "I exalt on high" (held by a *king); "Reduced, I descend"; "Lowest, I am ground by the wheel" (held by a prostrate figure). *Twelve additional figures more reflective of successive stages of the life *cycle border the *circle, from infancy through old age. The implication of an image which depicts a closed *cycle, a wheel that makes only one turn, taking the individual back to the point at which he started, is explained by Sears: "The implication is that a man should look beyond the worldly life, so transitory, so deceitful, to a spiritual existence which is not bound by time, the vagaries of chance, and the rhythms of growth and decay." (Sears, p. 145)

Another Wheel of Life, the "Psalter of Robert de Lisle", by the 14th-century English artist known as the "Madonna Master," depicts *ten stages of life, each with an accompanying verse, as follows:

Meek am I and humble, I live on pure milk.
Never shall I stumble, I measure my age.
A life worthy of the world is tested by the mirror.
Not the mirror's image, but life itself delights.
I am king, I rule the world, the entire world is mine.
I take up a staff for myself, at death's door.
Given over to decrepitude, death shall be my lot.
Given over to feebleness, I begin to fail.
I thought that I would go on living, life has deceived me.
I have been turned into ashes, life has deceived me.

whirlpool: As a combination of the spiral (representative of *cyclic movement) and *water, the whirlpool becomes a symbol of *time, as in Dylan Thomas' (1914-1953) "The Force that through the Green Fuse Drives the Flower": "The hand that whirls the water in the pool" (de Vries) The whirlpool serves as a similar image in Thomas' "It Is the Sinner's Dust-Tongued Bell," a poem in which the narrator "hears the hours chant" and "a whirlpool drives the prayerwheel."

wind: Wind is a symbol of *time and the process of aging, as in T. S. Eliot's (1888-1965) "Song for Simeon": "My life is light, waiting for the death wind"; and in Dylan Thomas' (1914-1953) "Should Lanterns Shine" where the narrator moves quickly in defiance of Time, "Whose beard wags in Egyptian wind." (de Vries)

windmill: The windmill incorporates the symbolism of the *wheel and thereby becomes symbolic of the *cyclic nature of *time. (de Vries) In Cervantes' *Don Quixote* (1605, 1615), the title character's attempt to "tilt with windmills" becomes a symbol of the folly of old age, of the attempt to deny and combat *time's passage.

wing: The wing is a symbol of *time and an attribute of *Fate. (de Vries) Early representations of *Time in the form of *Aion consisted of a winged figure with the head of a *lion and a human body entwined in *serpents. (de Vries) *Kronos, also symbolizig *time, is sometimes portrayed with *four *wings, two outspread as if preparing to fly, and two lowered, at rest.

Dylan Thomas (1914-1953) presents an image of *Time and age as winged in "Among those Killed in the Dawn Raid was a Man Aged a Hundred": "The morning is flying on the wings of his age."

winter: Winter symbolizes old age. Shakespeare employs winter as a symbol of both healthful, vigorous old age (Adam in *As You Like It*) and depleted, decrepit old age (Aegeon in *The Comedy of Errors*):

Therefore my age is as a lusty winter,
Frosty, but kindly.   (*As You Like It*, act 2, sc. 3)

. . . this grained face of mine be hid
In sap-consuming winter's drizzled snow.
                    (*The Comedy of Errors*, act 5, sc. 1)

In "Late Leaves," Walter Savage Landor (1775-1864) presents winter as a symbol of old age:

Winter may come: he brings but nigher
His circle (yearly narrowing) to the fire
. . .
And spring and summer both are past,
    And all things sweet.

In Shelley's (1792-1822) "Dirge for the Year," "White Winter" is a "rough nurse" who "Rocks the death-cold year to-day."

Wise Old Man: The Wise Old Man is a Jungian archetype expressive of the age-old wisdom of humanity and, in Jungian terms, the collective unconscious. In stories and dreams, he represents the spiritual element in humankind (or in the individual) which, in times of hardship, appears and lends assistance in the form of advice but never action. As an embodiment of the spiritual, he appears in dreams as magician, *doctor, priest, teacher, professor, grandfather, or a similar authority figure. Jung says: "The archetype of spirit in the shape of a man, hobgoblin, or animal always appears in a situation where insight, understanding, good advice, determination, planning, etc., are needed but cannot be mustered on one's own resources. The archetype compensates this state of spiritual deficiency by contents designed to fill the gap." (Jung, ACU, p. 216)

The Wise Old Man appears as the spirit-type in fairytales, as well, always when the hero finds himself in a dangerous situation to which there is no immediately apparent solution, a situation which requires application of cleverness or profound thought. Jung says: "The knowledge needed to compensate the dificiency comes in the form of a personified thought, i.e., in the shape of this sagacious and helpful old man." (Jung, *ACU*, p. 218)

The *old man often asks questions intended to stimulate reflection in the hero, with the result of "mobilizing the moral forces." Often he gives the hero "the necessary magic talisman, the unexpected and improbable power to succeed, which is one of the peculiarities of the unified personality in good or bad alike." (Jung, *ACU*, p. 220) He has a wicked side too, as seen in the Arthurian character *Merlin, who is sometimes goodness personified and at other times "the wicked magician who, from sheer egoism, does evil for evil's sake." (Jung, *ACU*, p. 227)

The Wise Old Man is connected with the unconscious when he appears as a dwarf—the homunculus in *alchemy, hobgoblins, brownies, gremlins, *elves, etc. Jung explains this phenomenon: "It seems to me . . . that this liking for diminutives on the one hand and for superlatives—giants, etc.—on the other is connected with the queer uncertainty of spatial and temporal relations in the unconscious. Man's sense of proportion, his rational conception of big and small, is distinctly anthropomorphic, and it loses its validity not only in the realm of physical phenomena but also in those parts of the collective unconscious beyond the range of the specifically human." (Jung, *ACU*, p. 224)

In contemporary popular culture, Obi Wan Kanobe of George Lucas' *Star Wars* series functions as the Wise Old Man. He gives advice to the stories' hero, Luke Skywalker, yet he never takes action himself. (Campell, PM)

witch: The stereotypical witch in Anglo-Saxon culture is portrayed as an old *hag who practices black magic and rides a broomstick. Her animal familiar is typically a *black *cat. Perhaps the best-known example from Western literature of this common image of the witch is found in Shakespeare's *Macbeth*. The *Weird Sisters' prophecy regarding Macbeth's future at the beginning of the play catalyzes his ambition, leading to a series of unscrupulous actions with unfortunate consequences. These three *crones, reciting strange incantations and propagating violence and misfortune, wield the malevolent power which has become identified as the witch's distinguishing characteristic. (Benet) Shelley (1792-1822) presents an image of the witch's mischief and malevolence in "The Witch of Atlas":

> These were the pranks she played among the
> > cities
> Of mortal men, and what she did to sprites
> And Gods, entangling them in her sweet ditties
> > To do her will . . .

Though witches are not necessarily old women, in representations from Western culture the witch has become identified with the *crone. The *crone, originally one aspect of the *Triple Goddess, became separated from the Virgin/Mother/*Crone complex. The Virgin and Mother aspects of the complex were assimilated to Christianity, but the *Crone, as a threatening and powerful image of death, was rejected and repressed. Separated from the complex, she took satanic form, becoming wholly malevolent in the form of the witch. Suppression of the *crone, which took most overt form in witchhunts, is viewed by some as reflecting a general suppression and denial of death in patriarchal culture. The *crone, as a figure whose physical form reflected the ravages of age and the inevitable decay of the body, was a too-potent reminder of the kind of aging and death that modern Western culture wished to repress: death as the result of slow degeneration and decline. Reduced to the witch, she became wholly a force of evil to be suppressed and eliminated. (Walker, *Crone*)

As the patroness of sorceresses, *Hecate became linked with witchcraft. In later Christian culture, she was Queen of the Witches. Becoming solely identified with her *crone aspect, *Hecate formed the prototype of the witch. She was subsequently portrayed as an ugly, witch-like old woman believed to cause lunacy. (Eliade, ER)

The witch as *crone has been a popular subject of visual artists. In *Mirth* (1815), Francisco Goya shows two witches dancing. (McKee and Kauppinen) In Sarah Paxton Ball Dodson's *The Bacidae* (1883), two *sorceresses, one a *crone and one a young woman, practice augury by examining a chicken's entrails. (Rubinstein, pp. 116-117, Plate 11)

wolf: In the *Ages of Man, the medieval artistic and literary convention dividing an individual's lifespan into *ten stages, a man of 60 is represented as a wolf.

A lamb between two wolves is a representation of *Susannah and the Elders*, a Biblical tale of the opposition of youth and old age. (de Vries)

wood: Wood is a symbol of wisdom. (de Vries) Burnt wood symbolizes wisdom and death. (Cirlot) "Old wood" in P. Sidney's (1554-1586)
"Old Age" is of higher value by virtue of age because it "doth yield the bravest fire." (Sohngren and Smith)

woodcutter: The woodcutter is often a variant of the *Wise Old Man, a Jungian archetype, since he appears in fairytales when the hero is in danger. True to the archetype, he gives advice but never takes part in the action himself. In many fairytales the father is a woodcutter. (de Vries)

In *Père Jacques* (1881) the French painter Jules Bastien-Lepage presents an image contrasting youth and age. An old woodcutter, stooped by a large load of sticks, stares out at us, while a young girl, apparently unaware of the viewer, gathers wildflowers.

Y

Yama-uba (Mountain-Woman): Japanese mythology is populated by a variety of ghostly beings. Among the many spirits of *mountains and forests is Yama-uba ("Mountain Woman"). She takes a variety of forms as she wanders her mountainous haunts, sometimes assuming the form of a beautiful young woman and sometimes that of a terrifying old *crone. She is often portrayed with her son (fathered by a warrior), Kintaro or Kintoki (sometimes called "Child of Nature"). Anesaki presents an example of Yama-uba in the Japanese lyric drama. She is described by the chorus in the following (Anesaki, pp. 289-292):

> She manifests herself in a wondrous figure of monstrous
>   size,
> Formed out of clouds and mists.
>   . . .
> She roams endlessly among the clouds of illusion;
> And see her figure like the mountains,
> Yet changing perpetually.
> She hovers around the peaks,
> Her voice is echoed from the dales.
> The figure close by only a moment ago
> Is passing away, moving up and down,
> To the right and the left, encircling the summits,
> Wandering along the ranges, flying and drifting,
> And finally leaving no trace behind.

Yama-uba and her son are portrayed in a work by the 18th-century Japanese artist Rosetsu, *Yama-uba, the Mountain Woman, and Her Son Kintaro, the Child of Nature*. (Anesaki, Plate XXXII)

year: The year, often represented in the form of an *old man's figure inscribed within a *circle, serves as a prototype of numerous representations of *cyclic processes. Two or three outer *circles divided into *twelve equal parts, labeled with the signs of the *zodiac, the months and depictions of work appropriate to each month, usually surround the inner *circle. (cf. tapestry of *The Creation*, Gerona cathedral; Cirlot)

Youth and Old Man: The Youth and Old Man image is symbolic of the rising and the setting *sun. (Cirlot)

Steven Marx in "'Fortunate Senex': The Pastoral of Old Age," notes a lack of middle-aged characters in pastoral poetry and drama; conversely, he points to a wealth of elders in such literature: Wordsworth's Michael ("Michael, A Pastoral Poem"), Robert Frost's "yankee farmers," and Virgil's Tityrus and Meliboeus. Marx explains the pastoral setting as representing a nostalgic desire for lost youth. Expressing a desire for a return to an Edenic state, this setting, removed from culture, presents old age as a phase of life similarly removed from societal constraints. It is, in Victor Turner's terms, a "liminal" state. Old age, as represented in pastoral literature, shares with representations of youth in such literature a lack of concern with the practical aspects of life. Marx says: "Old age shares with youth an exemption from the concerns that Hindu sacred texts allocate to the middle-aged, whose office it is to 'maintain the world.' Renaissance writers located such concerns within the purview of the 'life of action'—the *vita activa*—and specifically excluded that way of life from the pastoral realm." (p. 22) Consequently, such writers bring youthful and aged figures together in pastoral settings. Sharing in a feeling of exclusion from and lack of interest in "the world," they share common ground. (cf. Blake's *Songs of Innocence* and Virgil's *Eclogues*) Though often portrayed in harmonious relationships, they sometimes conflict. Such conflicts form the basis for articulation of the contrast of the "soft primitivist" and the "hard primitivist." The first, typically the youth, is attracted to the pleasures and release from societal constraints offered by the rural setting. The hard primitivist, on the other hand, is attracted to the discipline which is required of the individual who wishes to survive the harsh realities of the natural world.

William Sidney Mount presents an image contrasting youth and old age in *Boys Caught Napping in a Field* (1848). In this painting, an old man with a cane comes upon three boys napping under a tree.

Z

zodiac: The word "zodiac" is derived from *zoe* ("life") and *diakos* ("wheel"), indicating its definition as a *Wheel of Life. Zodiacal symbolism, though varied, can be found in many cultures, including Mesopotamian, Egyptian, Judean, Persian, Indian, Tibetan, Chinese, American, Islamic, Greek, and Northern European. (Cirlot)

The zodiac is based upon a view of the individual as a microcosm reflective of the macrocosm of the universe. The zodiac consists of a *circle divided into *twelve equal segments of 30 degrees each, orginally corresponding to and named for the succession of *twelve constellations through the sky. (cf. *Zodiac*, from MS., France, ca. A.D. 1000; von Franz, *Time*, Plate 14) These begin with Aries in the spring and progress through the seasons to Pisces in the *winter. Just as the *four seasons are believed to correspond to stages of an individual life, so the *twelve stages of the zodiac (representative of the *twelve months) are believed to correspond to an individual life's course. In this view, there are *twelve *ages of man progressing in *cyclic fashion (reflected in the zodiac's *circular form), the final stage followed again by the first in rebirth. Thus, the progression of the months each year and their accompanying process of birth and rebirth is viewed as instructive of the progression of a soul through successive physical incarnations.

Many *Wheels of Life from the later Christian era retained zodiacal imagery, although the *cyclic view of existence which they represented was not entirely compatible with a Christian view. Such zodiacal references, often in the form of animals corresponding to the different signs of the zodiac, are found in depictions of *Wheels of Life containing *twelve divisions. (Brewer; Cirlot; Sakoian and Acker; Sears)

Medieval education included instruction in the computas, a system of reckoning time. This training necessitated the production of texts for such instruction, typically consisting of numerous diagrams, tables, and dialogues

of varied authorship. As one of many systems of the division of time, the
*Ages of Man was commonly included in such compilations. One of the most
influential and widely read computistic texts was Bede's *De temporum ratione*
(A.D. 725). One of Bede's major schema was based on a tetradic cosmology.
He drew correspondences between the *four *seasons, the *four humors, the
*four temperaments, and the *four *ages of man. Bede's tetradic system
formed the basis for numerous later tracts, including *Byrhtferth's Manual*,
which contains numerous diagrams for clarification. He combines the major
tetradic divisions (*north, south, east, west; *winter, summer, spring, fall;
*four ages of man) with *twelve-fold divisions (*twelve months; *twelve signs
of the zodiac) in Latin and Old English. *Senectus*, or old age, appears in the
same quadrant as October/November/December and Libra/Scorpio/Sagitta-
rius (see Oxford, Bodleian Library, MS. Ashmolean 328, *Byrhtferth's Manual*;
Sears, Plate 9) Similar tetradic diagrams incorporating the zodiacal signs by
Byrhtferth appear in the "Ramsey Computus" (ca. 1090) and the "Peter-
borough Computus" (ca. 1122). (Sears, Plates 10 and 11)

Zorya: The Zorya are a version of the Three *Fates from Slavic mythology.
They guard a dog fettered by a chain to the constellation, the Little Bear. The
breaking of the chain will bring the end of the world. (Walker, WEMS)

Zurvan: Zurvan is the Persian half-masculine, half-feminine *crone figure,
who gave birth to God and the devil as twins. (Walker, *Crone*) Zurvanism,
which took its name from Zurvan, the "lord of light and darkness" (Lurker)
and the personification of infinite *Time, constituted the late period of
Zoroastrian religion in ancient Islam (3rd century B.C.). (Eliade, ER, pp. 296-
297) Zurvan also occurs as the four-faced god of the *four elements in
*Manichaeanism, a later movement heavily affected by Zoroastrian concepts
of *fate and *time.

Another of Zurvan's descriptions was "decrepitude" or old age. He was
also "creator of all the paths which lead to the Cinvat *bridge—the crossing-
point into the Beyond." (Lurker)

BIBLIOGRAPHY

Abramova. "Paleolithic Art in the U.S.S.R." *Arctic Anthropology* IV-2.

Anesaki, Masaharu. *The Mythology of All Races: Japanese*. New York: Cooper Square Publishers, Inc., 1964.

Asimov, Isaac. *The Annotated Gulliver's Travels by Jonathan Swift*. New York: Clarkson N. Potter, 1980.

Bachofen, J. J. *Myth, Religion, and Mother Right: Selected Writings of J. J. Bachofen*. Princeton, N.J.: Princeton University Press, 1967.

Barnstone, Willis, ed. *The Other Bible*. San Francisco: Harper & Row, 1984.

Benet's Reader's Encyclopedia, 3rd ed. New York: Harper & Row, 1987.

Boardman, John. *Greek Art*, revised ed. New York: Oxford University Press, 1973.

Boethius. *The Consolation of Philosophy*. Translated by V. E. Watts. New York: Penguin Books, 1969.

Boyle, Joan M. and James E. Morriss. *The Mirror of Time: Images of Aging and Dying*. Westport, Conn.: Greenwood Press, Inc., 1987.

Brewer, E. C. *Brewer's Dictionary of Phrase and Fable*. Centenary ed. (revised by I. H. Evans). New York: Harper & Row, 1981.

Briggs, Katharine. *An Encyclopedia of Fairies: Hobgoblins, Brownies, Bogies and Other Supernatural Creatures*. New York: Pantheon, 1976.

Buckley, J. H. and G. B. Woods, eds. *Poetry of the Victorian Period*, 3rd ed. Glenview, Ill.: Scott, Foresman & Co., 1965.

Budge, E. A. W., translator. *The Book of the Dead, The Papyrus of Ani, Scribe and Treasurer of the Temples of Egypt, about B.C. 1450*. New York, 1913.

Bunyan, John. *Pilgrim's Progress*. London: Methuen, 1905.

Burckhardt, Titus. *Alchemy: Science of the Cosmos, Science of the Soul*. Longmead: Element Books, 1986.

Butler, Robert N. "The Life Review: An Interpretation of Reminiscence in the Aged." *Psychiatry, Journal for the Study of Interpersonal Processes*, vol. 26 (1963).

Buttrick, George A., ed. *The Interpreter's Dictionary of the Bible*, 4 volumes. New York: Abingdon Press, 1962.

Cady, E., ed. *The American Poets, 1800-1900*. Glenville, Ill.: Scott, Foresman, 1966.

Campbell, Joseph. *Historical Atlas of World Mythology:* vol. 1, *Way of the Animal Powers*. New York: A. van der Marck Editions, 1983.

Campbell, Joseph. *The Masks of God: Occidental Mythology*. Middlesex, England: Penguin Books, 1964.

Campbell, Joseph. *The Mythic Image*. Princeton, N.J.: Princeton University Press, 1974.

Campbell, Joseph. *The Power of Myth*. New York: Doubleday, 1988.

Canaday, John. *The Lives of the Painters*, 4 volumes. New York: W. W. Norton and Co., 1969.

Cavendish, Richard, ed. *Mythology, An Illustrated Encyclopedia*. New York: Rizzoli, 1980.

Christian, John, ed. *The Last Romantics: The Romantic Tradition in British Art, Burne-Jones to Stanley Spencer*. London: Lund Humphries, 1989.

Cirlot, J. E. *A Dictionary of Symbols*, 2nd ed. New York: Philosophical Library, 1962.

Cooper, J. C. *An Illustrated Encyclopedia of Traditional Symbols*. London: Thames and Hudson, 1978.

Dahmus, Joseph. *Dictionary of Medieval Civilization*. New York: Macmillan, 1984.

Davidson, H. R. Ellis. *Gods and Myths of Northern Europe*. New York: Penguin Books, 1964.

Davidson, H. R. Ellis. *Gods and Myths of the Viking Age*. New York: Bell Publishing Co., 1981.

Davidson, Thomas. *The Philosophy of Goethe's Faust*. New York: Haskell House Publishers, 1969.

de Beauvoir, Simone. *The Coming of Age*. New York: Putnam, 1972.

De Santillana, Giorgio and Hertha von Dechend. *Hamlet's Mill: An Essay on Myth and the Frame of Time*. Boston: Gambit, 1969.

de Vries, Ad. *Dictionary of Symbols and Imagery*. London: North-Holland Publishing Co., 1984.

Dickens, Charles. *A Christmas Carol and Other Christmas Stories*. New York: Penguin, 1980.

Dieckmann, Lisolette. *Goethe's Faust: A Critical Reading*. Englewood Cliffs, N.J.: Prentice-Hall, 1972.

Diggle, J., ed. *Oxford Classical Texts: Euripides, Iphigenia in Taurus*. New York: Clarendon, 1981.

Draper, John W. *The Humours and Shakespeare's Characters*. Durham, N.C.: Duke University Press, 1945.

Draper, John W. "Shakespeare's Attitude Towards Old Age." *Journal of Gerontology*, vol. 1, no. 1, pt. 1 (1/1946), pp. 118-126.

Eco, Umberto. *Art and Beauty in the Middle Ages*. Translated by Hugh Bredin. New Haven, Conn.: Yale University Press, 1986.

Eliade, Mircea, ed. *Encyclopedia of Religion*. New York: Macmillan, 1987.

Eliade, Mircea. *Images and Symbols*. "The God Who Binds and the Symbolism of Knots." New York: 1961.

Eliot, T. S. *The Wasteland and Other Poems*. New York: Harcourt, Brace and World, 1930.

Erikson, Erik. *Insight and Responsibility*. New York: W. W. Norton, 1964.

Erikson, Erik. "Reflections on Dr. Borg's Life Cycle." *Daedalus*, vol. 105, no. 2 (Spring 1976), pp. 1-28.

Euripides. *Medea and Other Plays*. New York: Penguin, 1963.

Evans, Bergen. *Dictionary of Mythology, Mainly Classical*. Lincoln, Nebraska: Centennial Press, 1970.

Evelyn-White, H. G., translator. *Hesiod: The Homeric Hymns and Homerica*. New York: Macmillan, 1914.

Ferguson, John C. *The Mythology of All Races: Chinese Mythology*. Boston, 1928.

Fernandez, James. "Reflections on Looking Into Mirrors." *Semiotica*, vol. 30 (1980), pp. 27-39.

Flack, Audrey. *On Painting*. New York: Harry N. Abrams, 1981.

Forman, H. Buxton. *The Poetical Works of Percy Bysshe Shelley*, 5 volumes. London: George Bell and Sons, 1900.

Freedman, Richard. "Sufficiently Decayed: Gerontophobia in English Literature." In Spicker, Stuart, et al., *Aging and the Elderly: Humanistic Perspectives in Gerontology*. Atlantic Highlands, N.J.: Humanities Press, 1978, pp. 49-62.

Frost, Robert. *The Poetry of Robert Frost*. New York: Holt, Rinehart and Winston, 1969.

Grant, Michael and John Hazel. *Gods and Mortals in Classical Mythology*. Springfield, Mass.: G. and C. Merriam Co., Publishers, 1973.

Graves, Robert. *The Greek Myths*, 2 vols. New York: Penguin Books, 1955.

Graves, Robert. *The White Goddess*. New York: Farrar, Straus and Giroux, 1948.

Griffin, J. J. "The Bible and Old Age." *Journal of Gerontology*, vol. 1, no. 4 (October 1946), pp. 464-471.

Grimal, Pierre. *The Dictionary of Classical Mythology*. New York: Basil Blackwell, Inc., 1986.

Grimal, Pierre, ed. *Larousse World Mythology*. Seacaucus, N.J.: Chartwell Books, 1965.

Hammond, N. G. L. and H. H. Scullard, ed. *Oxford Classical Dictionary*, 2nd ed. Oxford: Clarendon Books, 1970.

Hankins, J. E. *Shakespeare's Derived Imagery*. New York: Octagon Books, 1967.

Harris, Joel Chandler. *Uncle Remus: His Songs and His Sayings*, revised edition. New York: Grosset and Dunlap, 1974.

Haskell, Molly. "Paying Homage to the Spinster." *New York Times Magazine*, April 1988.

Hawthorne, Nathaniel. *A Wonder-Book, Tanglewood Tales, and Grandfather's Chair*. Boston: Houghton, Mifflin and Co., 1883.

Heath, William, ed. *Major British Poets of the Romantic Period*. New York: Macmillan, 1973.

Herder, Boris. *The Herder Symbol Dictionary*. Translated by Boris Matthews. Wilmette, Ill.: Chiron Publications, 1986.

Hesiod. *Theogeny, Works and Days, Shield*. Introduction, translation and notes by Apostolos N. Athanassakis. Baltimore: Johns Hopkins University Press, 1983.

Hibbard, Addison, ed. *The Book of Poe: Tales, Criticism, Poems*. Garden City, N.Y.: Doubleday, Doran & Co., Inc., 1934.

Homer. *The Homeric Hymns*. Translated by Charles Boer. Chicago: The Swallow Press, 1970.

Homer. *The Iliad*. Chicago: University of Chicago Press, 1951.

Homer. *The Odyssey*. New York: Mentor, 1937.

Howatson, M. C., ed. *The Oxford Companion to Classical Literature*, 2nd ed. Oxford & New York: Oxford University Press, 1989.

The Interpreter's Bible. New York: Abingdon Press, 1956.

Irving, Washington. *Rip Van Winkle and the Legend of Sleepy Hollow*. Tarrytown, N.Y.: Sleepy Hollow Press, 1980.

Jung, Carl. *The Archetypes and the Collective Unconscious*, vol. 9, part 1, of *The Collected Works of C. G. Jung*. Edited by Herbert Read et al. Princeton, N.J.: Princeton University Press, 1969.

Jung, Carl. *Man and His Symbols*. Garden City, N.Y.: Doubleday and Company, 1964.

Jung, Carl. *Modern Man in Search of a Soul*. New York: Harcourt, Brace and Co., 1934.

Jung, Carl. *Mysterium Coniunctionis*, vol. 15 of *Collected Works of C. G. Jung*. Edited by Herbert Read et al. New York: Pantheon Books, 1953-1979.

Jung, Carl. "Paracelsus as a Spiritual Phenomenon" *Alchemical Studies*, vol. 14 of *Collected Works of C. G. Jung*. Edited by Herbert Read et al. Princeton, N.J.: Princeton University Press, 1953-1979.

Jung, Carl. *The Spirit in Man, Art and Literature*, vol. 16 of *Collected Works of C. G. Jung*. Edited by Herbert Read et al. New York: Pantheon Books, 1953-1979.

Jung, Carl. "The Stages of Life." *The Structure and Dynamics of the Psyche*, vol. 8 of *Collected Works of C. G. Jung*. Edited by Herbert Read et al. New York: Pantheon Books, 1953-1979.

Kirby, W. F., translator. *Kalevala: The Land of the Heroes*, 2 vol. New York: Dutton, 1974.

Larkin, P., ed. *The Oxford Book of 20th Century English Verse*. Oxford: Clarendon Press, 1973.

Lathem, Edward Connery, ed. *The Poetry of Robert Frost*. New York: Holt, Rinehart and Winston, 1969.

Leach, Maria, ed. *Funk & Wagnall's Standard Dictionary of Folklore, Mythology and Legend*. New York: Funk & Wagnall's, 1972.

Luke, David. "'How Is It That You Live, and What Is It That You Do?': The Question of Old Age in English Romantic Poetry." In Spicker et al. *Aging and the Elderly, Humanistic Perspectives in Gerontology*. Atlantic Highlands, N.J.: Humanities Press, 1978.

Luke, Helen M. *Old Age*. New York: Parabola Books, 1987.

Lurker, Manfred. *Dictionary of Gods and Goddesses, Devils and Demons*. London: Routledge and Kegan Paul, 1987.

Lyell, Ruth Granetz, ed. *Middle Age, Old Age: Short Stories, Poems, Plays and Essays on Aging*. New York: Harcourt Brace Jovanovich, 1980.

MacCulloch, John Arnott, ed. *The Mythology of All Races*, 13 vol. Boston: Marshall Jones Co., 1930.

MacCulloch, John Arnott. *The Mythology of All Races:* vol. 2, *Eddic*. Boston: Marshall Jones Co., 1930.

Marsh, Jean. *Pre-Raphaelite Women: Images of Femininity in Pre-Raphaelite Art*. London: Weidenfeld and Nicolson, 1987.

Martin, W. *Gerard Dou*. London: George Bell and Sons, 1902.

Marx, Steven. "'Fortunate Senex': The Pastoral of Old Age." *Studies in English Literature 1500-1900*, vol. 25, no. 1 (Winter 1985), pp. 21-44.

May, Herbert G. and Bruce M. Metzger. *The New Oxford Annotated Bible with the Apocrypha*. New York: Oxford University Press, 1977.

McKee, Patrick and Heta Kauppinen. *The Art of Aging: A Celebration of Old Age in Western Art*. New York: Human Sciences Press, 1987.

McKee, Patrick, ed. *Philosophical Foundations of Gerontology*. New York: Human Sciences Press, 1982.

Merritt, Howard S. *Thomas Cole*. Rochester, N.Y.: University of Rochester Press, 1969.

Myerhoff, Barbara. "Rites and Signs of Ripening: The Intertwining of Ritual, Time, and Growing Older." In Kertzer, David I. and Jennie

Keith, eds. *Age and Anthropological Theory*. Ithaca, N.Y.: Cornell University Press, 1984, pp. 305-330.

The New Yorker Book of Poetry (selected by the editors of *The New Yorker*). New York: Viking Press, 1969.

Olderr, Steven, compiler. *Symbolism: A Comprehensive Dictionary*. Jefferson, N.C.: McFarland, 1986.

Opie, Iona and Peter, compilers. *The Classic Fairy Tales*. London: Oxford University Press, 1974.

Opie, Iona and Peter. *The Oxford Dictionary of Nursery Rhymes*. London: Oxford University Press, 1951.

Ovid. *Metamorphoses*. Translated by A. D. Melville. New York: Oxford University Press, 1986.

The Oxford English Dictionary. Oxford: Oxford University Press, 1971.

Panofsky, Edwin. *Studies in Iconology: Humanistic Themes in the Art of the Renaissance*. New York: Oxford University Press, 1939.

Pierce, James Smith. *From Abacus to Zeus: A Handbook of Art History*. Englewood Cliffs, N.J.: Prentice-Hall, 1968.

Pigott, Juliet. *Japanese Mythology*. London: Paul Hamlyn, 1969.

Pliny. *Natural History*, 10 vols. W. Heinemann, ed. Cambridge: Harvard University Press, 1938-1963.

Pomeroy, Sarah B. *Goddesses, Whores, Wives, and Slaves: Women in Classical Antiquity*. New York: Schocken Books, 1975.

Porteous, Alexander. *Forest Folklore, Mythology, and Romance*. London: George Allen and Unwin, Ltd., 1928.

Radin, Paul. *The Trickster, A Study in Native American Mythology*. New York: Schocken Books, 1972.

Richardson, Bessie Allen. *Old Age Among the Ancient Greeks*. New York: Greenwood Press, 1969.

Rosenblum, Robert and H. W. Janson. *19th Century Art*. Englewood Cliffs, N.J.: Prentice-Hall and New York: Harry N. Abrams, 1984.

Rubinstein, Charlotte Streifer. *American Women Artists: From Early Indian Times to the Present*. New York: Avon, 1982.

Sakoian, Frances and Louis S. Acker. *The Astrologer's Handbook*. New York: Harper & Row, 1973.

Sawyer, John F. A. "The Ruined House in Ecclesiastes 12: A Reconstruction of the Original Parable." *Journal of Biblical Literature*, vol. 94 (December 1975), pp. 519-531.

Scofield, C. I., ed. *The New Scofield Reference Bible*. New York: Oxford University Press, 1967.

Sears, Elizabeth. *The Ages of Man: Medieval Interpretations of the Life Cycle*. Princeton, N.J.: Princeton University Press, 1986.

Shakespeare, William. *The Complete Works of William Shakespeare*. New York: Avenel Books, 1975.

Singleton, Charles S. *The Divine Comedy: Inferno, 2. Commentary*. Princeton, N.J.: Princeton University Press, 1970.

Sohngren, Mary and Robert J. Smith. "Images of Old Age in Poetry." *The Gerontologist*, vol. 18, no. 2 (1978), pp. 181-186.

Spicker, Stuart, Kathleen Woodward, and David Van Tassel. *Aging and the Elderly: Humanistic Perspectives in Gerontology*. Atlantic Highlands, N.J.: Humanities Press, 1978.

Stahmer, Harold M. "The Aged in Two Ancient Oral Cultures: The Ancient Hebrews and Homeric Greece." In Spicker, Stuart, et al., *Aging and the Elderly: Humanistic Perspectives in Gerontology*. Atlantic Highlands, N.J.: Humanities Press, 1978, pp. 23-36.

Stahmer, Harold M. *Old Age Among the Greeks*. New York: Greenwood Press, 1933.

Stapleton, Michael. *The Illustrated Dictionary of Greek and Roman Mythology*. New York: Peter Bedrick Books, 1978.

Stevens, Wallace. *The Palm at the End of the Mind: Selected Poems and a Play*. New York: Random House, 1967.

Stone, Merlin. *Ancient Mirrors of Womanhood: A Treasury of Goddess and Heroine Lore from Around the World*. Boston: Beacon Press, 1979.

Strayer, Joseph R., ed. *Dictionary of the Middle Ages*, vol. 1. New York: Charles Scribner's Sons, 1982.

Swift, Jonathan. *The Annotated Gulliver's Travels by Jonathan Swift*. Annotated by Isaac Asimov. New York: Clarkson N. Potter, 1980.

Tatz, Mark and Jody Kent. *Rebirth: The Tibetan Game of Liberation*. New York: Anchor Press, 1977.

Thomas, Dylan. *Collected Poems*. London: J. M. Dent, 1952.

Thompson, Stith, compiler. *One Hundred Favorite Folktales*. Bloomington: Indiana University Press, 1968.

Tripp, Edward. *Crowell's Handbook of Classical Mythology*. New York: Thomas Y. Crowell Publishers, 1970.

Tucci, G. *Tibetan Painted Scrolls*. Rome: Libreria dello Stato, 1949. Pages 158-159 on Urgyan-pa's Journey (from Tatz and Kent).

Turner, Victor. "Pilgrimages as Social Processes." In Turner, Victor. *Dramas, Fields and Metaphors: Symbolic Action in Human Society*. Ithaca, N.Y.: Cornell University Press, 1974, pp. 166-230.

Urdang, L. and F. G. Ruffner, Jr., eds. *Allusions—Cultural, Literary, Biblical, and Historical: A Thematic Dictionary*, 2nd ed. Detroit: Gale Research Co., 1986.

Von Franz, Marie-Louise. "Reflection." In *Parabola: Myth and the Quest for Meaning*, vol. v, no. 1 ("The Old Ones" issue).

von Franz, Marie-Louise. *Time: Rhythm and Repose*. London: Thames and Hudson, 1978.

Walker, Barbara G. *The Crone: Woman of Age, Wisdom, and Power*. San
    Francisco: Harper & Row, 1985.
Walker, Barbara G. *The Woman's Encyclopedia of Myths and Secrets*. San
    Francisco: Harper & Row, 1983.
Weston, Jessie L. *From Ritual to Romance*. Oxford: Cambridge University
    Press, 1920.
Williams, J. *English Renaissance Poetry: A Collection of Shorter Poems from
    Skelton to Jonson*. Garden City, N.Y.: Doubleday, 1963.
Wilstach, John Augustine. *The Works of Virgil*. Boston: Houghton, Mifflin
    and Co., 1884.
Woodward, Kathleen. *at last, The Real Distinguished Thing: The Late
    Poems of Eliot, Pound, Stevens, and Williams*. Columbus, Ohio: Ohio
    State University Press, 1980.
Woodward, Kathleen. "Instant Repulsion: Decrepitude, The Mirror Stage,
    and the Literary Imagination." *Kenyon Review*, vol. 5 (Fall 1983), pp. 43-
    66.
Woodward, Kathleen. "Master Songs of Meditation: The Late Poems of
    Eliot, Pound, Stevens, and Williams." In Spicker et al. *Aging and the
    Elderly*. Atlantic Highlands, N.J.: Humanities Press, 1978, pp. 181-202.
Woodward, Kathleen and Murray M. Schwartz. *Memory and Desire:
    Aging—Literature—Psychoanalysis*. Bloomington: Indiana University
    Press, 1986.
Wordsworth, William. *The Complete Poetical Works of William Wordsworth*.
    London: Macmillan and Co., 1894.
Yakima Nation Media Program. *The Challenge of Spilyay*. Toppenish,
    Wash.: Yakima Nation Museum, 1984.
Zimmerman, John Edward. *Dictionary of Classical Mythology*. New York:
    Bantam Books, 1964.

About the Authors

JENNIFER McLERRAN is an art critic and painter in Seattle, Washington. She
received her Master of Fine Arts from Colorado State University and a Master
of Humanities from the University of Colorado.

PATRICK McKEE is Professor and Chair of the Department of Philosophy at
Colorado State University.